W9-AJO-161

THE LANGUAGE OF SPANISH DANCE

The Language of Spanish Dance

By

MATTEO

(Matteo Marcellus Vittucci)

With

CAROLA GOYA

Foreword by RICHARD CRAGUN

Drawings by LOUIS GIOIA

Flamenco Guitar Music by PETER BAIME

Piano Arrangements by MARC SAINT-GERMAIN

UNIVERSITY OF OKLAHOMA PRESS : NORMAN AND LONDON

Labanotation by Jane Marriett
Checked by Ann Hutchinson Guest
Autography by Carol Elsner

Published with the assistance of The Program for Cultural Cooperation Between Spain's Ministry of Culture and United States' Universities; the Vice Provost for Research Administration, University of Oklahoma; and the National Endowment for the Humanities, a federal agency which supports the study of such fields as history, philosophy, literature, and languages.

Library of Congress Cataloging-in-Publication Data

Matteo.
    The language of Spanish dance / by Matteo (Matteo Marcellus Vittucci) with Carola Goya ; foreword by Richard Cragun ; drawings by Louis Gioia ; flamenco guitar music by Peter Baime ; piano arrangements by Marc Saint-Germain. — 1st ed.
        p.   cm.
    English and Spanish.
    Includes bibliographical references.
    ISBN 0-8061-2257-9 (alk. paper)
    1. Dancing—Spain—Terminology.   I. Goya, Carola.   II. Title.
GV1673.M35   1990
793.3'1946'014—dc20   89-48953
                                                           CIP

The paper in this book meets the guidelines for permanence and durability of the Committee on Production Guidelines for Book Longevity of the Council on Library Resources, Inc. ∞

To
Josephine Grisham Renzulli
&
Judith Hankins

Dancing as an art, we may be sure, cannot die out, but will always be under-going a rebirth. Not merely as an art, but also as a social custom, it per-petually emerges afresh from the soul of the people . . .

HAVELOCK ELLIS

Contents

Illustrations

Foreword

By Richard Cragun

WITH this book Matteo, in cooperation with Carola Goya, has successfully wrested the rich tradition of Spanish dance terminology from the perils of extinction. For in our present space age of constantly changing modes and conventions, it was surely only a question of time before this most important and colorful dance heritage slipped into the realm of obscurity. We of the dance community, scholars, and the general public can therefore feel indebted to these authors for a remarkable achievement, for a bridge has been created linking the history of Iberian dance with present developments, thus forming a solid basis upon which present and future generations may continue to add to their traditions. Furthermore, apart from providing an astute and comprehensive analysis, in codifying the myriad aspects of a fascinating yet complicated dance technique (there are hundreds of different forms), this definitive volume gives the reader an invaluable acquaintance with an intricate ethnic dance vocabulary and also unifies an area which formerly lay in fragments.

As a classical ballet dancer, I have always valued the importance of preserving all forms of dance tradition. Owing to lack of documentation, countless details pertaining to various aspects of style, schools, and choreography have been lost through modification by individual whim or, worse, through commercial exploitation, leaving after a few short generations a mere skeleton of the original form. For this reason it was particularly gratifying as part of my final education period at the Royal Ballet School in London to be among the first generation to study, under Rudolph and Joan Benesh, their own newly developed system of dance notation, the purpose of which was to preserve just those traditions and to safeguard current dance developments for posterity. The Benesh System and its New York counterpart, Labanotation, became the two internationally recognized methods of documenting all forms of dance and theater movement.

In the nick of time Matteo's labor of love, along with skillful use of notation, has arrived to resuscitate the ethnic dance tradition of Spain, which, owing to its specialized nature, has endured in recent years an exhausting and often fruitless struggle to survive. We realize that the loss of that tradition would have been tragic when we stop to consider the importance of the role which this art has played down through the ages in forming much of the inner character and outward profile of the Spanish people, not to mention the influence it has had in other areas of dance around the world, particularly in classical ballet.

Recently, while observing a performance of Antonio Gades, one of the foremost classical Spanish dancers of our day, I was again reminded of the many underlying similarities in our two fields. There is the heroic quality conveyed in Gades's use of the head and neck, in the sculptured epaulement of the shoulders, and in the position of his finely arched torso, as well as the expressive, almost delicate use of the hands, poetic statements in themselves. Even the five basic foot positions from which the choreography in ballet develops, though seen in their character equivalent, are a reminder of how closely related are the principles behind Prince Siegfried's movements and those of his princely flamenco counterpart. Perhaps much of that inner combustion which we sense building behind the premier danseur's preparation before he rockets across the stage in a fiery solo was at one time inspired by his Spanish colleague as the latter prepared at the same point in his flamenco solo a brilliant *farruca*.

The Spanish temperament appears to have been destined to express itself through dance. With its innate sense of rhythm and magnificent ability to convey the entire gamut of human emotion in concise movements plus its wonderful use of costumes, the Iberian dance culture has contributed immeasurably to the overall development of the dance.

As we know, the cradle of what we now call classical ballet was the royal court of seventeenth-century France, particularly under the patronage of Louis XIV, the "Sun King," or the "Dancing Monarch," as he was referred to by his contemporaries. It is also known that the Italian court dance masters of the time contributed greatly to the dance vocabulary with their specialty, *batteria*, or little beats, more often than not having borrowed them from the local folk dancers. But while history books seldom refer to the Spanish dance influence at this time, we can well assume that its role was not a minor one, for shortly thereafter many references to steps from the Spanish *sevillana* and *jota* began to appear in the northern courts. As ballet emerged from the royal courts and became accessible to the masses, it was the charm of the Spanish dances which drew the greatest number of spectators into the theater.

In the nineteenth century, as classical ballet reached its zenith, the lure of the Spanish dance increased rather than diminished. As a result, far off in Saint Petersburg in 1847 the exotic rhythms of castanets echoed throughout the famed Marinsky Theater in *Paquita*, act 2, by Marius Petipa. This was followed in 1855 by the ballet *Star from Granada*. Although Petipa's *Zoraiya, the Moorish Woman in Spain*, has not survived, there is practically no stage today in the ballet world which has not witnessed a production of his famous classic *Don Quixote*, created in 1871. This ballet, which exalts the wonderful world of Cervantes, makes perhaps more choreographic references to actual Spanish dance vocabulary than any other ballet of its kind to date.

We are all well aware of the tremendous impact that Spanish painters and their schools have had on contemporary art and theater design. Contemporary choreographers have also felt the magnetic pull of the Iberian culture and its unique rhythms, as we see in the brilliant *Three Cornered Hat*, by Leonide Massine, of 1919 or in the little-known in the West but nonetheless powerful act 3 of *Laurencia* (1939), created by yet another of Russia's illustrious choreographers, Tchabukiani.

It would be pointless to extend the list, which is considerable. Suffice it to say that, while Spanish themes and dance forms stemming from their ethnic background have left their mark in all areas throughout the years, these fragments have lain scattered throughout Spain awaiting unification into what can truly be called the Spanish school. Over the years and without the assistance of notation it became increasingly difficult to retain the purity of even those fragments, and with the deaths of the few dancers and teachers qualified to speak authoritatively about their art, the threat of further disintegration intensified.

With *The Language of Spanish Dance* that threat has been halted, and, as is often the case in the battle of preservation, these results have been achieved because clearly the authors' intentions were governed not only by a deeply felt love for and commitment to their mission but also by a scholarly background with which to complete their task.

The soul of the Spanish people has always been woven into the steps of their dances. This book traces the patterns of those steps and brings us closer to understanding their message.

Acknowledgments

I am grateful to the New York State Council on the Arts, which provided public funds that helped to support research for this book.

I also wish to express my deep appreciation to the following performing artists and educators in the world of dance who have encouraged me to undertake this project of documenting an art form that is no longer the sole possession of a single nation but belongs to dancers around the world: the late Walter Terry, Genevieve Oswald, Deborah Jowitt, Anna Kisselgoff, Kirsten Ralov, Dame Alicia Markova, the late Ben Sommers, Martha Hill, José de Udaeta, Doris Hering, Walter Sorell, Carlos Surinach, P. W. Manchester, Jennie Schulman, Lydia Joel, William Como, Laura Toledo, Hector Zaraspe, Marian Horosko, Wendy Hilton, Patricia Rowe, Carleton Sprague Smith, and Dame Marina Keet.

I wish especially to thank Jerane Michel for the many sessions of repetition necessary to illustrate the many *compuestos* of *escuela bolera*.

For the painstaking job of Labanotation I wish to thank Jane Marriett for serving as notator: Ann Hutchinson Guest for overseeing and final checking; and Carol Elsner for camera-ready autography.

I express my thanks to Louis Gioia for his exacting and indispensable drawings and to Peter Baime for his original transcriptions for the flamenco guitar.

For his helpful suggestions, his preparation of piano sequences, and his yeoman's service in endless hours of manuscript preparation, I am grateful to Marc Saint-Germain. To Doris Radford Morris and Sarah Nestor for their invaluable editing and suggestions for format, I am especially indebted.

I am grateful for the encouragement of all the maestros and maestras throughout Spain, many of whom are no longer alive, who allowed me the privilege of observing many hours of class instruction and of sitting in on private lessons and who graciously gave much of their time to answering my questions. Their spirit and cooperation always reflected their attitude that such a book would do honor to their dance.

Finally, I am grateful to my wife, Carola Goya, without whose loving encouragement, ceaseless cooperation, and unwavering faith this volume would never have seen the light of day.

MATTEO

New York City

Introduction

AS early as 1820, Antonio Cairón wrote in the preface of his dance manual, *Compendio de las principales reglas del baile*, "It is to be hoped that this work will stimulate some teacher more knowledgeable to publish another work of this kind, more expansive, more intelligible and useful, guiding all to avoid a thousand arguments occasioned only by ignorance." In 1912, Spain's most respected teacher of Andalusian dance, José Otero of Seville, echoed the same sentiment in his *Tratado de bailes*. No single person or volume could possibly cover the multifaceted subject of Iberian dance. *The Language of Spanish Dance* is only a link in the choreographic chain to help reinstate the dignified language which the Iberian dance once employed.

Throughout the many years I spent preparing this book, I was often confronted with the question, "Why bother with the names of steps? Spanish dancing is to be performed, not spoken." *The Language of Spanish Dance* has been designed to help preserve the authenticity of Spanish dance and its technique without detracting from its creativity. The definitions are intended to be flexible rather than rigid; they are meant to expand the dancer's vocabulary, not to confine it. My purpose is to give Spanish dance an international language comparable to the French terminology used in classical ballet. Some eight hundred terms are listed, together with illustrations, musical examples, and notes on the accoutrements (such as costumes, shoes, and castanets) of each style of dance.

Spanish dance is a complex art that can be subdivided into four styles: *folklórico* (folk or regional), *escuela bolera* (eighteenth-century classic), Andalusian, and flamenco. The characteristic movements which identify each of these styles have evolved because of their environment, clothing, and social customs.

Folklórico dances encompass the complete Iberian panorama of fifty-three provinces with an endless array of colorful regional costumes and hundreds of folk dances, many of which are seldom seen outside their homeland. Many of these dances, stemming from Greek, Phoenician, Celtic, and Moorish origins, employ strange steps, patterns, and props such as wooden shoes, water pitchers, flower arches, maypoles, stilts, swords, and kerchiefs.

The *escuela bolera* (bolero school) possesses today the refinement of eighteenth-century academic dancing. Elegance was and still remains the hallmark of this distinguished balletic form of dance performed in soft slippers (*zapatillas*) and fashioned by the Italian and French dancing masters of the time. Based on the principles of classical ballet, including a modified turn out of the legs, its technically brilliant jumped, beaten, and flying steps, coupled with delightful adornments in the use of the arms and castanets, require arduous and systematic training for the sheer strength and coordination it demands.

Generally speaking, the dance style of Andalusia (*baile andaluz*) is the style most people associate with Spanish dancing. Andalusians refer to their dances as *airoso y alegre* (gracious and happy). These dances are characterized by the proud uplifted chest of the male and the arched back and fluid, sensuous arm movements of the female performed to the sound of castanets. For many years it was in this Andalusian style (*estilo andaluz*) that such dances as *malagueñas, seguidillas, fandangos, el vito, panaderos,* and *farruca* were taught by the revered maestros, often in rechoreographed forms that were later seen on concert stages and in nightclubs around the world.

In contrast to the above dance styles, flamenco, with its ambiance of merriment (*jaleo*), singing (*cante*), and rhythmic hand clapping (*palmas*), which often involve the audience, has a highly charged level of dynamics. Because it is essentially a solo dance with strong eastern and Moorish influences and can be performed in four different manners—melancholy (*baile grande*), tragic (*jondo*), somewhat reserved (*baile intermedio*), and happy, carefree (*baile chico*)—and because of its overtness, pacing, and dramatic airs, flamenco is accessible to the responses of most viewers. These qualities make for exciting theater and entertainment. This form has undergone the most dramatic change, now finding itself the vehicle for production numbers and complete ballets using an entire company of dancers, thus creating still another theater style, *baile teatral*.

From north to south the four principal styles of dance can also be identified by the indigenous music which accompanies each. The sounds range from skirling bagpipes (*gaitas*), metalic triangles (*triangolos*), jingling tambourines (*panderetas*), flutes (*flaviols*), and castanets to the familiar rhythmic hand clapping (*palmas*) and flamenco guitar.

There have been only a few attempts to identify, analyze, and classify the terms used in these four styles of Spanish dance, in part because of the current system of teaching the art form using only a handful of terms. Spanish dance lexicons of the eighteenth and nineteenth centuries list many terms which have fallen into disuse. By combining written sources with the results of intensive interviews with today's teachers, it has been possible to resurrect many of these terms. A major task of *The Language of Spanish Dance* has been to define these terms with clarity and precision and to identify the *pasos* (steps) to which they pertain, as well as the *compuestos* (dance units, phrases, or combinations) in which they are involved. The definitions have been tested for clarity both by leading teachers and by students at various levels of proficiency.

This book is designed and structured to fill a void in the teaching of Spanish dance, which for decades has propagated the "dance routine" method of instruction using improvised-on-the-spot onomatopoeic expressions such as "Ta tum pa pim pam" because of the paucity of written terminology. Many reputable teachers have conscientiously devoted their lives to handing down their favorite dances to younger generations of Spaniards, as well as to countless foreign students. Lacking terminology and notation, in time many of those dances have been forgotten, adjusted, or rechoreographed. Teachers and students can now learn the names of the steps which they have performed and taught for many years. Imagine classical ballet, with the greatest popularity it has enjoyed in years, being taught to thousands throughout the world without its standardized French terminology!

The Language of Spanish Dance is an unprecedented compendium of information about the four styles of Spanish dance. I believe it will become indispensable to the dancer, the teacher, the choreographer, the researcher, the critic, and the *aficionado*. For teachers this book provides a comprehensive, item-by-item curriculum. For dancers it clarifies details and gives practical information for performance. For scholars and *aficionados* it will be a stimulating resource. For every reader it is a book that will encourage greater appreciation of all styles of Spanish dancing.

It is important to remember, however, that no book on dancing can make one into a dancer. This book is designed to define and illustrate the "tools" used in Spanish dancing and, as in ballet, to establish the proper identification of a step for teaching, recalling, notating, and documenting. For each term the entry provides the following:

1. The traditional or commonly accepted name;
2. Its phonetic pronunciation (shown by the method of transliteration adopted by the Academia Real, the Royal Academy of Madrid);
3. Its meaning and derivation;
4. Visual aids (drawings and photographs);
5. Detailed, succinct, count-by-count directions describing each term;
6. The origin, derivation, application, and folklore regarding the term;
7. Examples of the term's traditional or applied musical counterpart;
8. Detailed choreographic representation in Labanotation.

For convenience, after a section on "Basic Positions and Techniques" that defines and describes the fundamental body, arm, foot, and hand movements of Spanish dancing, the entries and cross-references appear in English-style alphabetical order. Thus all pertinent information may be found quickly and easily. *The beginner reading the instructions should first observe the counts down the left-hand side of a page, repeating them aloud several times. Thus one can establish the basic pulse and "flow" of the movements that follow.*

Due to the varied nature of Spanish dance, I am presenting each term in one of three different ways:

(1) As a definition, giving a broad overview of the indispensable dance-related terms that are basic to all styles of Iberian dance;

(2) As a direction, for movements that are not very difficult and can be adequately conveyed by word descriptions, counts, and Labanotation and do not require detailed drawings;

(3) As an illustrated term with drawings, detailed directions, Labanotation, samples of typical music, and historical footnotes. These more technically difficult *pasos* and *paseos* (steps and phrases of movement) may involve coordination of stepping, bending, gliding, leaping, turning, and hopping with arm or hand movements.

An unusual feature may be found in the appendix, "Basic Flamenco Rhythms." Each *compás* (rhythmic phrase) appears in *cifra,* the traditional notation for the Spanish guitar music that is the accompaniment for flamenco dancing.

One of the innovations of this work is the selection, quality, and volume of its illustrative materials, which include many drawings that show the action in progress. The exact movement is duplicated in Labanotation to represent such important minutiae as sustained timing, energy flow, indirect space, and weight pressure, which otherwise would require supplementary terminology to give the proper characterization. The Labanotation system overcomes the occasional problems of semantics and can be deciphered universally.

The illustrations were executed by Louis Gioia, who worked with live dancers under rehearsal and performance conditions. Because Spanish dancing is based on the spiraling effect produced by oppositional movement of the arms, legs, and torso at various speeds, it is important to outline anatomically the precise placement of these body parts. This is an especially difficult task in the case of a female dancer in costume. For clarity the artist has portrayed the body line through a transparent dress that reveals the movement in relation to the garment.

The photographs are accurate reproductions of Spanish dancing of the past and present. Carefully selected to exemplify the topics covered in the text, they range from eighteenth- and nineteenth-century paintings, lithographs, and etchings to photographs of contemporary theatrical productions.

Although every effort has been made to obtain information from the most authoritative sources, it must be acknowledged that the most renowned dancers may be neither the most capable teachers nor the most dependable scholars. Diverse opinions and inconsistencies in the nomenclature and the manner of dance execution are inevitable. Hence the familiar Spanish saying, *Cada maestrito tiene su librito* ("each teacher has his own little book"). In recognition of this I have presented more than one version wherever appropriate.

A bibliography has been provided for scholars and *aficionados* who wish to pursue further the many aspects of Spanish dance. The most extensive compilation on Spanish dance to date, it will prove especially useful in the study of flamenco, which has been described as "a way of life of those who sing and dance their sorrows and joys." Flamenco is the most popular form of Spanish dance, but it cannot be thoroughly appreciated or understood solely by learning and imitating dance steps.

It is my sincere hope that, after years of performing, rehearsing, and teaching many forms of ethnic dance, the all-inclusive format I have evolved will pioneer a much-needed guide for other forms of ethnic dance. With the rapid advancement of dance education and pedagogy, I believe that the choreographic terms presented in this volume will serve as a textbook for those who wish to reconstruct, maintain, or ultimately create dances from one of the richest and most varied countries the world of dance has ever known, ESPAÑA.

THE LANGUAGE OF SPANISH DANCE

BRAZOS BASICOS *(BRAH-thos BAH-see-cohs)*
(Basic arm positions)

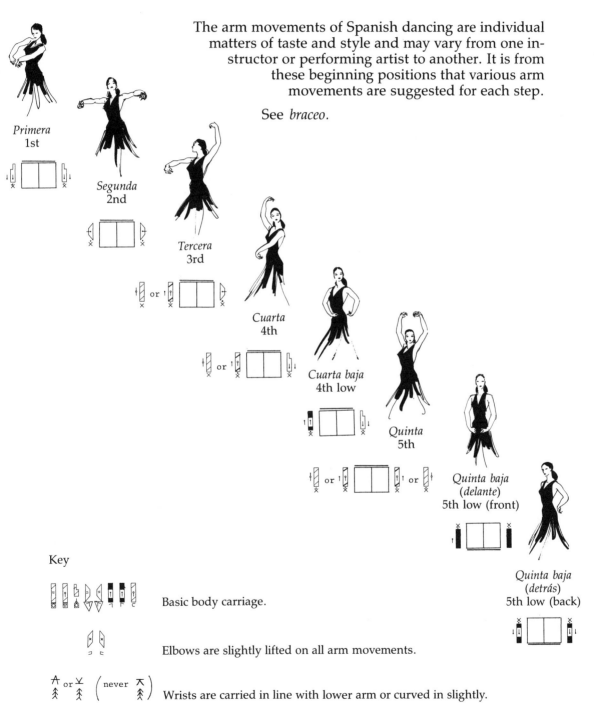

The arm movements of Spanish dancing are individual matters of taste and style and may vary from one instructor or performing artist to another. It is from these beginning positions that various arm movements are suggested for each step.

See *braceo*.

Primera
1st

Segunda
2nd

Tercera
3rd

Cuarta
4th

Cuarta baja
4th low

Quinta
5th

Quinta baja
(delante)
5th low (front)

Quinta baja
(detrás)
5th low (back)

Key

Basic body carriage.

Elbows are slightly lifted on all arm movements.

or (never) Wrists are carried in line with lower arm or curved in slightly.

3

PIES *(pee-EHS)*
(Positions of the feet)

Unlike movements of the arms (*braceo*), which can vary according to individual taste, positions of the feet are more defined and precise. Though interchangeable, those pictured on the left pertain mostly to the *escuela bolera* (bolero school) and *folklórico* (regional) styles. Those on the right are basic to most Andalusian and flamenco dance.

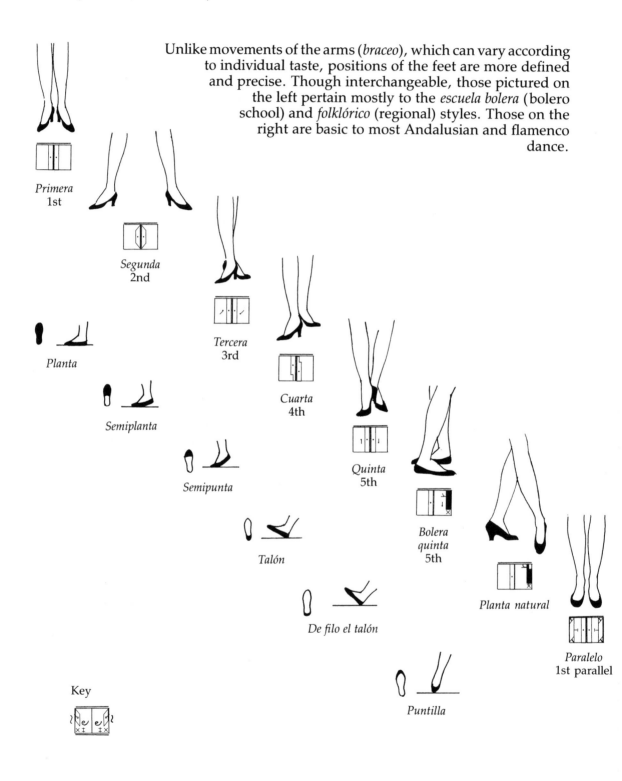

Primera
1st

Segunda
2nd

Planta

Tercera
3rd

Semiplanta

Cuarta
4th

Semipunta

Quinta
5th

Talón

Bolera quinta
5th

De filo el talón

Planta natural

Puntilla

Paralelo
1st parallel

Key

PALMAS, PITOS, Y CASTAÑUELAS *(PAHL-mahs, PEE-tohs, ee cahs-tah-nyoo-EH-lahs)*
(Rhythmic hand claps, finger snaps, and castanets)

Shown below, left to right, are the folkloric and classic styles of playing castanets, the method of finger snapping (*pitos*), and positions for attaining muffled (*sordas*) and dry (*secas*) rhythmic clapping (*palmas*) in Andalusian and flamenco dancing.

See *basic castanet rhythms, carretilla, chasquear los dedos, palmas, pitos.*

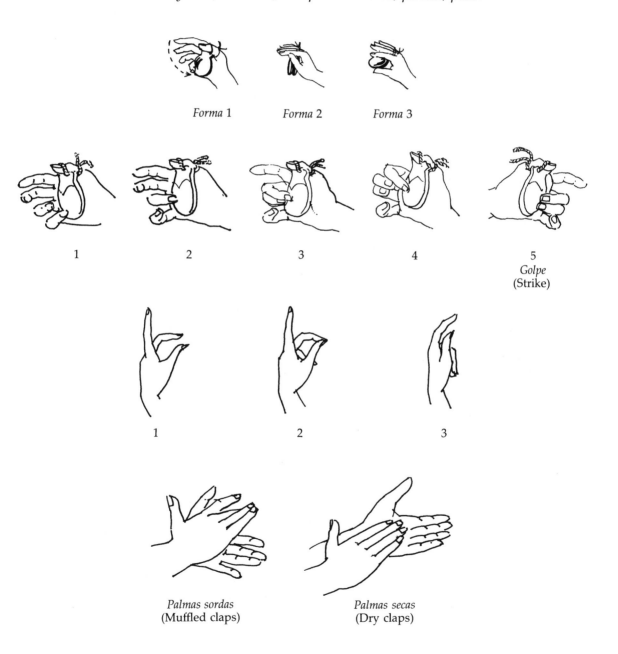

Forma 1   Forma 2   Forma 3

1   2   3   4   5
Golpe
(Strike)

1   2   3

Palmas sordas
(Muffled claps)

Palmas secas
(Dry claps)

MOVIMIENTOS DE LAS MANOS *(moh-vee-mee-EHN-tos deh lahs MAH-nohs)*
(Movements of the hands)
Also called *muñecas* (wrists) or *filigranas* (ornamental, delicate movements) in
    flamenco.

These flowing movements, of Eastern origin, are characteristic only of the
bailaora or *bailarina* (female dancer) in flamenco and Andalusian dance. The
male dancer uses his hands sparingly, if ever, keeping his fingers together
with very little rotation of the wrists. Escudero, the most famous of flamenco
dancers, was adamant on this point.

Beg pos   Ct 1   Ct 2   Ct 3

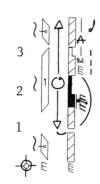

Beg pos	Arms—in any position, palms facing outward.
Ct 1	With fingers slightly separated and vitalized, circle hands outward, leading with middle finger.
Ct 2	Continue to circle hands, curving fingers toward palms.
Ct 3	Uncurl fingers as circle is completed.
	Movements above are also done in reverse, rotating inward.

Movimientos de las manos

See *decálogo, filigranas, muñecas.*

PICA TACON *(PEE-cah tah-COHN)*
(Pierce, or puncture, heel)
Also called *punta tacón.*

The forward jabbing action "into" the floor (not a tapping on the floor) is basic
to all rhythmic footwork (*zapateado*) and gives this action its name.

Ct 1

Ct &

Beg pos Feet—1st parallel.
Arms—optional.

Preparation: Lift foot backward from
knee.

Ct 1 Stab ball of foot into floor.
Ct & From established position drive heel
firmly downward.

Repeat on other foot.

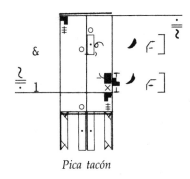

Pica tacón

Pesante

Ct: 1 &   2 &

REDOBLE ANDALUZ *(reh-DOH-bleh ahn-dah-LOOTH)*
(A redoubling four-sound drum roll—Andalusian)

This is a basic foot rhythm (*zapateado*) of prime importance in Andalusian and flamenco dancing.

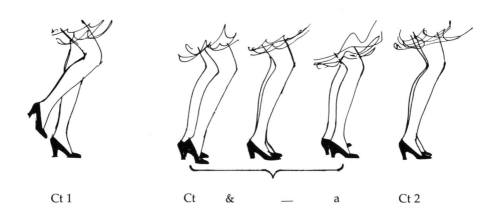

Ct 1   Ct   &   —   a   Ct 2

Beg pos	Feet—1st parallel. Arms—optional.
Ct 1	Lift R foot backward from knee.
Ct &	Strike ball of R foot. Drop R heel, taking weight. Strike back edge of L heel. (These three sounds make a musical triplet.)
Ct 2	Follow immediately with stamp on L foot (*planta*).

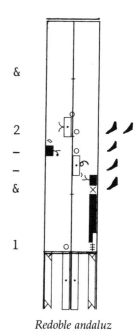

Redoble andaluz

REDOBLE FLAMENCO *(reh-DOH-bleh flah-MEHN-coh)*
Also called *remate*.

Beg pos   See *redoble andaluz*, above.

Ct 1   Lift R foot backward from knee.
Ct &   Stamp R foot beside L, taking weight. Strike back edge of L heel. Stamp on L foot. (These three sounds make a musical triplet.)
Ct 2   Follow immediately with stamp on R foot (*planta*).

See *pica, remate, tacón, tacón raspado*.

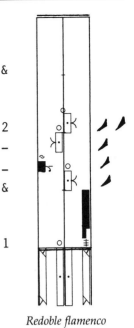

Redoble flamenco

ABANIQUEO *(ah-bah-nee-KEH-o)*
(Fanning, swinging motion, gesturing)

A feminine technique that lends charm and subtlety to gesture and movement in dances such as *caracoles, guajira,* and *la maja y el torero.* The term derives its name from *abanico* (fan). There is a tendency to overuse the technique by featuring groups of dancers with oversized fans that move constantly, are fluttered, and are opened and closed with no apparent motivation. Once the fan is opened, it should be used with rhythmic discretion. The movements are inwards (*por adentro*) and are coordinated with the speed of the heel work (*zapateado*). If the heel work is lively, the accompanying fan action should be slow, and vice versa.

ABRIR Y CERRAR *(ah-BREER ee theh-RAHR)*
(To open and close)

As described below, this step is executed in the style of the *escuela bolera.* It is repeated several times, the feet being reversed each time. Except for the pointed toes, the step is also seen with various degrees of height and energy in many *folklórico* dances.

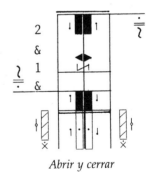

Abrir y cerrar

Beg pos	Feet—5th R front.
	Arms—5th.
	Preparation: Bend knees slightly (*demiplegado*).
Ct & 1	Spring vertically, pointing toes and landing in broad 2nd position (*cuadrada*).
Ct & 2	Spring into air again, returning to 5th R foot back.
	Repeat above counts, but return to 5th R foot front.

See *cambiamientos bajos y altos.*

A CABALLO
See *caballo folklórico.*

A CAPRICHO *(ah cah-PREE-choh)*
(Capricious, at one's whim)
Also called *improvisación*.

A free style in dance *(baile)* referring to improvised movements or rhythms interpolated into certain sections of a dance. These usually result from the performer's experience or sense of what will please him or her and the audience. Such innovations are also employed in solo guitar playing *(toque)*.

See *falseta, improvisación.*

ACCENTUACION *(ahc-thehn-too-ah-thee-OHN)*
(Accentuation, emphasis)

The various accents within a rhythmic phrase or cycle *(compás)*. Also, a term in castanet playing signifying the varying accents, which may change from phrase to phrase, depending on the musicality of the artist. This term is not to be confused with *golpeo* (a constant, repetitious beating of the left-hand castanet).

See *golpeo, pulsación.* See also Appendix: Basic Flamenco Rhythms.

ACTITUD *(ahc-tee-TOOD)*
(Attitude, pose)

A sudden, static position in the midst of continuous action.

ADELANTE
See *direcciones básicas.*

ADENTRO *(ah-DEHN-troh)*
(Within, inside)

A movement in which the foot begins a circular pattern toward the supporting leg and then moves backward and away from the supporting leg. The foot completes the circle, returning to the sustaining leg. If the right foot is used, the direction is counterclockwise; if the left, the direction is clockwise. *Adentro* is similar in meaning to the balletic term *en dedans.*

See *afuera, rodazán.*

AFANDANGADO *(ah-fahn-dahn-GAH-doh)*
(In the manner of a *fandango*)

A term applied to a nineteenth- or twentieth-century social *danza* (dance) which required the expression or rhythmic character of a *fandango*. Even the courtly minuet of Versailles succumbed to the animated spirit of the then-popular Spanish *fandango,* as did many ballroom and drawing-room dances of that period. The minuet was referred to as *minué afandangado.*

See *fandango.*

AFICIONADO *(ah-fee-thee-oh-NAH-doh)*
(An enthusiast, fan, "lover of")

An enthusiastic supporter of a particular activity, including *cante, baile,* or *tauromaquia* (bullfighting). Such individuals range from the uninformed to the cognoscenti, but a true *aficionado* is imbued with a strong fondness for and knowledge of the subject.

AFIRMACION *(ah-feer-mah-thee-OHN)*
(Affirmation, assurance)

The confident, positive manner in which a dancer presents himself or herself on stage, probably the most important ingredient in Spanish theater dance.

AFUERA *(ah-FWEH-rah)*
(Out, outside)

A movement in which the foot begins a circular pattern forward and away from the supporting leg and then continues and completes the circle by returning toward that leg. If the right leg is used, the direction is clockwise; if the left, the direction is counterclockwise. *Afuera* is similar in meaning to the balletic term *en dehors.* The term also applies to carriage of the arms.

See *adentro, rodazán.*

AGARRADINO *(ah-gah-rrah-DEE-noh)*
(Grasped, held)

In folkloric dances, position in which a man puts his arm around his partner's waist.

AGITANADO *(ah-hee-tah-NAH-doh)* or AGITANAO *(ah-hee-tah-NAH-oh)*[1]
(Gypsylike; from *gitano,* gypsy)

The more popular of the two basic styles of *flamenco* dance. *Agitanado* style is an energized, outward display of noise, shouting, stamping, and frenzied movements. It is especially suited to shorter dancers of smaller, more compact stature, whereas taller dancers generally tend toward the opposite, calmer, more classic style, *reposao.*

See *reposao.*

AIRE *(AH-ee-reh)*
(Carriage, gait, appearance)

An air or quality of pride or aloofness that emanates from the artist. *The term also refers to the overall character, feeling, or atmosphere created by the major or minor key in which music is played or sung.*

See *manera, reposao.*

---

[1] So pronounced by Flamencos. It is characteristic of Flamencos to drop the *d* sound.

AIROSO *(ah-ee-ROH-soh)*
(Airy, graceful, lively)

A nimble, fleet, airborne quality like that characterizing eighteenth- and nineteenth-century classical dances and regional dances such as *seguidillas*, *boleros*, and *sevillanas*.

See *más saltadora*, *sevillanas*.

AL AIRE *(ahl AH-ee-reh)*
(In the air)

A term indicating that a foot making a movement (such as a *rodazán*) is not touching the floor but is at any level in the air. It is similar to the balletic term *en l'air*.

ALEGRIAS *(ah-leh-GREE-ahs)*
(From *alegría*, joy)

If one were to ask the average flamenco dancer which dance is the one most often performed, in all probability the answer would be the *alegrías*. There is good reason for this, because the *alegrías*, as we now view or perform it, though constructed on firm rules, is not confined to the point that it cannot "breathe." Since it first emerged from the Gypsy quarter, the Barrio Santa María of Cádiz, after the turn of the century as a woman's solo, it has slowly evolved with added footwork (*zapateado*), energy, and speed. In spite of recent changes, including being danced by men, the dance has managed to maintain its identity and continues to be the perfect vehicle for an artist's personality, showmanship, and technique. Because of its steady evolement and popularity in nightclub (*tablao*), concert-hall, and legitimate theater, it has likewise evolved a sequence that can be defined with terminology as can other flamenco dances of this type.

Although there are several versions of the *alegrías* of varying lengths, all of them fall into the category of dances counted in a rhythmic cycle (*compás*) of twelve counts with accents falling on the counts of 3, 6, 8, 10, and 12. The artist may choose to add extra phrases (*compases*) for improvisations (*improvisaciones*) in certain sections or eliminate sections completely, except the indispensable *castellana*, with its unique traditional melody.

Often a beginning section (*salida*), a vocal warm-up is a very characteristic flamenco high-pitched "*ay*" or "*la, la, la!*" or the onomatopoetic strumming of a guitar, "*tarata tran*" or "*tirita tran*," to set the mood for the dancer. Following is the basic choreographic structure of the *alegrías*. The *llamadas* (signals or calls) that alert the guitarist and act as a "break" into a new tempo, phase, or section of the dance are in parenthesis: *entrada, paseo* (*llamada*), *silencio* (*llamada*), *castellana* (*llamada*), *escobilla* (sometimes a *silencio* or a *puente* [bridge] is inserted here with or without accompaniment), and lastly a *desplante* or a *salida de bulerías* to *jaleo* or *paso final*.

It is very likely that the addition of *bulerías* rhythm as an ending together with rhythmic footwork (*zapateado*) and handclapping (*palmas*), which makes it the liveliest part of the dance, may have evolved when the dance moved from its birthplace, the *barrio,* to its new home, the theater. In the old version, *alegrías antiguas,* the climax (*jaleo*) was reached by accelerating the tempo to which lighthearted or humorous (*por chufla*) steps and gestures were performed. Several other dances which maintain the same basic rhythm structure (*compás*) are derived from the *alegrías* and continue in the same happy mood. They are the *romeras, caracoles, mirabrás, rosas,* and *cantiñas.*

It is said that the *compás* of the *alegrías* was "born to be danced." In spite of its antiquity, it was only at the turn of the century that its song (*cante*) became accepted as a solo song in its own right.

See *castellana, desplante, escobilla, farfulleos, llamada, paseo, salida, silencio.* See also Appendix: Basic Flamenco Rhythms.

A LO ALTO *(ah lo AHL-toh)*
(Aristocratic, eminent)

Usually applied to social or period *danzas* (dances) in which manners and decorum are of primary importance.

See *alta danza, bailes palaciegos, danza, manera, postura.*

A LO LLANO *(ah loh LYAH-noh)*
(Even, smooth)

An easy, unadorned, modest manner in which a step or dance is performed. It is the opposite of the term *vistoso.*

See *vistoso.*

AL SUELO *(ahl SWEH-loh)*
(On the ground)

A term indicating that the foot making the movement is in contact with the floor. It is similar to the balletic term *a terre.*

ALTA DANZA *(AHL-tah DAHN-thah)*
(High, elevated, or eminent dance)

A term for the aristocratic dance of the seventeenth and eighteenth centuries.

See *a lo alto, bailes palaciegos.*

A MATA CABALLO *(ah MAH-tah cah-BAH-lyoh)*
(At breakneck speed; literally, to kill a horse)

A satirical term used mostly in reference to regional dances such as the *jota aragonesa* which feature spectacular feats of technique performed at top speed. A flamenco dancer, in an attempt to win applause, performs the last portion of his dance *a mata caballo.*

A MEDIO PASO *(ah MEH-dee-oh PAH-soh)*
See *bolero, robado.*

AMPURDANESA *(ahm-poor-dah-NEH-sah)*
(Of or from a district in Catalonia)

One of the two major styles of dancing the Catalonian *sardana*. This style moves clockwise, to the left, while the Selvata style moves in the opposite direction. The names are derived from the districts in which the styles originated.

See *sardana*.

ANDADURA *(ahn-dah-DOO-rah)*
(Gait, amble)

The character of the dancer's walk in performance.

ANDALUZ *(ahn-dah-LOOTH)*
(Of or from Andalusia; from the Arabic al-Andalus, Land of the Vandals)

Pertaining to Andalusia (or Andalucía), a region in southern Spain once comprising the kingdoms of Sevilla, Córdoba, Jaén, and Granada and now including the provinces of Almería, Cádiz, Córdoba, Granada, Huelva, Jaén, Málaga, and Sevilla. The region was named by the invading Moors.

ANTREXATA
See *cuarta*.

A PALO SECO *(ah PAH-lo SEH-coh)*
(To the accompaniment of a dry stick)

In flamenco dancing, signifying a dance performed to the sound of hand clapping (*palmas*), finger snapping (*pitos*), and general merrymaking (*jaleo*). Flamenco dances were originally performed without guitar music, and the term referred to the tapping of a cane or staff (*báculo*) on the floor, scraping the rungs of a wooden chair, or knocking on a tabletop with the knuckles to accompany the dance.

ARABESCO *(ah-rah-BEHS-coh)*
(In Arabic fashion)

A fanciful or ornamented movement reflecting Eastern influence.

See *filigrana, gracia, movimientos de las manos* (Basic Positions and Techniques)

ARIN-ARIN *(ah-REEN-ah-REEN)*
(light-light, agile-agile; Basque)
Also called *Basque jota*

A vital dance reflecting the Basque spirit of rejoicing. Although it is usually the last dance in the *aurresku*, a traditional suite of Basque dances, at times it is performed independently as part of a concert of Spanish dances.

See *aurresku*.

ARRODILLAR *(ah-roh-dee-LYAHR)*
(To kneel)

This term is applied generally to any kneeling action. It is used by men and women in all styles of Spanish dancing. The character of the action can range from a *caída* (sudden drop) onto one or both knees by a man in flamenco, to a gracious *reverencia* by a female bolero dancer (*bolera*), to a ritual of courtship in folk dancing.

See *arrodillarse, caída, reverencia baja.*

ARRODILLARSE *(ah-roh-dee-LYAHR-seh)*
(To set one's knee down, kneel)

A vigorous step, typical of the *jota aragonesa*, performed mostly by males. The movement is often used as a final step (*paso final*), as illustrated below.

Beg pos   Ct 3–1–2   Ct 1–2   *Paso final*

Beg pos	Feet—2nd; partners face each other. Arms—between 2nd and 5th (*folklórico*).
Ct 3–1	Turn left, dropping R knee to floor as R shoulder almost touches partner's R shoulder and R forearm moves across chest.
Ct 2	Hold.
Ct 3–1	Turn quickly to right on balls of both feet, staying low, until L shoulders almost touch; drop L knee to floor, changing arms to opposite positions (L across chest).
	Repeat all movements, reversed, keeping body low; do not rise and fall.

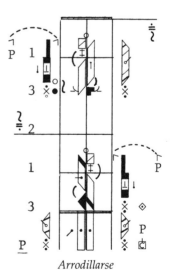

Arrodillarse

Males often perform the movement by first leaping into the air as a preparation to landing on one knee (ct 1). When performed in a series, the leap occurs only once, at the beginning. See *caída, reverencia al suelo, rodillazo, vuelta de rodillas*.

Ct: 3   1   2   3   1   2   3

ARTASI-OTSIKO *(ahr-TAH-see-ot-SEE-koh)*
(Scissors)

This energetic Basque step is the counterpart of a Spanish *fibraltada*, generally known as a hitch kick. *Artasi* is a low preparatory kick of the right leg followed by *otsiko*, a high kick of the left leg. Because of its extreme height and energy, it is performed only by men.

See *pasos vascos básicos, vuelta fibraltada*.

ASAMBLE
See *asamblé natural o sencillo*

ASAMBLE BATUDA *(ah-sahm-BLEH bah-TOO-dah)*
([The feet] joined while beating; *asamblé* borrowed from French *assemblé*)
Also called *paso unido*.

This beaten movement is typical of the *escuela bolera*.

Beg pos   Feet—5th L front.
          Arms—4th L up, head turned slightly
          to right.

  Ct &   Brush R leg to side, springing into air.
  Ct 1   Land 5th R front.
  Ct &   Spring into air, beating R leg back,
          L front.
  Ct 2   Land on L leg extending R leg to side.
          Step may move slightly to left.

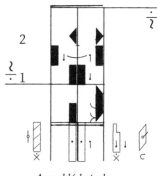

Asamblé batuda

See *batidos*

ASAMBLE HACIA ATRAS *(ah-sahm-BLEH AH-thee-ah ah-TRAHS)*
(Joined together by way of the back)
Also called *paso unido*.

The movement can be performed slowly and with much decorum, as in old court dances (*bailes palaciegos*). In this case the standing leg is bent (*semi-doblada*) during the side extension, then both knees straighten on the count of one, or vice versa. It can also serve as a link or to shift the weight between foot movements.

Beg pos Feet—3rd R front.
         Arms—4th L up.

   Ct & Extend R leg low to side.
   Ct 1 Close R leg into 3rd behind.

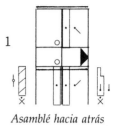

Asamblé hacia atrás

This movement can also be performed as in ballet, with a hop (*salto*) during the preparatory extension.

See *paso unido*.

ASAMBLE HACIA DELANTE *(ah-sahm-BLEH AH-thee-ah deh-LAHN-teh)*
(Joined together by way of the front)
Also called *paso unido*.

Beg pos Feet—3rd L front.
         Arms—4th L up.

   Ct & Extend R leg low to side as a
        preparation.
   Ct 1 Close R leg into 3rd front.

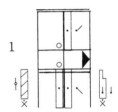

Asamblé hacia delante

This movement can also be performed as in ballet, with a hop (*salto*) during the preparatory extension.

See *asamblé hacia atrás, paso unido*.

ASAMBLE NATURAL O SENCILLO *(ah-sahm-BLEH nah-too-RAHL o sehn-THEE-lyoh)*
(Brought together, joined in a natural or easy manner; Hispanicized French)
Also called *paso unido* or simply *asamblé*.

A term describing a position in which the feet are brought together (usually into 1st, 3rd, or 5th position) from any previous position. These positions were used by the early dancing masters mostly in social dances (*danzas*) in which the exact positions of the feet and floor patterns (*caminos*) were more important than the arm movements. This term is not to be confused with the usual balletic term *asamblé*, which in Spanish dance would be called *asamblé saltado*. *Asamblé* is frequently used and is short for *asamblé natural o sencillo*.

ASENTADO *(ah-sehn-TAH-doh)* or Asentao *(ah-sehn-TAH-oh)*[1]
(Seated)

A basic stance, with relaxed or slightly bent knees, typical of Andalusian and flamenco dancing. The easy freedom in the knees makes possible the spiral flow of the body and the intricate rhythmic footwork (*zapateado*) typical of southern Spain. The term does not apply to folkloric dances or dances of the *escuela bolera*.

ASPULSAR *(ahs-pool-SAHR)*
(To shake, dust off; Catalonian)

A movement of the lower leg in which the knee is lifted forward and the foot is rhythmically shaken while the dancer hops on the opposite foot. This step, unique in Catalonian folk dancing, derives its name from the action of the foot, as if it were shaking off dust from the shoe. It is not to be confused with a *sacudida*.

See *sacudida*.

ATABALILLOS *(ah-tah-bah-LEE-lyos)*
(Little kettledrums)

This is an eighteenth-century step typical of the *seguidillas boleras*. Presumably the name is derived from the similar alternating pounding action of an *atabalero*, a player of tympani or kettledrums.

Beg pos Feet—1st.
         Arms—5th or between 2nd and 5th
         (*folklórico*).

   Ct 1 Step back on L foot extending R leg
         sideways, knee slightly bent.
   Ct 2 Make small hop (*saltito*) on L leg.
   Ct 3 Step back on R foot, swinging L leg
         sideways as in ct 1.
   Ct 4 Hop on R foot.
 Ct 5–6 Repeat first 2 cts.

   Arms

   Ct 1 Begin outward circle with L arm,
         passing through 2nd to low 5th front,
         beginning to incline torso very
         slightly to left.

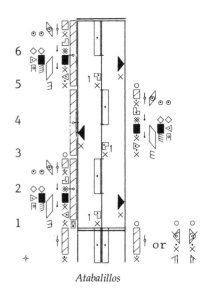

Atabalillos

[1]So pronounced by Flamencos. It is characteristic of Flamencos to drop the *d* sound.

Ct 2   Complete circle with L arm, arm mov-
       ing directly up center body line to
       5th, as torso completes inclination.
Ct 3   Begin outward circle with R arm,
       passing through 2nd to low 5th front,
       beginning to incline torso very
       slightly to left.
Ct 4   Complete circle with R arm, arm
       moving directly up center body line
       to 5th, as torso completes inclination.
Ct 5–6   Repeat first 2 cts.

When *folklórico* arm positions are used, the arms do not move, and the castanets are played in that position.

ATRAS *(ah-TRAHS)*
(Behind, in back of)

Describing the position of one foot in respect to the other or to positions of dancers in relation to each other. It is similar to the balletic term *derrière*.

ATZESKU *(ah-TSEHS-koo)*
(Left hand; Basque)

The last, or "tail," person in a line of male dancers, who sometimes link themselves together by holding hands or handkerchiefs.

See *aurresku*.

AURRESKU *(ah-oo-RREHS-koo)*
(From *aurre*, in front, before, and *ku*, hand; Basque)

Aurresku is a dance of greeting which introduces most Basque festivals. Its name is derived from the leading man (*aurresku*) in a line of dancers. His counterpart, on the end, is the *atzesku* (left hand, in Basque).

See *arín-arín, atzesku, cap y cua*.

AVANZAR *(ah-vahn-THAR)*
(To advance)

A term indicating that a step or a combination moves forward.

AVISO *(ah-VEE-soh)*
(Notice, warning)

In flamenco, a cue from the dancer warning the guitarist of a forthcoming change of rhythm. Such cues are usually previously rehearsed but can be spontaneous and may include any audible or visual signal, such as a stamping of the foot (*golpe de pie*), a hand wave, or a shout (*grito*).

See *llamada*.

BAILADORA *(bah-ee-lah-DOH-rah)*
(Female Gypsy dancer)

A seldom used term for a female who does Gypsy dancing instinctively, without formal training, and does not perform in legitimate theaters or concert halls. A *bailador* is the male equivalent.

BAILAORA *(bah-ee-lah-OHR-rah)*
(Female flamenco dancer)

One who specializes in flamenco dance. She may be a professional or an amateur, native-born or foreign. A *bailaor* is the male equivalent.

BAILARINA *(bah-ee-lah-REE-nah)*
(Female dancer)

A female dancer who has studied with more than one master and has a broad background, including years of study for a professional career, in several forms of Spanish dance (usually classical ballet, *escuela bolera, folklórico,* and often flamenco). A *bailarín* is the male equivalent.

BAILE *(BAH-ee-leh)*
(Dance)

The term *baile* has taken on a broader connotation since its original use in the 1800s. At that time a *baile* was a dance of a regional or *folklórico* type in which the upper torso and arms were used freely, almost at will, making air designs to accompany the actions of the feet *(pasos)*. It was distinguished from the word *danza,* which also meant dance, but one performed by the aristocracy and with more restricted action of the upper torso and limbs. Today *baile* no longer carries the early meanings. Social ballroom dancing or a Saturday night disco dance is referred to as *baile,* and a square dance is called *baile de figuras.* Dances presented in a theater are now called *danzas.*

See danza.

BAILE CHICO *(BAH-ee-leh CHEE-coh)*
(Little dance, light in quality)

A term applied to Andalusian and flamenco dances and songs which are light and gay in mood. These include *bulerías, farruca, guajira, rumba gitana, tanguillo, tientos canasteros, zambra, zarongo gitano,* and *alboréas. Baile chico* is the antithesis of *baile jondo* or *baile grande.*

BAILE CONTEMPORARIO
See *baile estilizado.*

BAILE CROTALORIO *(BAH-ee-leh croh-tah-LOH-ree-oh)*
(Dance with castanets)

Archaic term for *baile de palillos.*

See *baile de palillos, crotalogía.*

BAILE DE CASTAÑUELAS
See *baile de palillos.*

BAILE DE COFRADIA *(BAH-ee-leh deh coh-frah-DEE-ah)*
(Dances of brotherhood, sisterhood, confraternity)

Pilgrimage dances belonging to the church. These were slow, solemn processional dances performed as the dancers carried holy images or relics from one shrine to another. They were unlike any of the other dances of Spain, including those of the nobility (*bailes palaciegos*), or the recreational (*folklórico*) dances of the people. *Bailes de cofradía* were not always subdued and serious. Religious faith, with its many facets, is a principal characteristic of the Spanish people, and dances of joy, and at times grotesqueness, were not uncommon. To this day on major feast days choirboys, since the sixteenth century called *los Seises* (the Sixes)—although there are actually ten—still dance in period costumes while playing castanets at the high altar before the Holy Sacrament in the Cathedral of Seville.

BAILE DEL CANDIL *(BAH-ee-leh dehl cahn-DEEL)*
(Dance by candlelight; literally, dance of the oil lamp)[1]

This picturesque term refers to the dances of the eighteenth and nineteenth centuries, such as *sevillanas, seguidillas, boleros,* and *fandangos.* They were not dances of the theater but were first performed in small areas such as Andalusian patios and inns where friends and neighbors would gather on warm summer evenings. These intimate gatherings were later transformed into outdoor spectacles, and they have met worldwide acceptance as theater dances in today's repertoires.

BAILE DE PALILLOS *(BAH-ee-leh deh pah-LEE-lyohs)*
(Dance with castanets)
Also called *baile de castañuelas.*

This term refers especially to those Andalusian dances in which castanet playing has been an integral part since the eighteenth century.

See *baile crotalório.*

---

[1] Originally a *candil* was a wick placed in oil in a small vessel which was attached to a wall bracket or suspended overhead to give light for the improvised dancing. The present-day term for footlights is *candilejas.*

BAILE DE PLAZA *(BAH-ee-leh deh PLAH-thah)*
(Dance of the plaza, or square)

Originally a dance performed by the people outdoors in the plaza or village square. Many such dances were later adapted for the theater.

BAILE DE PRESENTACION *(BAH-ee-leh deh preh-sehn-tah-thee-OHN)*
(Dance of presentation)

A dance in vogue during the first part of the twentieth century. It was an introductory dance in which a female artist (or a couple) would present the opening number as an overture, so to speak, allowing the audience to gain an impression of her charm, wardrobe, personality, and demeanor. The *presentación* (presentation) was usually performed in an eye-catching costume, often with a large comb and lace mantilla which the artist would discard before beginning the main part of the dance.

See *compostura, gracia.*

BAILE DE ZAPATILLAS *(BAH-ee-leh deh thah-pah-TEE-lyahs)*
(Dance with pumps or heelless slippers)

Such a dance was so called because of the shoes the dancers wore. The slippers (*zapatillas*) were typical of the footwear worn in eighteenth- and nineteenth-century dances of the court and ballroom and later the theater. *Zapatillas* were light, soft, and pliable and were seldom expected to make an audible sound (*zapateado*). They were the forerunners of present-day pleated ballet slippers (which, incidentally, Spaniards call *zapatillas*).

BAILE ESTILIZADO *(BAH-ee-leh ehs-tee-lee-THAH-doh)*
(Stylized or contemporary dance)
Also called *baile contemporario, baile teatral.*

A term loosely used to refer to a style or "school" of Spanish dancing based on traditional folk, classic, or flamenco dances. Originally dances in this genre were choreographed for the concert stage to music that was not composed for dancing (*para bailar*). La Argentina (Antonia Mercé) in Europe and Carola Goya in America were the first to interpret the music of Isaac Albéniz, Enrique Granados, Ernesto Halffter, Joaquín Turina, and Manuel de Falla. Such dances were earlier referred to as "neoclassic" or "departures" but are now classified as *baile estilizado.*

Using this genre, many choreographers subsequently staged major ballets that were presented internationally by the companies of La Argentinita (Concepción López), Carmelita Maracci, Roberto Ximénez and Manolo Vargas, Luisillo, Roberto Iglesias, Antonio Gades, Antonio, and others. It is not to be inferred that this style is limited to group works. The limitations of this book prevent the acknowledgment of many choreographers and solo works that have been and are continuing to be created in *baile estilizado.*

BAILE GRANDE *(BAH-ee-leh GRAHN-deh)*
(Grand dance)
Also called *baile jondo* ("deep," serious, or profound dance).

A flamenco term for a dance that is of a primarily serious or profound mood. Examples are *cañas, polo, siguiriyas, soleares, taranto, tientos antiguos, rondeñas,* and *cerranas.*

BAILE INTERMEDIO *(BAH-ee-leh een-tehr-MEH-dee-oh)*
(Intermediate dance)

A term for flamenco dances, music, or songs which are neither wholly serious (*jondo, grande*) nor frivolous (*chico*) but whose character falls somewhere in between. These include *alegrías, peteneras, zapateado, caracoles, mirabrás, cantinas, rosas.*

See *baile chico, baile grande.*

BAILE JONDO
See *baile grande.*

BAILE NACIONAL *(BAH-ee-leh nah-thee-oh-NAHL)*
(National, native, or domestic dance)

Spain consists of fifty provinces that culturally overlap each other, and each district is proud of its local variation of the regional dance. *Baile nacional* includes an endless array of regional dances, such as *fandangos, jotas, boleros, seguidillas,* and their many variations. For centuries these very old folkloric dances were handed down from generation to generation and most of the time were performed outdoors. They were an integral part of all social and religious occasions such as holidays (*fiestas*), carnivals (*verbenas*), fairs (*ferias*), and religious pilgrimages (*romerías*). In time *baile nacional* became an important element of Spanish musical dramas (*zarzuelas*) and remains so today. Unlike the many solo flamenco and Andalusian dances of southern Spain, *baile nacional* for the most part consists of couple and group dances. Because of their immense variety of steps, rhythmic patterns, indigenous music, and regional costumes, the dances are adapted for the stage and included in most Spanish dance repertoires.

See *baile, baile de plaza, danza.*

BAILES PALACIEGOS *(BAH-ee-lehs pah-lah-thee-EH-gohs)*
(Dances of the palace or court)

Dances from as early as the fifteenth century which were performed indoors and were especially designed for the spacious rooms of the aristocracy and the royal court. Many of the dances were physically demanding. They were not limited to slow, measured steps; in fact, the rhythm of a *pavana* was usually followed by a spirited *gallarda.* It was not uncommon for male dancers to execute variations with high jumping and beating steps, spins, and somersaults for the admiration of the ladies. They were often accompanied by lute or harp or even with song or poetry.

See *danza, graves y breves, pavana.*

BAILE TEATRAL
See *baile estilizado*.

BALANCEADO *(bah-lahn-theh-AH-do)*
(Balanced, rocked)

A movement that shifts the balance from one foot to the other in waltz rhythm while remaining in place.

Beg pos   Feet—From any previous movement.
          Arms—Optional.

Ct 1   Step only slightly to side on R.
Ct 2   Step into 5th behind, taking weight
       on ball of L foot.
Ct 3   Step directly into 5th front, taking
       weight on R foot. Maintain even body
       level throughout. Do not bob up and
       down.

       Repeat to opposite side.
       Entire step is done in place (*en sitio*).

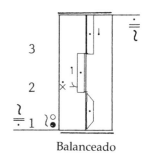

Balanceado

BALANCEADO CRUZADO *(bah-lahn-theh-AH-doh croo-THAH-doh)*
(Balanced, swayed in a crossed manner)

A movement which oscillates broadly and smoothly from side to side in waltz rhythm.

Bet pos   Feet—From any previous movement.
          Arms—Optional.

Ct 1   Step to side on R (*paso de lado*).
Ct 2   Cross L behind and beyond R taking
       weight on ball of L foot.
Ct 3   Return weight directly in place
       onto R.

       Maintain even body level throughout.
       Do not bob up and down.

       Repeat to opposite side.

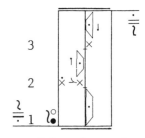

Balanceado cruzado

BALANCEO Y VAIVEN *(bah-lahn-THEY-oh ee vah-ee-VEHN)*
(Balancing and swaying)

Subtle movements typical of the female flamenco dancer (*bailaora*) which usually correspond to the more melodic sections (*falsetas*) of the guitar. These movements include inclining the torso in all directions, performing undulating movements of the rib cage (at times with a rhythmical accentuation), swaying gently from side to side, and slightly quivering the shoulders.

See *expresión, temblor de hombros, zarandeo.*

BALONE *(bah-loh-NEH)*
(Bounced or ball-like; from the French *ballonné*)

A step preferred by women, as it gracefully flourishes the skirt.

Ct &   1   2   3

Beg pos	Feet—in 3rd. Arms—in 4th L up.
Ct &	(Preparation) Extend R leg diagonally front with slight spring (*saltito*) into air.
Ct 1	Land on L as R foot flicks inward to L knee.
Ct 2	Slide R foot to right, taking weight (*sacado*).
Ct 3	Draw L foot to R 3rd back (*asamblé*).

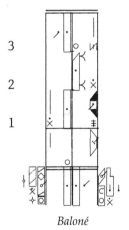

Baloné

Technically speaking, the first two counts comprise the *baloné*. However, it may be combined with other movements which travel in the direction of the raised foot (*progresivo*), such as that illustrated above, which was performed in nineteenth-century ballroom *danzas* as a *paso de mazurca*. It is similar to a balletic *ballonné*.

See *mazurca, retirado, sacado.*

Ct: &   1   2   3

BAMBOLEO *(bahm-boh-LEH-oh)*
(A swinging, swaying, or rocking)

An individual physical response to the rhythm of the music as one might react when watching others perform or awaiting one's turn to join in.

See *balanceo y vaivén, continencia, zarandeo.*

BASIC CASTANET RHYTHMS
Vals (Waltz)   3/4
   Both   Left   Roll
    1   2   &3

Sevillanas   6/8
   Left   Roll   Roll   Right
    1   &2   &3   &

Bolero   3/4
   Both   Left   Roll   Left   Roll   Both
    1   &   2   &   3   &

Pasodoble   2/4
   Both   Left   Roll   Both
    1   &   2   &

See *carretilla; golpe; palmas, pitos y castañuelas.* (Basic Positions and Techniques).

BASICO *(BAH-see-coh)*
(Basic, fundamental)

A term used to describe any exercise or dance movement in its simplest form. *Básico* is used interchangeably with *sencillo* (simple) or *natural* (natural).

See *natural, sencillo.*

BASICOS *(BAH-see-cohs)*
(Basics)

A term referring to those techniques required for learning rhythmic footwork (*zapateado*), arm movement (*braceo*), castanet playing (*toque*), various rhythms (*compases*), etc. *Básicos* are the rudimentary or fundamental movements needed in early dance curricula that can be identified, practiced, and mastered, first as simple variations and later with more complicated variations.

Although they are taught as warm-up and stamina-building exercises during the first lessons of Spanish dance, they are reviewed and "remastered" in daily technique classes on all levels.

See *ensayo al medio, natural, sencillo*. See also Appendix: Basic Flamenco Rhythms.

BASQUE JOTA
See *arín-arín*.

BATA DE COLA *(BAH-tah deh COH-lah)*
(A dress with a tail; a trailing gown)
Also called *traje de cola*.

The costume of a flamenco dancer (*bailaora*). It was originally a simple, full-length garment, usually with sleeves and with a small train (*cola*) and sometimes with a single narrow ruffle at the bottom edge. As with all other dresses of the Flamencas, the materials were limp and sagging. After the arrival of flamenco in the theater, a drastic evolution took place in the dress. The torso became extremely form-fitting and decolleté, while the skirt and *cola* were made of wide ruffles (*volantes*) which were at times so excessive in number and stiffness that, during the quiet portions of a dance, the rustling became distracting to the audience. The revealing lines of costumes was a radical departure from the modesty of the original *bata de cola*. In the most recent development, the shape of the skirt has returned to the soft flow of its original lines.

BATIDO *(bah-TEE-doh)*
(Beaten)

An all-inclusive term which classifies movements that can be beaten. It was applied to steps, mostly of the eighteenth and nineteenth centuries, which involved a simple beating of ankles or calves and required little or no elevation but were performed with rapidity and brilliance. Many of these fancy bits of footwork were done in such dances as the *seguidillas boleras* and other regional dances in everyday street shoes.

See *batimán, briseles, danza, seguidilla*.

BATIDOS *(bah-TEE-dohs)*
(Beaten steps)

The term *batidos* refers to steps which require technical training. They are for virtuosic display in the theater and are typical of the *escuela bolera*. Many dances were originally done with little or no beaten steps, but during the second half of the eighteenth century they were greatly influenced by the classical Italian school of ballet, and they soon began to acquire more elevation and beating steps (*batidos*) without losing the typical arm style and use of castanets.

See *batido, batuda, escuela bolera, vistoso*.

BATIMAN *(bah-tee-MAHN)*
(Beating, striking, or flapping motion)

The delicate, quick-beating movement about the ankle resembles a balletic *petit battement sur le coup de pied.*

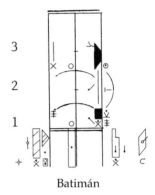

Batimán

Beg pos   Feet—Weight on L foot.
          Arms—4th L up, head turned slightly
          right, toros inclined sidewise over
          R leg.

    Ct 1   Lift R leg, ankle slightly flexed, and
          touch heel just below the L calf in
          back.
    Ct 2   Move R foot around to front, the heel
          touching just above the L ankle.
    Ct 3   With R leg touch ball of foot to right
          side, as L knee bends slightly.

BATIMAN CORTADO *(bah-tee-MAHN cor-TAH-doh)*
(Beating and cutting away action)

A cutting movement used in *escuela bolera* and regional (*folkórico*) dances.

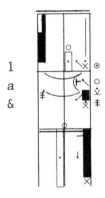

Batimán cortado

Beg pos   Feet—5th R front, weight on L.
          Arms—Optional.

    Ct &   Lift R foot, slightly flexed, to front
          of L ankle.
    Ct a   Move R foot around to behind
          L ankle.
    Ct 1   Step back onto 3rd with knee slightly
          bent, undercutting L foot, which extends forward and low.

BATIMAN SALTADO *(bah-tee-MAHN sahl-TAH-doh)*
(Beating, striking, or flapping with a hop)

This movement is the same as *batimán* except that a small hop (*saltito*) is made on each count on one foot while the other does the beating action. It is usually part of a longer phrase of steps as used in a *seguidilla.* The delicate, quick-beating movement near the ankle resembles a balletic *petit battement sur le coup de pied.*

Beg pos   Feet—Weight on L foot.
          Arms—4th L up, head turned slightly
          right, torso inclined sideways over   3
          right leg.

   Ct 1   Hop L (*saltito*) lifting R leg, ankle   2
          slightly flexed, and touching heel just
          below calf in back.
                                                       1
   Ct 2   Hop L moving R foot around to front,
          the heel touching just above the
          L ankle.
   Ct 3   Hop L extending R foot to right side
          as L knee bends slightly.

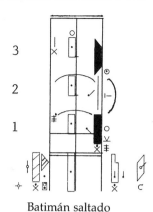

Batimán saltado

See *batimán*.

BATTUTA DEL CANARIO *(bah-TOO-tah dehl can-NAH-ree-oh)*
(Rhythmic beating step of the *canario;* from Italian *seguito de battuta* [series of
    stamps, scuffs, and brushes])

This step is of historical interest to the Spanish dance aficionado. It comes
from a popular sixteenth-century dance, the *canario,* which was characterized
by audible rhythmic footwork. This animated dance was said to have come
from the Canary Islands and was adapted by the Spaniards as a spirited dance
with advances and retreats. It is claimed to be the father of the *jota* and is included in many opera ballets by Raymond Lully. Its animated 3/8, 6/8, and
3/4 rhythm is that of the present-day *zapateado.*

Although eighteenth-century texts indicate that the movement for making
the audible stamping step (*battuta*) was a scuffing action similar to that of
pushing the foot into a *pantoufle* (a platform shoe or clog several inches high
capable of producing sound), one must surmise that with the development of
the heeled shoe this basic foot action evolved into the brushlike step *escobilla*
and later into the basic movements of today's rhythmic footwork (*zapateado*)
called *pica* or *punta.*

See *redoble andaluz* (Basic Positions and Techniques), *tacón raspado, tejida,*
    zapateado.

BATUDA *(bah-TOO-dah)*
(Springboard jumping contest)
Also called *tejido* (woven).

This term applies to a series of steps that involve beating the calves or ankles
and require considerable elevation.

See *bolero, cambiamientos bajos y altos, cuarta, vuelta volada.*

BIEN HECHO (*bee-EHN EH-choh*)
(Well done!)

A complimentary phrase audibly addressed to a soloist. After the dancer performs a sudden tour de force, such as spinning on the ball of one foot while executing a double broken turn (*vuelta quebrada doblada*) or quickly recovering from a drop to the floor (*caída*) to a vertical position or concludes a sequence of complicated footwork (*zapateado*), one will undoubtedly hear the exclamation, "¡Bien hecho!"

See *grito*.

BIEN PARADO (*bee-EHN pah-RAH-doh*)
(well stopped)

An expression referring to a sudden stop or suspension of movement— "posed action." It can occur within or at the end of a dance but traditionally comes at the end of each verse (*copla*) of partner dances such as *sevillanas* or *seguidillas*. It is usually preceded by a quick turn (*vuelta*) ending with partners facing each other at a slight angle, with left shoulders almost touching, arms in the fourth position with right arms up, the ball of the left foot slightly forward (*planta natural*).[1] In some old-style (*estilo antiguo*) dances the couples assumed the same pose, ending side by side facing front (*afrente*). "¡Bien parado!" is also used as an audible expression (*grito*) of approval.

See *estet, grito, planta, seguidilla, vuelta y figura*.

BISCAS (*BEES-cahs*)
(Crossed or squinted eyes)

A movement named after a Gypsy dancer of the late 1920s called La Bisca. It is a swaying movement (*zarandeo*) in which the knees, bent and held together, oscillate from side to side as the dancer advances on the balls of the feet. Technically this position, with bent knees together, is often referred to as *rodillas dobladas* (folded or bent knees).

See *zarandeo*.

BOLADILLO (*boh-lah-DEE-lyoh*)
(Meaning uncertain, possibly of Italian origin)

An archaic term for a turn or spin.

BOLERA (*boh-LEH-rah*)
(A female bolero dancer)

BOLERAS
See *bolero*.

---

[1] It is interesting to note that on the last note of the final step (*paso final*) in similar dances farther north, such as *seguidillas manchegas* (from which the Andalusian *las sevillanas* derived), one foot is held in the air.

BOLERO (*boh-LEH-roh*)
(From *volar*, to fly)

By the end of the eighteenth century the popularity of this dance was nothing less than phenomenal, reaching the proportions of a mania. There were *bolero* academies throughout southern Spain. Young and old were possessed by the bravura of its steps, and it was just as popular in the ballroom as it was on the stage. Originally it was a dance of the people performed in triple meter and at a moderate speed. Castanets were played, and the dance usually consisted of four verses (*coplas*). Soon the Italian dancing masters began to superimpose balletic technique on this popular dance, adding jumps, beats, flying turns, and much adornment, refining and polishing it to the point that by the time it reached the theater it had become a brilliant execution of highly developed steps by trained dancers. The *bolero* was such a historic milestone in Spanish dance that it was considered Spain's national dance; hence the term *escuela bolera* (bolero school, or style).

The forms of the *bolero* are many and varied, and their names are legion, each depending on the time and place of origin, the music, the choice of steps, and the maestro who choreographed it. However, in its basic form the dance is divided into three parts: (1) *introducción* (introduction, beginning), which consists of the dancer's first appearance making a promenade (*paseo de salida*) before actually beginning the dance, followed by a turn and getting into position (*vuelta y colocación*); (2) *adorno* (adornment, embellishment), the dancer's favorite steps of the *escuela bolera* in combinations of his or her choice; and (3) *exaltación* (exaltation, elevation), the final phase of the dance, which displays several tour de force steps, including jumps, leaps, and beaten and spinning steps.

As a theater dance, the *bolero* was often danced by women in toe shoes (*en puntas*), a direct influence of the Italian and French classical schools.

As a theater presentation, the classical bolero (*bolero clásico*) can be performed either solo or alternating with a partner or by several couples performing alternately and adjusting the tempo to the variation being performed. When dancers alternate their variations, the style is referred to as stolen (*robado*) or at half pace (*de medio paso*).

The term *boleras* is different from *bolero,* although the timing of *boleras* is taken from the latter, and it is generally used in the theater to represent Andalusians or happy, animated people. *Boleras* are in the nature of dance songs, and *bolero* is the dance proper. The terms are not unique to Spain. Both are common in Mallorcan dance.

See *baile de palillos, batidos, batuda, cambiamientos bajos y altos, escuela bolera, lazos, liso, oposiciones, paso del demonio, robado.*

BORDONEO (*bor-doh-NEH-oh*)
(Embroidery; pretty, artistic movements)

One of the most delicate of Spanish dance steps and typical of Valencia, this step was often referred to as the "lace maker's step" because the minute heel-toe action depicted the dainty lace border on a petticoat or dress. Still in use, it is one of the best-remembered steps of Fanny Elssler in her famous "La

Cachucha." In some folkloric dances the body is allowed to oscillate, causing the woman's skirt to sway.

| Beg pos | Ct 1 | Ct 2 | Ct 3 |

Beg pos Feet—3rd or 5th, R front.
          Arms—4th, L up; torso inclined from
          waist over R thigh.

Ct 1 Step L to side.
Ct 2 Pivoting on R heel, face R toe inward.
Ct 3 Pivoting on R sole, end R heel in 3rd
      or 5th.

      Repeat above several times, traveling
      to left.

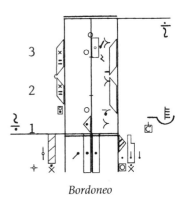

Bordoneo

Allegretto

Ct: 1 2 3

BORNEO *(bohr-NEH-oh)*
(Swinging, twisting)

A general term applied to body movements or steps such as *bordoneos, paraditas,* and *tortillés* which display the action of swinging, turning, or twisting.

See *bordoneo, paraditas, torcido.*

BOSQUEJO *(bohs-KEH-hoh)*
(Sketch)

An intimate, lifelike theatrical representation of regional characters and situations re-created in traditional scenes of village life. The greatest contributor of such miniature masterpieces to the concert stage was La Argentinita (Concepción López).

BRACEAR *(brah-theh-AHR)*
(To swing the arms)

To swing the arms in a free style or manner that is typically Spanish and, in spite of its apparent ease, is difficult to perform. Often accompanied with castanet playing, it is used mostly by women in a *paseo de gracia, entrada,* or *salida.*

See *entrada, paseo de gracia, paso doble, salida.*

BRACEO *(brah-THEH-oh)*
(Movement or carriage of the arms)

Probably the most obvious element that gives Spanish dance, especially Andalusian dance, its unmistakable ethnic or national character is the style in which the arms are held or moved—its *braceo.* This term has at least four meanings:

1. Continuous movement of one or both arms passing from one position to another or through a series of positions.[1]

2. A classroom term for a set of exercises to help the arms move in a flowing and harmonious manner, an action which should originate not from the shoulder socket but from the center of the back (between the shoulder blades).[2]

3. A certain section of a dance (such as a *paseo* or a *castellana* following various patterns of rhythmic footwork in an *alegrías*) which features the arms (*brazos*) and upper torso.

4. A traditional or characteristic manner in which the arms are held, as in many regional (*folklórico*) dances.[3] Such folkloric positions of the arms vary from one region or province to another. They include those in which the arms are (*a*) held aloft and widespread (between second and fifth positions), (*b*) held shoulder-high and squared off at the elbows, with forearms held ver-

[1] Whereas in ballet the arms often pass through a central position nicknamed the "gateway" (a curved position of the arms in front of the chest commonly known as first position), in Spanish dance they do not. If Andalusian dance were to have a similar "key" through which most arm movements pass, it might be thought of as fifth (*quinta* or *corona*), above the head. This is true of the *escuela bolera.* Although this style is based on classical-ballet technique, it maintains its Spanish identity through the distinctive carriage of the arms (*braceo*).
[2] Each instructor has his or her own approach in teaching *braceo.* It can vary from an extemporaneous "follow-the-leader" method using improvised movements or free-style carriage of the arms with delicate, subtle movements of the wrists and fingers (*filigranas*) in teaching flamenco, to an organized series of exercises set to music and performed with castanets in teaching Andalusian and classical dance.
[3] Although generally not considered basic classic positions, each typifies the indigenous character of its particular region.

tically, (*c*) hanging down at the sides with elbows slightly bent and palms up when playing castanets, and (*d*) with elbows bent and hands resting on the hips (*en jarras*).

Although the term refers to moving the arms in a harmonious manner, the connotation is usually female. Most of the great entertainers of the past (many of whom were *tonadilleras*, female singers of light, witty songs such as Pastora Imperio, Raquel Meller, and Lola Flores) were immortalized by Spaniards for the beauty and artistry of their *braceo*. The term has its counterpart or function in ballet as *port de bras*.

See *baile nacional, braceo de escuela bolera, brazos básicos* (Basic Positions and Techniques), *corona, escobilla, silencio, tonadillera.*

BRACEO DE ESCUELA BOLERA *(brah-THEH-oh deh es-CWEH-lah boh-LEH-rah)*
(Movement or carriage of the arms of the *escuela bolera*)

The arm movement (*braceo*) accompanying all steps and combinations (*pasos y compuestos*) of the eighteenth- and nineteenth-century *escuela bolera* is synonymous with the balletic *port de bras* in its own usage and style.

Beg pos   Feet—5th or 3rd.
          Arms—5th (*corona*).

          Circle curved arms out and down, passing through 2nd; then rotate lower arms out so that backs of hands face each other (not touching)[1] as they reach low 5th (front) (*quinta baja afrente*). Continue to move them directly up midline of body, returning to 5th overhead (*corona*).

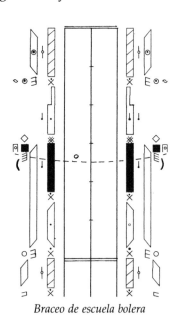

Braceo de escuela bolera

See *braceo, brazos básicos,* (Basic Positions and Techniques), *corona.*

---

[1]This flexed position of the hands back to back is often seen during practice classes when the instructor counts aloud with no music and castanets are not being played. In reality, during the actual dance, as seen in lithographs and photographs of this period, the wrists maintain a slight curve while the dancer plays castanets.

BRAZOS BASICOS
See page 3.

BRINCO
See *salto*.

BRINCOS *(BREEN-cohs)*
(Leaps, jumps, hops, bounces)

A term for the leaping, hopping actions in folkloric dances.

BRISE *(bree-SEH)*
(Broken; French)

This movement is similar to a balletic *brisé*. The footwork and term were introduced to classical Spanish dancing by French and Italian dancing masters. In Spanish terms, it is fundamentally an *asamblé saltada al diagonal batuda*, and, as in classical ballet, it is one of the many *brisé* variations of the *escuela bolera*.

Beg pos	Feet—Standing on L foot, R leg extended diagonally forward right. Arms—4th L up, head slightly turned to right.	
Ct &	Spring into air extending L leg diagonally forward, beating it behind R leg.	
Ct 1	Land on R foot, L leg remaining extended.	

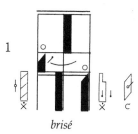

brisé

See *batido*, *batuda*.

BRISELES *(bree-SEH-lehs)*
(Breakings, broken movements; from French *brisé*, Hispanicized as plural noun)

One of the several *brisé* combinations of the *escuela bolera*.

Beg pos	Feet—5th R front. Arms—5th.
Ct &	Extend R leg low to side.
Ct 1	Close R into 5th behind and extend L leg low to side.
Ct &	Spring into air, beating legs underneath, L leg front, R leg behind.
Ct 2	Land to left side in 5th R front.
Ct &	Spring into air, beating R leg behind, L leg front.
Ct 3	Land on R foot, extend L leg low to side.

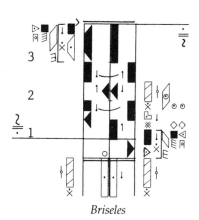

Briseles

Arms

Ct &–1   Circle R arm out and down, passing through 2nd to 5th low front.

Ct &–2   Move R arm up midline of body, returning to 5th.

Ct 3   Circle L arm out and down, passing through 2nd.

Repeat reversed from ct 1.

See *brisé*.

BRISELES DEL SOUSSOU *(bree-SEH-lehs dehl soo-SOO)*
(Hispanicized version of French *brisé dessus dessous*, broken over under)

The names of several classical ballet beating steps (*batidos*) were incorporated into the *escuela bolera*, but with changes in their execution.

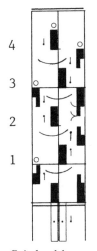

Beg pos   Feet—5th R front.
Arms—Optional.

Preparation—Lift R leg forward and spring into air, lifting L leg to beat R leg from behind.

Ct 1   Land on R leg, L leg remaining extended forward.

Ct &   Spring into air, lifting R leg forward to beat L leg from behind.

Ct 2   Land on L, R leg remaining extended forward.

Ct &   Swing R leg back and spring into air, lifting L leg back to beat R leg from front.

Ct 3   Land on R, L leg remaining extended behind.

Ct &   Spring into air, lifting R leg back to beat L leg from front.

Ct 4   Land on L, R leg remaining extended behind.

Briseles del soussou

BULERIA FLAMENCA *(boo-leh-REE-ah flah-MEHN-cah)*
(*Bulería* rhythm in Gypsy fashion)

A fancy version of a bulería rhythm with a syncopated effect. Usually performed as a closing step at a quickened speed.

Beg pos | Feet—1st parallel, facing slightly to left.
Arms—5th.

Ct 5 | Touch L heel slightly diagonally forward.
Ct 6 | Step on ball of L foot behind R heel.
Ct 1 | Step on R foot in front of L foot.
Ct 2 | Step on L beside R foot.
Ct 3 | Drag ball of R foot, taking weight behind L heel.
Ct 4 | Step on L foot in front of R foot.

Repeat all to opposite side. Rhythmic emphasis is on cts 5 and 6, which should begin entire rhythmic pattern (*compás*), i.e., 5, 6, 1, 2, 3, 4, etc.

Arms
Cts 2 3 | With R arm make complete outward
4 5 6 1 | circle, passing through 2nd, 5th low front, returning up midline of body to 5th, body turning slightly to right, head facing front.

Bulería flamenca

See *bulerías, compás de bulerías*.

BULERIAS *(boo-leh-REE-ahs)*
(Ridicule, mockeries, laughs, jokes)
Also called *fiesta*.

Bulerías are among the most jovial and happiest items in the flamenco repertory and are often presented as a vivacious combination of song and dance performed in a gay, frivolous (*baile chico*) manner. Their structure resembles the *jaleo* from Jerez, the city whose Gypsies are credited with having a special flare for performing them. The *bulerías* lend themselves to improvisation (*improvisación*) more than any other dance in flamenco. Their meter is in triple time, their tempo is lively, and guitarists agree that their performance (*toque*) requires maintenance of the most intricate and technically demanding rhythm (*compás*) in flamenco dancing. It is difficult to believe that as late as 1898 the flamencologist Francisco Marín called *bulerías* a vulgarization of flamenco. The term *por bulerías* refers to a departure from the traditional way of playing *bulerías* and indicates that some element of popular Latin American song has been adapted to its catchy rhythm.

See *bulería flamenca, chico, chufla*. See also Appendix: Basic Flamenco Rhythms.

BULERIA SENCILLA *(boo-leh-REE-ah sen-THEE-yah)*
(Basic *bulería* step)

A basic rhythmic foot pattern (*zapateado*) used when the rhythm of *bulerías* is introduced and from which more complicated variations (*variaciones*) can follow.

Beg pos   Feet—1st parallel.
          Arms—Man grips the edge of his jacket, elbows out; woman uses free style (*filigranas*), head turned slightly to right.

Ct 1   Step R.
Ct 2   Step on ball of L foot (beside R foot).
Ct &   Drop heel of L foot.
Ct 3   Step R.
Ct 4   Step on ball of L foot (beside R foot).
Ct &   Drop heel of L foot.
Ct 5   Step R.
Ct 6   Stab L heel beside R foot.

The step is done in place (*en sitio*), but the dancer may move on a very slight curve (*media luna*) right, accenting cts 6 and 1.

Repeat reversed.

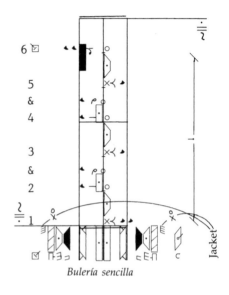

Bulería sencilla

See *bulerías, tiempo de, tiempo de bulería.* See also Appendix: Basic Flamenco Rhythms.

BURPIL
See *pasos vascos básicos (grabiletia).*

CABALLITO *(cah-bah-LYEE-toh)*
(Little horse, pony)

This step is typical of some *jotas.* When performed at a lively tempo, it resembles the galloping action of the small animal for which it is named.

Beg pos   Feet—From any previous action.
          Arms—L between 2nd and 5th
          (*folkórico*), R in 1st, but lower, chest
          inclined slightly left and diagonally
          back, head turned slightly right.

Ct 1   Step L into 3rd behind.
Ct 2   Give small hop (*saltillo*) on L as
       R knee bends and lifts.
Ct 3   Step diagonally forward on heel of
       R foot.

       Repeat above several times, traveling
       diagonally (*al diagonal*) to right.

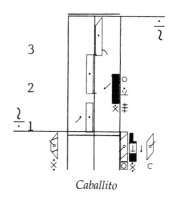

Caballito

CABALLO
See *campanela*.

CABALLO FOLKLORICO (*cah-BAH-lyoh folk-LOH-ree-coh*)
(Horse step in folkloric style)
Also called *a caballo* (on horseback).

This step is typical of the *jota aragonesa*.

Beg pos   Feet—3rd R front, partners facing.
          Arms—L arm a little lower than 1st,
          R arm between 2nd and 5th
          (*folklórico*).

Ct 1   Stepping on R, lift L knee hip height.
Ct 2   Hop on R, turning one-quarter right
       until left side is toward partner's left
       side.
Ct 3   Step forward on L.
Ct 4   Stepping on R, lift L knee hip height.
Ct 5   Hop on R, turning one-quarter left
       until facing partner.
Ct 6   Close L into 3rd behind.

       Ct 1 and ct 4 are heavily accented
       (*marcado*), and knees are very slightly
       bent throughout.

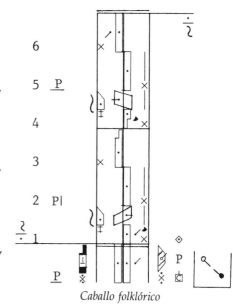

Caballo folklórico

CABRIOLA (*cah-bree-OH-lah*)
(Goat leap, caper)
Also called *zapateta* (slap on sole of shoe or leap).

This step is one of the most energetic in all of regional Spanish dancing and is often used as the most spectacular (*más vistoso*) by dancers doing it in a series (*corrida*), advancing downstage in a crescendo as the last step (*paso final*).

Ct 1   Ct 2   Ct 3   *Cabriola entera*

Beg pos Feet—From any previous action.
         Arms—Between 2nd and 5th
         (*folklórico*).

Ct 1   Step L across R (*paso cruzado*) and ex-
         tend R leg, knee bent, to side.
Ct 2   Spring high into air, beating L heel to
         R heel.
Ct 3   Land on L.
         Repeat above, reversed.

         The male *cabriola*, in contrast to the
         female, is higher (*entera*), the dancer
         often striking the soles of his sandals
         (*alpargatas*) together. The female
         cabriola is lower (*media*), and she
         strikes her heels.

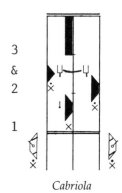

Cabriola

See *a lo alto, cabriola entera, más saltadora.*

CABRIOLA ENTERA *(cah-bree-OH-lah en-TEH-rah)*
(*Cabriola* done in a robust, vigorous way)

One of the most spectacular (*vistoso*) steps in folkloric dance, in which the male jumps high into the air, beats the soles of his sandals (*alpargatas*) together and completely extends one leg (*entera*) before returning to the floor. It is illustrated under the entry for *cabriola*, above.

Beg pos   Feet—From any previous action.
               Arms—Between 2nd and 5th
               (*folklórico*).

   Ct 1   Step L across R and extend R leg,
            knee bent, to side.
   Ct 2   Spring high into the air beating the
            sole of L foot against sole of R foot.
   Ct &   Extend R leg completely, high to side.
   Ct 3   Land on L.

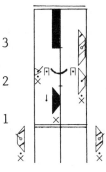

Cabriola entera

See *cabriola* (plate).

CACHUCHA *(cah-CHOO-chah)*
(Small cap, a term of endearment)

A dance of the early nineteenth century made famous by the Austrian ballerina Fanny Elssler, who first danced it in 1836 at the Paris Opera. She was hailed as "the Spaniard from the North," and her vivacity, passionate temperament, and skillful actions in winning an audience (*provocativos*) made her the legendary figure she is today. The *cachucha* not only electrified audiences but also became dance history involving many imitators and romantic (but true) accounts of rivalry, jealousy, and competition. It is danced in the balletic style of the eighteenth century (*escuela bolera*) in 3/8 time, and although it was not, choreographically speaking, spectacular (*vistoso*), Charles de Boigne, in his *Petit memoires de l'opera* (Paris, 1857), told how this simple but charming dance won its way to fame: "The real public needed several performances to become accustomed to the *Cachucha*. The contortions, the movements of the hips, the provocative gestures, the arms which seem to seek and embrace an absent lover, the mouth crying out for a kiss, the thrilling, quivering, twisting body, the captivating movements, the castanets, the strange costume, the shortened skirt, the low cut, half-open bodice, and all Elssler's sensual grace, lascivious abandon and plastic beauty were very much appreciated by the opera-glasses of the orchestra stalls and side boxes. The public, the real public, found it more difficult to accept those choreographic audacities, those exaggerated looks, and it can be said that it was the *loges infernal* which forced the success on this occasion. The French Cachucha is not a natural, inborn taste; it is an acquired taste."

The *cachucha* was saved for posterity by Friedrich Zorn in his own form of notation and published in 1887. Fortunately, after Elssler's retirement in 1851 and more than a century in oblivion, the original Zorn notation was painstakingly deciphered and translated into Labanotation, staged many times as a theater piece, and taught in dance education curricula by Ann Hutchinson. The dance is fully recorded in her *Fanny Elssler's Cachucha* (New York, 1981).

See *paso de cachucha, provocativo*.

CADENA *(cah-DEH-nah)*
(Chain)
Also called *pasamano* (banister, literally, passing of hands).

A term for a movement similar to the European and American "grand right and left" used in eighteenth- and nineteenth-century social dances (*danzas*) and regional folk dances.

CADENCIA
See *cierre*.

CAIDA *(cah-EE-dah)*
(Fall, drop)

There are many kinds of *caídas*, especially for men in flamenco and Andalusian dance. They are seen mostly in *farrucas*. Some are preceded by a rapid turn (*vuelta*) to make the fall (*caída*) even more effective. In another version the dancer (*bailaor*) takes a few very short running steps (*carrerillas*), falls, and slides some distance on both knees. This was an applause-getting stunt popular in the 1950s. Another variation occasionally seen in the past was one in which both feet were thrown out to one side as the dancer plummeted to the floor, where he landed sidelong on the hand of the opposite side with his free hand extended upward. Fortunately such cheer-evoking gimmicks have, for the most part, disappeared from the repertory.

By no means are *caídas* used exclusively by men as show stoppers. Women use them, although usually less abruptly, by employing a circular movement (*vuelta*), then descending in a less forceful fashion than men, allowing their skirts to lie dramatically on the floor encircling their kneeling figures.

CAMADA *(cah-MAH-dah)*
(Kick; Catalonian)

A kicking or leg-swinging action.

CAMADA RODEÑA *(cah-MAH-dah roh-DEH-nyah)*
(Circular kick; Catalonian)

A circular or fanlike kick or swinging of the leg. The *camada rodeña* can be done both inwardly (*adentro*) and outwardly (*afuera*).

CAMBIAMIENTOS *(cahm-bee-ah-mee-EHN-tohs)*
(Exchanging, switching [of the feet])

A springing step. From either 3rd or 5th position the dancer springs into the air, changing his feet, and then lands gently in either 3rd or 5th position with the opposite foot in front. *Cambiamientos* can be low (*bajos*) or high (*altos*) and may be compared with balletic *changements de pieds*. Although these buoyant movements are usually associated with dances of the *escuela bolera* and certain folkloric dances, the same action is at times adapted into flamenco, when it is performed on the balls of the feet (*media planta*) and close to the floor in groups of two followed by a brief hesitation. It is used for an audible rhythmic accentuation rather than elevation. The term is short for *cambiamientos de pies* and in turn is usually shortened to *cambios*.

See *cambiamientos bajos y altos, saltado*.

CAMBIAMIENTOS BAJOS Y ALTOS *(cahm-bee-ah-mee-EHN-tohs BAH-hos ee AHL-tohs)*
(Changing [of the feet] low and high)
Also called *paso de exaltación* (step of exaltation, elevation, excitement).

This step is usually performed with much bravura (*vistoso*), especially in the *bolero*. It resembles a balletic *pas ciseaux* or *écart en l'air*. It is often performed in more complicated patterns than those shown below, such as three low (*bajos*) and one high (*alto*), the legs making a pattern of four movements against the triple meter of the music. This exhausting step, with arms alternating from 4th to 5th, is accompanied by the dancer playing a marked rhythm on the castanets, making it a virtuosic and spectacular last step (*paso final*) and establishing it as a tour de force, evoking applause and "exaltation."

Ct & 1 & 2 & 3   & 4 & 5 &   6

Beg pos   Feet—5th R front, firmly pointed
           when in air.
           Arms—4th to 5th to 4th.   6

Ct &   Jump into air.
Ct 1   Land in 5th L front.   5
Ct &   Jump into air.
Ct 2   Land in 5th R front.   4
Ct &   Jump into air.
Ct 3   Land in 5th L front.
Ct &   Jump into air, throwing legs apart.   3
Ct 4   Land in 5th R front.
Ct &   Jump into air, throwing legs apart.   2
Ct 5   Land in 5th L front.
Ct &   Jump into air, throwing legs apart.   1
Ct 6   Land in 5th R front.

See *bolero, paso final, robado, variaciones.*

Cambiamientos bajos y altos

Ct: &   1   &   2   &   3   &   4   &   5   &   6   &

CAMBIAMIENTOS DE PIES
See *cambiamientos.*

CAMBIO *(CAHM-bee-oh)*
(Change, shift)

Any change (*cambio*) in dance accompaniment, such as singing (*cante*), music
(*toque*), and hand clapping (*palmas*) which alters or modifies the pace, rhythm,
or mood of a dancer's movements. When used in the plural (*cambios*), the term
also refers to a series of quick alternating strokes of the right and left castanets.

   Choreographically, the term indicates a jump from third or fifth position to
the same position with the other foot in front.

CAMBIOS
See *cambiamientos, diferencia.*

CAMBIOS BAJOS *(CAHM-bee-ohs BAH-hohs)*
(Low changes [of the feet])

A movement similar to the balletic *petit changement de pieds.*

Beg pos	Feet—5th R front.	
	Arms—5th or 4th L up.	
	Preparation—Knees slightly bent.	

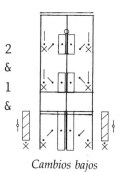

Cambios bajos

Ct &	Jump vertically into air, just clearing floor.
Ct 1	Land in 3rd L front.
Ct &	Jump vertically into air, just clearing floor.
Ct 2	Land in 3rd R front.

CAMINO (cah-MEE-noh)
(Path, road)

A term applied to the various floor patterns used in society, ballroom, and court dances (*danzas*) of the eighteenth and nineteenth centuries. These sometimes elaborate floor patterns were used in such early ballroom dances as *contradanzas* and *cuadrillas* as well as in partner or solo dances such as *folies d'espagne*. The term is derived from the chalk markings drawn by the dancing master on the floor indicating the direction or path (*camino*) the dancer was to follow in learning a dance. *Caminos* could vary from single circles (*ruedas*) to exotic forms bearing the names *amores y ventanillos* (amours and little windows), *la pirámide* (the pyramid), *la copa de champagne* (the champagne glass) and patterns depicting *las flores* (the flowers), *cadena japonesa* (Japanese chain), and *molino de viento* (windmill). Manuscripts of the period in which these *caminos* were recorded have become invaluable guides for the reconstruction of many forgotten dances.

See *figura*, *mudanza*.

CAMPANAS (cahm-PAH-nahs)
(Bells)

Musical notes (usually four, played by the guitarist during an *alegrías*) which resemble the gentle ding-dong sounds of bell ringing (*campaneo*) before variations of rhythmic footwork on the same theme are introduced.

CAMPANELA (cahm-pah-NEH-lah)
(Bell, bell shape)
Also called *caballo* because its circular leg-lifting action resembles that of mounting a horse (*caballo*).

The action below is the classical version of Esquivel de Navarrho (a nineteenth-century Spanish dancing master), deriving its name from the leg motion outlining the circumference of a bell-shaped farthingale. Another classical version, that of the sixteenth-century Italian Fabritio Caroso, suggests that the straight leg swings forward and back like the clapper of a large bell similar to a balletic *battement en cloche*.

Beg pos   Ct 1–2   Ct 3   Ct 4–5   Ct 6

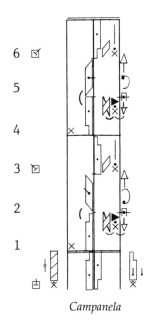

Beg pos   Feet—4th R back, facing audience,
          knees slightly bent.
          Arms—4th L up.   6 ☑

  Ct 1–2 Step on L in place and pivot left (to   5
          face left downstage corner) as R leg,
          knee bent, lifts and describes a large
          semicircle.   4

    Ct 3 Step onto R, bending knee slightly.
  Ct 4–5 Reverse above semicircular pattern
          with R leg by stepping onto L in place   3 ☑
          and pivoting right (to face downstage
          right corner).   2

    Ct 6 Step R back, bending knee slightly.

          The folkloric version of *campanela* has   1
          a small hop on ct 2 and on ct 5.

Campanela

See *caballo folklórico, campanela folklórica.*

Ct: 1 2 3   4 5 6

CAMPANELA FOLKLORICA *(cahm-pah-NEH-lah folk-LOH-ree-cah)*
(Bell-like step in regional style)

This regional (folkloric) version of the *campanela*, with its side-to-side swinging motion, resembles that of a bell or its clapper.

Beg pos   Feet—R knee raised forward to hip
             level, foot hanging relaxed.
             Arms—between 2nd and 5th
             (*folklórico*).

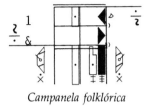

Campanela folklórica

   Ct &   Knee remains in place as lower leg
             swings to right.
   Ct 1   Lower leg swings to left.
             Repeat above.

             In a variation called *salto y campanela*
             the dancer gives a small hop (*saltillo*)
             on each ct 1.

See *campanela*.

CAMPANEO *(cahm-pah-NEH-oh)*
(Bell ringing)

A gait or sway used in mime or character dancing. Its name is derived from the to-and-fro swinging motion of a bell (*campana*).

CANARIO
See *battuta del canario*.

CANTAOR
See *cante jondo*.

CANTE JONDO *(CAHN-teh HOHN-doh)*
(Deep, serious, profound song, singing)
Also called *cante grande*.

The foundation or cornerstone of flamenco dance. *Cante jondo,* vocal flamenco music, must be constructed on principles of aesthetics and logical sequence, namely the setting, the lead into the theme, the development of the theme or inciting force, the climax, and the denouement. The following structure is apparent to the aficionado if not to the average audience:

1. *Temple:* a warming up to the basic rhythm without using words, only modulations on the sound "Ay!"
2. *Planteo* or *tercio de entrada:* the plan, statement, or entrance section.
3. *Tercio grande* (large section): the major part and theme.
4. *Tercio de alivio* (section of alleviation, relief): an easing of the emotional involvement in the main section.

5. *Tercio valiente* or *peleón* (section of evaluating, quarrel or struggle): the personal touch leading to the conclusion.
6. *Cambio* or *remate* (change or closing): the closing either with a variation of the basic theme or a change to a similar song (*cante*) to terminate it.

In flamenco singing (*cante flamenco*) it is characteristic to elongate certain words at times beyond recognition, using many notes to maintain the basic rhythm (*compás*) and still create a dramatic effect. This type of singing is called *melisma*.

Complete mastery of and personal involvement in these aspects, along with an untrained, rasping voice known as *voz afilla* or *voz raja*, are the ideal tools for *cante flamenco*.

See *duende, expresión, farfulleos, jondo, letra, tonadillera, zarzuela.*

CAP Y CUA *(CAHP ee COO-ah)*
(Head and tail; Catalonian)

The first or "head" dancer and the last or "tail" dancer of a group.

CARACOL *(cah-rah-COHL)*
(Snail)

A floor pattern (*camino* or *figura*) named for the coiling, spiraling design of a snail's shell. In flamenco the term refers to a choreographed pattern of encircling, intertwining, passing, and repassing movements (frequently a figure eight) which one or two dancers follow while maintaining the slow basic rhythm (*compás*) of dances such as *soleares*. The term is also applied to a favorite spiraling floor pattern in certain eighteenth- and nineteenth-century set dances (*danzas*) of the ballroom. These *caracoles* required numerous people to perform them.

See *camino, figura, mudanza.*

CARACOLES *(cah-rah-COH-lehs)*
(Snails)
Also called *mirabrás.*

A *baile intermedio* with a rhythmic cycle (*compás*) similar to an *alegrías* but with a less set structure and conditioned by the song (*cante*) of twelve counts. Its name may have come from the old song "La Caracolera" ("The Snail Vendor"). The term is also used as a friendly exclamation (*grito*) of wonder, surprise, or pleasure by a *jaleador* in behalf of a performing artist.

See *alegrías, baile intermedio, flamenco, grito, jaleador.* See also Appendix: Basic Flamenco Rhythms.

CARAMILLO *(cah-rah-MEE-lyoh)*
(Small flute, flageolet)

A small but very important folk instrument used to accompany folkloric dances. It is sometimes used alone and sometimes as a companion to other instruments with quite different timbres. Its clear pastoral sound usually alerts the dancers to assemble or to prepare for the introductory steps of a dance (*salida*). It has its counterpart in various northern regions of Spain in the Catalonian *flaviol* and the Galician and Basque *txistu*.

CAREO *(cah-REH-oh)*
(Meeting face to face)

Although this step is used in other Spanish dances, it is traditionally performed four times at the end of the fourth *copla* of the *sevillanas*.

| Beg pos | Ct 1 | Ct 2–3 | Ct 6 |

Beg pos   Feet—3rd L front, couples stand as shown. Directions are for dancer facing upstage (with back to reader). Arms—4th, partners look at each other.

Ct 1   Step sideways onto L foot.

Ct 2   Draw R foot to 3rd position behind L, taking weight on ball of foot.

Ct 3   Step in place, L foot taking weight.

Ct 4   Step forward R, beginning to make a half turn left.

Ct 5   Continuing left turn, step L 3rd back on ball of foot.

Ct 6   Step into 3rd position, R foot front (facing audience).

Arms

Ct 1–3   Lift L arm to 5th as R arm makes a complete circle, moving outward and downward through 2nd to low 5th front, and up through 1st, returning to 5th.

Ct 4–6   Repeat ct 1–3 with L arm.

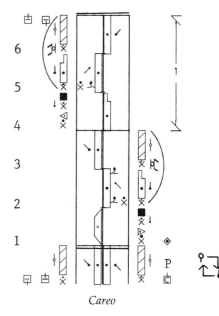

Careo

See *sevillanas*.

Ct: 1 2 3   4 5 6

CAREO DEL BESO *(cah-REH-oh dehl BEH-soh)*
(From *careo*, face to face, and *beso*, kiss)

A sudden face-to-face passing of dancers so close and with such abandon that they appear to exchange a kiss while moving into each other's place. The term is no longer in use, but its action is graphically preserved in the vivid lithographs of such artists as Gustave Doré.

See *pasos enfrentados.*

CARGADO *(cahr-GAH-doh)*
(Weighted, loaded)
Also called *Cortado* (cut).

Derived from the action of cutting away and taking the weight *(cargo)* on the foot that does the cutting. The term was used mostly in social dances *(danzas)* of the eighteenth and nineteenth centuries.

See *cortado.*

CARRERA
See *carrerilla.*

CARRERILLA *(cah-rreh-REE-lyah)*
(Short run, race)
Also called *carrera* and *carrerita.*

A series of small running steps in a dance similar to a balletic *pas couru.*

CARRERITA
See *carrerilla.*

CARRETILLA *(cah-reh-TEE-lyah)*
(Little cart)

A term in castanet playing signifying the continuous rolls made with the four fingers of the right hand. Although the *carretilla* is almost always played with the right hand, some manuscripts give specific directions for playing them with both hands in certain baroque dances. Its name comes from the soft rumbling sound of a pushcart (*carretilla*) over cobblestone streets. Today a single *carretilla* or roll consists of five beats. The first four are played with each finger of the right hand in succession and followed immediately with a single beat (*golpe*) on the left. When several of these five-stroke rolls are played in succession, they are called *carretillas seguidas*.

See *palmas, pitos, y castañuelas* (Basic Positions and Techniques); *seguidos*. See also Appendix: Basic Flamenco Rhythms.

CASTAÑETEAR *(cahs-tah-nyeh-teh-AHR)*
(To play castanets)

This term includes castanet playing by a dancer making a rhythmic accompaniment while performing, by a *tonadillera* (a female professional singer of light, charming songs) accompanying herself as she sings, or by onlookers marking the rhythm (*jaleo*) to encourage (*animar*) dancers during the general merrymaking at fiestas. The term also means to snap one's fingers rhythmically.

The most recent development in the evolution of castanet playing is their use as a solo instrument in concert. As a result of this new art form the term *castañetista* is now emerging.

See *chasquear los dedos, crotalogía, palillera, pitos, tonadillera.*

CASTAÑUELA *(cahs-tah-nyew-EH-lah)*
(Castanet)

A Castilian term for the castanet used throughout Spain. It is derived from *castaña* (chestnut), which suggests the general shape of the instrument.

See *palillos, pitos, postiza, pulgaretes.*

CASTELLANA *(cahs-teh-LYAH-nah)*
(Castilian, a stanza in old Spanish poetry)

A short section in an *alegrías*, usually of four *compases*, which precedes the *escobilla*. The slow, flowing quality of the music lends itself to the swinging of arms (*braceo*), especially by women, and to steps (*paseos*) that travel back and forth across the stage. It formerly had no rhythmic footwork (*zapateado*), but today occasional stamps for accenting are used.

CASTIZO *(cahs-TEE-thoh)*
(Authentic, traditional, pure, as opposed to false, imagined, or contrived)

A term applied to any traditional Spanish art form (dance, song, music) in its purest Iberian manifestation.

See *españolado.*

CEASE Y CONTRACEASE ANDALUZ *(seh-ah-SEH ee cohn-trah-seh-ah-SEH ahn-dah-LOOTH)*[1]

(Origin uncertain; see *seasé y contraseasé de escuela bolera,* note 2)

This action is similar to a balletic *glissade changée.*

Beg pos   Feet—3rd.
                Arms—Low 4th L front.

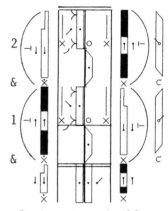

   Ct &   Step to side on R.
   Ct 1   Slide L into 3rd front as knees bend slightly.
   Ct &   Step to side on R.
   Ct 2   Slide L into 3rd behind as knees bend slightly.

            In another interpretation of this step, ct &–1 moves to right and ct &–2 moves to the left *(contra).*

            The knees straighten after each bend, allowing a small rise and fall of the head level.

Ceasé y contraceasé andaluz

Arms and head
 Ct &–1 Swing out arms slightly, changing them to low 4th R front while turning head slightly to right.
 Ct &–2 Reverse above action of arms and head.

See *seasé de escuela bolera, seasé y contraseasé de escuela bolera.*

CERDAÑA
See *sardana.*

CERRADO *(theh-RAH-doh)*
(Closed)

A term used to describe a step or movement indicating that the feet are in a closed position or that they are brought to a closed position at the end of the movement. Not to be confused with *cierre.*

See *asamblé natural o sencillo, paso unido.*

CHACONA *(chah-COH-nah)*
(Chaconne, old dance)

A dance of the eighteenth and nineteenth centuries in slow triple meter utilizing castanets. It was a dance of the Spanish nobility.

---

[1] This is Maestro José Otero's version and spelling. The term is also spelled *seasé y contraseasé.*

See *Bailes palaciegos.*

CHAFLAN *(chah-FLAHN)*
(A squaring off, slanting, beveling)

A sharp, affirmative step of punctuation used in rhythmic footwork (*zapateado*).

Beg pos   Feet—3rd L front, knees slightly
          bent.
          Arms—Optional (man often holds
          edges of his jacket).

    Ct &   Strike tip of R toe behind L heel.
    Ct 1   Raising L heel, stamp R foot, replac-
          ing L heel, simultaneously shifting
          ball of L foot very slightly forward.

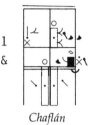

Chaflán

CHAPATEO
See *choqueteo, posticeo.*

CHASQUEAR LOS DEDOS *(chahs-keh-AHR lohs DEH-dohs)*
(To snap the fingers)

A unique sound accomplished by snapping the middle or second and middle fingers successively. Although used in some folkloric dances, it is associated mostly with traditional flamenco dancing. Until relatively recent times, castanets were not used in flamenco dancing. Despite their general acceptance today, the purist feels that the female dancer (*bailaora*) sacrifices much of the lyric beauty of her undulating wrists and fingers when she is manipulating *castañuelas. Chasquear los dedos,* when executed properly, can make a sound (*repique*) that will be remembered and admired as much as that of castanets. In fact, the literal term *castañetear* (to play castanets) also means to snap the fingers. The action is most commonly called *pitos.*

See *palmas, pitos, y castañuelas* (Basic Positions and Techniques); *pitos.*

CHETE *(cheh-TEH)*
(Thrown; Hispanicized French *jeté*)

An antiquated seventeenth- and eighteenth-century term, now called *echado.*

See *echado.*

CHICO
(Small, little)

A term applied to types of dance (*baile*), song (*cante*), and guitar playing (*toque*), such as *bulerías, tanguillo, jaleo, romeras, sevillanas,* and *rumba gitana,* the basic nature of which is light, happy, positive, and at times humorous. It is the antithesis of *jondo* or *grande.*

CHINCHINES *(cheen-CHEE-nehs)*
([Coll.] drizzling rain)
Also called *platillos* and *crótalos.*

Small, high-pitched brass finger cymbals used in old Moorish-influenced *zambras.* The onomatopoeic name given to them refers to the thin, tinkling, metallic sound they emit. This sound is a familiar one in Middle East dancing and may very well have been another Arabic influence on Andalusian dance.

See *zambra.*

CHIRIMIA *(chee-ree-MEE-ah)*
(Flute or flageolet player)

The intricate fast-moving footwork of the *escuela bolera* suggests the rapid finger movements of a flute player. It is also a seldom used synonym for *lazos.*

See *lazos.*

CHOQUE
See *Choqueteo.*

CHOQUETEO *(cho-keh-TEH-oh)*
(Collision, clashing movement)
Also called *choque* and sometimes *chapateo* in Seville.

The action of striking castanets together with a single stroke. If they are struck in a careless or crude manner, a fine pair of castanets can be cracked or split, thus ending their professional life.

See *golpe, posticeo.*

CHUFLA *(CHOO-flah)*

This flamenco term is applied to a light, happy, high-spirited *(chico)* dance when it is used as a vehicle for humor or to titillate an audience. Such treatment of a dance, called *por chufla,* usually lends itself favorably to a closing number or encore, leaving the audience in a happy and positive mood. It can involve not only the dancer but also the singer, the *palmista,* and even the guitarist, who sometimes jokingly move along with the featured dancers.

See *chico.*

CIERRE *(thee-EH-reh)*
(Act of ending, closing)
Also called *cadencia.*

A flamenco term applied to the closing of a rhythmic phrase *(compás)* or section of a dance. It is a type of *llamada.*

See *llamada.*

CIFRA *(SEE-frah)*
(Method of notation for guitar music using numbers)

The flamenco guitarist, as a soloist or as an accompanist for singing (*cante*) and dancing (*baile*), must memorize many musical forms. For years one *flamenquisto* taught another an interesting variation by playing the passage over and over until the student had committed the sound and fingering to memory. Even today this method is used by some. Its main drawback is that what is learned may also be forgotten. Today, to maintain a permanent record of a variation, many guitarists write the form of notation called *cifra*. Musical notation, using letters and symbols, had existed for many centuries, but Spain was the first country in the fifteenth century to use numbers to notate music.

Based on a staff of six lines, this system has evolved into a most valuable method of documenting for posterity any melody, its rhythm, mode, harmony, tempo, key, and all the *rasgueados* and *falsetas* that are employed as accurately as ordinary music notation.

See Appendix: Basic Flamenco Rhythms.

CIGUEÑA *(thee-GWEH-nyah)*
(Stork)

A typical pose in various *jotas* which the dancer holds for two counts, poised on the half toe of one foot, with the opposite knee bent, raised, and crossed in front of the standing leg while the upper body, with arms raised, twists in opposition to the lifted leg, somewhat resembling an *attitude croisé devant*. The term takes its name from the indigenous stork of the region poised on one foot with its wings spread. In flamenco it refers to a pose in which one knee is bent and lifted in front, the foot of the same leg being placed close to the other knee. Another variation of *cigüeña* is a step used in *farruca* and *bulerías* in which the dancer (in the latter position) advances with small sliding or shifting (*resbalada*) steps on the other foot, making a syncopated rhythm.

See *vuelta cigüeña*.

CIMBRADO *(theem-BRAH-doh)*
(A quick bending movement in dance)

The term indicates typical low-bending movements of the waist and torso that give a very lyrical and supple quality. *Cimbrados* are seen mostly in Andalusian, flamenco, and *escuela bolera* styles and are less common in regional or *folklórico* dances.

See *sostenido*.

CINGARO *(theen-GAH-roh)*
(Flamenco term for a non-Gypsy flamenco dancer)

Many of the finest exponents of flamenco dance (*baile*), song (*cante*), and guitar playing (*toque*) are not of Gypsy origin.

See *castizo*.

COBLA *(COH-blah)*
(Catalonian *sardana* orchestra)

A Catalonian orchestra specifically for playing music to accompany *sardanas*. The modern *cobla* generally comprises four woodwinds, four brasses, and a double bass. The solo instrument is a *tenora*, a combination of wood and brass whose timbre is a clear, nasal sound that is characteristic of Catalan *sardana* music.

See *sardana*.

COLETAZO *(coh-leh-TAH-thoh)*
(A strike with the tail)

A female flamenco dancer's sudden sidewise movement with her train *(cola)*.

COLETILLA *(coh-leh-TEE-lyah)*
(Little tail, ending, queue)
Also called *juguetillo, estribillo*.

A flamenco term referring to the few extra lines of sung words *(letras)* which are sometimes added to a stanza *(copla)* or are sung separately between the stanzas, as in *alegrías*.

COLOCARSE *(coh-loh-CAHR-seh)*
(To place, collect oneself)

An individual or unique manner of presenting oneself affirmatively when performing. The expression "pull oneself together" is common.

See *compostura, vuelta y figura*.

COMPAS *(cohm-PAHS)*
(Rhythmic cycle, measure of time)

Compás is the foundation upon which all dance *(baile)*, especially flamenco, is based. A thorough understanding of each rhythmic cycle *(compás)* with its individual accents and harmonic sequences is essential. The many flamenco *compases* can be divided into two general groups or rhythmic families: the even, those in 4/4; and the odd, those in 3/4 and 6/8. To be *en compás* implies both to have complete mastery of the *compás* and to be self-contained (to have *compostura*).

See *ritmo*. See also Appendix: Basic Flamenco Rhythms.

COMPOSTURA *(cohm-pohs-TOO-rah)*
(Composure)

The quality of self-assurance, ease, and calmness which the true artist emanates.

See *colocarse*.

COMPUESTO *(cohm-PWEHS-toh)*
(Compound, mixture)

Used in the *escuela bolera* to describe a formalized arrangement of steps employed in its syllabus. Each *compuesto* is made up of a small combination of steps (*pasos*). Some *compuestos*, known by a single name and composed of several steps (units of movement) are quite long and often uneven in phrasing. *Compuesto* is similar to balletic *enchaînement*.

CONCHAS *(COHN-chahs)*
(Shells, shell-like shapes)
Also called *hojas* (leaves).

One of the two halves of wood or plastic or synthetic material (*fibra*) which are laced together to make a pair of castanets. A pair is played in each hand except in an orchestra, where the *conchas* are fastened to a handle which, for convenience, is shaken. Their size, shape, concavity, and material determine their quality and pitch.

See *castañuela*.

CON GOLPE *(cohn GOHL-peh)*
(With a strike, stamp, tap)

Designates an accent with any part of the foot, but not a mere transfer of the weight onto one foot. This accent (which can be silent or audible) is found in all forms of Spanish dance, from those performed in soft ballet slippers (*zapatillas*) to those in which boots (*botas*) with hard leather heels are worn.

CONTINENCIA *(cohn-tee-NEHN-thee-ah)*
(Self-control, abstinence, moderation)

A graceful bow performed while dancing. The term is most commonly used in reference to eighteenth- and nineteenth-century *danzas*. Not to be confused with *continenza*, a Renaissance Italo-Hispanic step of court dancing involving a small sidewise shift of balance with a slight sway of the hip.

See *compostura, danza*.

CONTONEO *(cohn-toh-NEH-oh)*
(Affected gait, manner of walking, strut)

A female style of walking in Andalusian and flamenco dance. The term is also applied to a character in the mime section of a ballet or sketch (*bosquejo*) or to a mannerism of the performing artist.

CONTRADANZA
See *camino*.

CONTRAPASO *(cohn-trah-PAH-soh)*
(A step backward)

A step to the back which carries the weight of the body onto it. A term used in all styles of Spanish dance in place of the longer term *paso sencillo atrás*. Not to be confused with *contrapás*, a Catalonian linked dance composed of skipping steps.

CONTRAPAS XINXINA *(cohn-trah-PAHS cheen-CHEE-nah)*
(Contrapás of Xinxina; Catalonian)

A typical Catalonian step similar to *embotados*, in which the knee is lifted to the side as each foot alternately takes a step backward (*contrapaso*).

See *embotado*.

CONTRATIEMPO *(COHN-trah tee-EHM-poh)*
(Against time or count)

The audible counter-rhythm, accentuation, and syncopation (*jaleo*) that add to the excitement and heighten the interest of the merrymaking that is indispensable to flamenco dancing. The dancer sometimes produces these rhythmic effects (on the off beat or between the beats) by stamps (*golpes de pies*) or by rhythmic floorwork (*zapateado*) in countertime to his or her own hand clapping (*palmas*) or to that of the assisting *jaleadores*.

See *jaleador, jaleo, martillo, palmas*.

CONVULSION *(cohn-vool-see-OHN)*
(Convulsive action)

One of the various contortions and writhings of the torso, arms, hands, and face of a flamenco dancer during a dance. Such movements are often reflections of the dancer's mental state and involvement in the dance being performed.

See *duende, expresión, fruncimientos de entrecejos, grande, ondulado*.

COPLA *(COH-plah)*
(Stanza, couplet, popular song, ballad)

Spanish dances are generally accompanied by several verses (*coplas*). Their sentiments range from the lighthearted and frivolous to the serious and tragic. The music for *coplas* can be either played alone or sung, but it was the sung *copla* that first inspired the dance. The sequence of steps in *sevillanas*, *fandangos*, and *seguidillas* adheres to a set choreographic form, but the length of a *copla* depends on the song that accompanies a particular dance.

See *letra, seguidilla*.

CORONA *(coh-ROH-nah)*
(Crown or halo)

The 5th position (*quinta*) of the arms, in which they encircle or frame the head, as in the style of *escuela bolera*.

See *brazos básicos* (Basic Positions and Techniques), *media corona*.

CORRIDA *(coh-REE-dah)*
(Course or running, in a series, without stopping)

A constant repetition of a step. *De corrida* means at full speed.

See *seguida*.

CORRIENTE *(coh-ree-EHN-teh)*
(Running, flowing)

A term describing an uninterrupted movement or series of movements.

CORTADO *(cor-TAH-doh)*
(Cut, cutoff)
Also called *troncado*.

A term describing the action of one foot releasing and replacing the other either from behind (*por detrás*) or to the side (*al lado*). It is similar to a balletic *coupé*.

CORTESIA SENCILLA
See *reverencia sencilla*.

CORTO
See *curt*.

COSTADO *(cohs-TAH-doh)*
(Side)

A term used to indicate an action that moves to the side (*de costado*), either right or left. *De costado* is similar to the balletic *de côté*.

CROTALOGIA (croh-tah-loh-HEE-ah)
(The art of castanet playing; from *crótalo* [castanet, rattle])

Castanets are an ancient percussion instrument, the antecedents of present-day castanets having been in use in Egypt as early as 3000 B.C. They have long been used as a rhythmic accompaniment to Spanish dancing, and their musical potential is today being recognized and developed by dancers and musicians. New techniques in playing and various new systems of notation especially for castanets are now being realized. See Matteo, "Woods That Dance" [a history of castanets], *Dance Perspectives* [New York], no. 33 (1968).

See *castañuela, palillera*.

CROTALOS
See *chinchines*.

CRUCES
See *pasada*.

CRUZA *(CROO-thah)*
(A crossing, passing)
Also called *travesía.*

A shortened form of *cruzamiento,* a term for a crossing in a floor pattern *(camino)* in folkloric dances.

CRUZADILLO *(croo-thah-DEE-lyoh)*
(A little crossing or passing)

A folkloric term for *esplante cruzado* or *paso de vasco,* in which one foot passes over or crosses the other.

See *esplante.*

CRUZADO *(croo-THAH-doh)*
(Crossed, in a crossed position)

A term describing the position rather than the movement when limbs begin to be crossed or become crossed during or after the completion of a step. The term also applies to the positions of partners or lines of dancers who have exchanged places. However, it does not have the same meaning as the balletic term *croisé,* which describes an angle of the upper torso and shoulders.

CRUZADO POR DELANTE *(croo-THAH-doh por deh-LAHN-teh)*
(Crossed by way of the front)

This is a position or placement in which either foot is crossed (with slightly flexed ankle) over the opposite ankle. The degree to which the foot is flexed or lifted depends on the period and style of the dance, which, in turn, is greatly influenced by the kind of footgear worn, whether soft heelless slippers *(zapatillas),* pumps with small heels, gentlemen's boots *(botas),* or country people's rope-soled canvas sandals *(alparagatas).*

CRUZADO POR DETRAS *(croo-THAH-doh pohr deh-TRAHS)*
(Crossed by way of the back)

A position or placement in which one foot is crossed (with slightly flexed ankle) at the calf or behind the knee of the opposite leg.

See *cruzado por delante.*

CRUZAMIENTO
See *cruza.*

CUADRADA *(cwah-DRAH-dah)*
(Squared, framed)

A broad second position with the knees bent. It can begin or end a step.

See *cuarta cuadrada*.

CUADRILLA
See Cuadro, Figura.

CUADRO *(CWAH-droh)*
(A square)

A square formation with two or four people on each side. A basic formation (*figura*) in old social figure dances (*danzas*).

See *cuadro flamenco*, Figura.

CUADRO BOLERO *(CWAH-droh boh-LEH-roh)*
(A square; a frame or setting for *bolero* dancers)

A small group of dancers dressed in period costumes who present classic dances of the eighteenth and nineteenth century such as *boleros, seguidillas,* and *panaderos.*

See *baile de zapatillas, escuela bolera.*

CUADRO FLAMENCO *(CWAH-droh flah-MEHN-coh)*
(A square; a frame or setting for flamenco)

As entertainment in the early *cafés cantantes,* a *cuadro flamenco* was a small tableau of dancers, singers, and guitarists who gathered for a good-time *jaleo* and to compete in skills for the entertainment of the guests. Later this form of entertainment moved from the night club to the theater. On a concert program it is usually the *grande finale* in which all the artists who have previously appeared on the program assemble to perform their favorite steps, with each succeeding dancer trying to top the previous one. It all makes for an exciting climax, which often brings the audience to its feet with shouts of approval.

See flamenco, *jaleo, tablao.*

CUARTA *(CWAHR-tah)*
(A fourth, quarter)
Also called *trenzado* (braided) and *antrexata* (Basque).

A movement originally of Basque origin, later adopted by the French and Italian ballet schools as the *entrechat quatre.* It was "created" and introduced to these ballet styles by the legendary Marie Anne Camargo, whose father was a Basque.

| Beg pos | Ct & | Ct 1 |

Beg pos   Feet—5th R front, knees slightly
          bent.
          Arms—5th.

Ct &   Jump vertically, simultaneously ex-
          changing position of legs in midair.
Ct 1   Land in original position (5th R
          front).

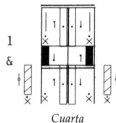

Cuarta

Ct: &   1

CUARTA CUADRADA *(CWAR-tah cwah-DRAH-dah)*
(A fourth, squared off)

Because it is similar in appearance, this regional step is often confused (both in nomenclature and in execution) with the *hecho y deshecho* of the *escuela bolera*. Both steps are technically demanding when castanets are played simultaneously.

Ct &   Spring vertically into the air.
Ct 1   Land in 2nd, move arms to 2nd, turn-
          ing head slightly to right.
Ct &   Spring vertically into the air, beating
          the L calf behind R, moving arms to
          4th R up, returning head to normal.
Ct 2   Land in 5th L front.

          Repeat above, reversed.

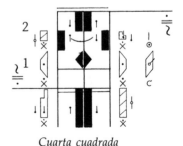

Cuarta cuadrada

CUATRO PELOS *(CWAH-troh PEH-lohs)*
(Four hairs)

Cuatro pelos is the Spanish name given to this Basque step. *Pelo* also means hairbreadth, a trifle, or the hairspring of a watch or firearm. The inferred analogy is the quick, minute, to-and-fro actions of the moving foot.

Beg pos Feet—3rd R front, knees straight but not braced.
Arms—Hanging straight at sides.

Ct 8 & a Stamp L foot as ball of R foot begins to draw quarter clockwise circle with ball of foot on ground (*cuarta rodazán a fuera al suelo*), traveling to right and taking weight on R.

Ct 1 Close L foot to 3rd front.

Ct & a 2 Move R foot closely in front and behind L with ball of foot and behind L with ball of foot on ground, lowering R heel in 3rd pos back, taking weight on R.

Ct & a 3 & a 4 Repeat & a 1 & a 2, reversed (to left).

Ct & a 5 & a 6 Repeat & a 1 & a 2 (to right).

Ct & a 7 Repeat & a 1 (to left).

Ct & a Lift L foot from 3rd back to 3rd front.

Ct 8 Hold.

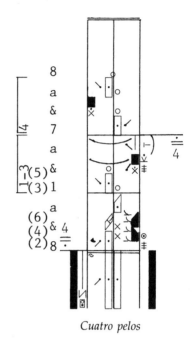

Cuatro pelos

The first and only stamp comes at the end of the previous phrase. The step seems to skim over the floor and is typical of Basque dances frequently in the repertoire of Spanish dance companies.

CUNA *(COO-nah)*
(Cradle)

Prominent in some *jotas,* this step takes its name from the rocking effect caused by shifting the weight from the ball of one foot to the other. For obvious reasons, the quick, delicate rocking motions danced on high half toe (*semipunta*) are conveniently referred to as *cunitas* (little cradles). This step of northern Spain resembles those seen in hornpipes and Scottish dances and may well be of Celtic origin. Danish choreographer, Agust Bournonville, who was enamored of Spanish dance, used *cuna* steps effectively in several Spanish variations of his ballets.

Beg pos   Ct 1–2   Ct 3

Beg pos   Feet—On half toe, crossed at ankles
          R over L, knees relaxed.
          Arms—*Folklórico* (as shown above).

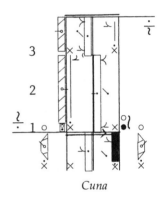

Ct 1–2   While on half toe, drop R heel, taking
         entire weight on sole of R foot.

Ct 3   Change weight onto sole of L foot
       causing feet to "rock" from left to
       right; allow torso to move very
       slightly from side to side with each
       movement.

Cuna

A variation of above is to remain on
half toe and "rock" from side to side
on every count in quick tempo, holding torso erect and steady. Ankles
and knees must remain flexible
throughout, moving with ease from
side to side. Do not bounce up and
down.

Ct: 1   2   3

CUNA EN VUELTA *(COO-nah en VWEHL-tah)*
(Performing a *cuna* [rocking or tilting motion] while making a turn)

A variation of *cuna*, a typical *jota* step. This action is made in place (*en sitio*),
but the momentum of the rocking action causes it to revolve slowly.

See *cuna*.

CUNITAS
See *cuna*.

CURT *(COORT)*
(Short; Catalonian)

A typical step of a Catalonian *sardana* of Ampurdan. It is used in combination with its opposite, *llarg* (long). The Spanish term for *curt* is *corto*.

Beg pos   Feet—1st (dancers standing in a circle).
        Arms—Holding hands low to sides.

Ct 1   Point L foot forward on the ground (*punto en suelo*).
Ct 2   Step L to left.
Ct 3   Point R toe forward on ground.
Ct 4   Step R foot into 1st position.

See *llarg, punt, sardana*.

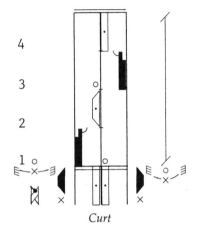

Curt

DANZA *(DAHN-thah)*
(Dance)[1]

Danza and *baile*, both meaning dance, are terms which over many years have almost interchanged meanings. Technically speaking, they should not be used synonymously. As early as 1865 dancing master González de Sales differentiated between the two, stating that a *danza* consisted of more measured *pasos* (steps) than a *baile*. It was implied that refined people performed *danzas* conditioned by the type of clothing they wore and by the indoor surroundings of the courts, ballrooms, and *salones de fiesta* in which they danced. *Danzas* (as they were called and taught in the sixteenth through nineteenth centuries), unlike *bailes*, focused attention on the legs and feet and gave primary attention to such details as bracing the knees, the proper degree of turning out the feet,

---

[1]Please note that the original meaning of this term, referring to the early nontheatrical society dances, is used throughout this volume.

and the etiquette, exactitude, and neatness of stepping and memorizing complicated floor patterns (*caminos*). In the old *danzas* only the feet moved; the rest of the body was quite still, and the arms were often held in a fixed and determined position, such as the hands on the hips (*en jarras*). Intricate sequences which required a good memory, much practice, and supervision were woven into the simpler old dances and were called *danzas de figuras*. The foot technique of Spanish *danzas* became a complicated feature. The nobility participated in *bailes palaciegos*, which were often part of the elaborate theatrical performances given at the palace. Books and printed musical scores for dances of the court, ballroom, drawing room, and salon as late as the nineteenth century refer to these society dances as *danzas*. In contemporary Spain the word *danza* implies a dance performance at public festivals, and ordinary dances are called *bailes*. A square dance is referred to as a *baile de figuras* or *baile de cuenta*.

See bailes, *bailes palaciegos, paso.*

DEBOLES *(deh-boh-LEHS)*
(Rolling motions of a ball; Hispanicized French *déboulés*)

An eighteenth-century term indicating half turns executed alternately on each foot while moving in one direction; now called *vuelta de pasos*. It is similar to balletic *tours chaînés* or *demi-tour*.

See *vuelta de pasos.*

DECALOGO *(deh-CAH-loh-goh)*
(A Decalogue)

Vicente Escudero, Spain's acknowledged greatest flamenco dancer, felt so deeply about the true qualities of the male flamenco dancer that in 1951 he published a pamphlet entitled *Decalog on the Pure Flamenco Dance*, in which he set forth the ten basic laws (*decálogo*) of behavior and performance that are still associated with his name:

1. Dance as a man
2. Sobriety
3. Turn the wrists from the inside outward, with the fingers together
4. Hips quiet
5. Dance *asentado* (seated, serenely) not in a circusy manner
6. Harmony of the feet, arms, and head
7. Esthetic and plastic purity
8. Style and accent
9. Dance in the traditional garb
10. Achieve a variety of sounds through the inner emotional interpretation of the dramatic character of the dance, without metal taps on the shoes, or inlaid wood on the stage or other externals

See *aire, asentado, castizo, expresión, macho, movimientos de las manos* (Basic Positions and Techniques), zarandeo.

DE CUADRADO *(deh cwah-DRAH-doh)*
(Face to face, squared)

The face-to-face position of partners or couples as they begin or end a movement in a *baile* or a *danza*.

See *careo, de frente, pasos enfrentados*.

DE ESCUELA *(deh ehs-CWEH-lah)*
(From the school)

A term used to distinguish those dances (other than indigenous folk dances) which were taught in the various dancing schools (*escuelas del baile*) of Spain at the turn of the twentieth century. These "school" dances included all types, from the courtly *pavana* to the then contemporary *garrotín*. The dances were choreographed in the form of routines set to traditional or composed music arranged for piano accompaniment.

DE FIGURAS *(deh fee-GOO-rahs)*
(With or of figures, patterns)

Set dances (*danzas*) of the seventeenth-through-nineteenth-century courts, ballrooms, and drawing rooms. These dances, such as *cuadrillas*, included series of elaborate figures or floor patterns (*figuras*). A contemporary square dance is called *baile de figuras*.

DE FILO EL TALON
See *talón*.

DE FRENTE *(deh FREHN-teh)*
(Opposite; literally, from the forehead)
Also called *de cuadrado*.

A term indicating the relationship of a person or line of dancers opposite, in front of, or across from one another in folk dances and *danzas*.

See *pasos enfrentados*.

DE FRENTE POR DETRAS *(deh FREHN-teh pohr deh-TRAHS)*
(From the front, by way of the back)
Also called *vuelta por delante y por detrás*.

A term describing an action of the feet, performing a turn (*vuelta*), which is initiated with one foot in front. The turn is completed then repeated in the same direction by first placing the other foot behind. The term is similar to the balletic *dessus dessous*.

See *vuelta por delante, vuelta por delante y por detrás*.

DE LADO DERECHO
See *direcciones básicas*.

DE LADO IZQUIERDO
See *direcciones básicas.*

DELANTE *(deh-LAHN-teh)*
(Before, in front of)

A term, indicating the position of one foot or person, couple or line of persons in relation to another. *Delante* is an adverb describing the direction of a step. It may also refer to placing a limb in front of the body. When the term is used to modify an action (that is, *vuelta por delante*), it indicates that the limb initiating the movement is in front.

DEMI
See *medio.*

DE PALILLOS *(deh pah-LEE-lyohs)*
(With castanets)

A term describing Andalusian dances of the eighteenth and nineteenth centuries whose main feature was the use of castanets. They were called "castanet dances" (*bailes de palillos*) to distinguish them from other regional or flamenco dances. Dances of the *escuela bolera* are always *de palillos.*

DERECHAS *(deh-REH-chahs)*
(Rights)

An early term used in social dances (*danzas*) that referred to a repetition in reverse of the figures or patterns (*mudanzas*) in order to return to the starting point. A similar term used in the *escuela bolera* is *deshecho* (undone, untied), meaning reversed action.

See *hecho y deshecho, mudanza.*

DESCANSO *(dehs-CAHN-soh)*
(Rest, quiet, repose)

A term applied to the short musical intervals between *coplas,* or verses, of vigorous regional dances such as *jotas* and *seguidillas.* These intervals are designed as brief rest periods to enable the dancers to catch their breath, to regain their energy, or simply to chat in preparation for the oncoming and difficult variations before the last step (*paso final*). When such dances are adapted to the stage, this brief interval (*descanso*) is often omitted, and the stanzas (*coplas*) are danced without interruption (*corrida*). When the movement is incessant and these effective stops (also called *pausas* or *paradas*) are disregarded, the dance loses much of its character.

See *bien parado, parada, pausa.*

DESLIZ *(dehs-LEETH)*
(Slip, slide, glide)
Also called *resbalamiento.*

A term applied to a step with a slipping or sliding motion along the floor.

See *ceasé y contraceasé andaluz, glisada, glisés, lisada por detrás de escuela bolera, sacado.*

DESPLANTE *(dehs-PLAHN-teh)*
(Movement from a fixed or established plan or posture)

In Andalusian and flamenco dancing, *desplante* is the dancer's signal to the guitarist to indicate a rhythmic break, change, or link in a dance and is performed with a series of foot stamps *(golpes de pie),*[1] which in turn leads into a different rhythm and/or change of mood. It may be best compared to what is known as a "break," in which a step or rhythm, after being established *(plantado)* by several repetitions, is uprooted or eradicated *(desplanté)* to continue on to a new rhythm. The term comes from the Spanish art of fencing *(esgrima),* which gentlemen of nobility studied along with the art of dancing.

See *aviso, llamada.* See also Appendix: Basic Flamenco Rhythms.

DESTAQUE *(dehs-TAH-keh)*
(From *destacar,* to bring out, make conspicuous, emphasize)

Describing the action of a straight or bent leg lifted into the air. Although it resembles a balletic *battement,* the accent is upward rather than downward.

See *puntapié.*

DESTAQUE ADELANTE RETIRADA *(dehs-TAH-keh ah-deh-LAHN-teh reh-tee-RAH-dah)*
(From *destacar,* to bring out, make conspicuous, forward and drawn back)

Beg pos   Ct 1   Ct 2   Ct 3

[1]Marked on counts 1, 2, 3, as in *bulerías.*

Beg pos   Feet—From previous action, facing
          diagonally right.
          Arms—4th L up.

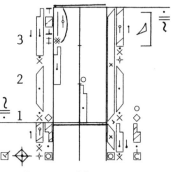

  Ct 1   Step forward on R.
  Ct 2   Lift L leg forward (*destaque*).
  Ct 3   Sharply draw back lower leg toward
         body as knee flicks up skirt (major ac-
         cent) and upper torso back.

  Arms
  Ct 1–3 Swing through 2nd to 4th R up.

Destaque adelante retirada

See *destaque, direcciones básicas, retirado, vistoso.*

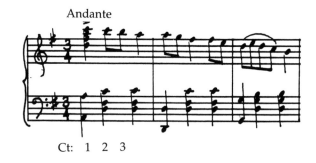

Ct: 1   2   3

DESTAQUE CON VUELTA *(dehs-TAH-keh cohn voo-EHL-tah)*
(From *destacar,* to bring out or emphasize, with a turn)

A compound movement in which the lifting of a leg (*destaque*) is followed immediately by a turn (*vuelta*) toward the standing leg and executed in a smooth,
connected manner. In the *escuela bolera* it is called *vuelta con destaque,* and the
initial movement is to the side (*de lado*).

See *destaque, vuelta por delante.*

DESTAQUE EN DOS TIEMPOS *(dehs-TAH-keh ehn dohs tee-EHM-pohs)*
(From *destacar,* to bring out, emphasize, in two counts)

This action, which resembles a balletic *developpé,* is essentially the same as
vacío but is performed more quickly and in a more staccato manner, thus fore-
going any soft, flowing quality. It can be performed either to the front (*delante*)
or diagonally forward (*en diagonal anterior*).

DETOURNE *(deh-toor-NEH)*
(Turning away; French *détourné*)

An about-face turn in the direction of the back foot, reversing the position of
the feet. Such turns may be a complete turn or a half turn (facing the opposite
direction) in which the back foot becomes the front foot. When performed in

the *escuela bolera* style, they are done on half-toe (*semi punta*). These turns are also called *vuelta por detrás* and *media vuelta por detrás,* respectively.

See *media vuelta, vuelta por detrás.*

DETRAS DE *(deh-TRAHS deh)*
(Behind, in back of)

A term denoting the position or action of one limb of the body behind the other. It also defines one's position in relation to a partner or in a group. It is similar to the French term *derrière.*

DEYA *(DEH-yah)*
(Call; Basque)

A stamp given as a signal during a dance which precedes a change in melody and rhythm in Basque music, usually from 5/8 to 6/8 or 2/4. This term may be compared with the Spanish *llamada.*

DE ZAPATILLA *(deh tha-pah-TEE-lyah)*
(With slipper)

A term referring to dances of the eighteenth and nineteenth centuries such as *seguidillas* and *boleros,* which are light, gracious, often with complicated footwork, and performed in soft, flexible slippers (*zapatillas*). All *escuela bolera* dances are *de zapatilla.*

DIAGONAL *(dee-ah-goh-NAHL)*
(Diagonal)

A term indicating that the movement is performed in an oblique direction.

See *direcciones básicas.*

DIFERENCIA *(dee-feh-REHN-thee-ah)*
(Change, difference, variation)
Also called *cambio, variación.*

Changes or variations in a dance or the stanzas of a song.

See *cambio.*

DIRECCIONES BASICAS *(dee-rehc-thee-OH-nehs BAH-see-cahs)*
(Basic or fundamental directions)

There are eight basic directions in which the dancer, who begins in place (*en sitio*), may move:

1. Forward (toward the audience)—*adelante*
2. Backward (away from the audience)—atrás
3. To his/her right side—*de lado derecho*
4. To his/her left side—*de lado izquierdo*
5. Diagonally forward to his/her right—*en diagonal anterior derecha*

6. Diagonally forward to his/her left—*en diagonal anterior izquierda*
7. Diagonally back to his/her right—*en diagonal posterior derecha*
8. Diagonally back to his/her left—*en diagonal posterior izquierda*

It must be remembered that these floor directions do not apply to the position or angle of the dancer's body, arms, or head in relation to the audience. Such details would vary not only with the four major styles of Spanish dance but also with regional differences and personal interpretations. For the most part they apply to the directions in which the feet move.

DOBLADA *(doh-BLAH-dah)*
(Bent, doubled, folded)

A term applied to a part of the body, such as the arms, waist, or knees.

DOBLE *(DOH-bleh)*
(Combination of two)

A castanet stroke in which the right-hand castanet is struck (*golpe*) quickly two times, making a double sound (*doble*), usually followed immediately by a single beat on the left castanet. Together the three sounds make the rhythm of a triplet (*trecillo*).

DUENDE *(DWEHN-deh)*
(Elf, fairy, the "magic" of being involved)

The "soul" of true flamenco dance (*baile*) and music (*toque*), without which an audience is entertained but not involved. Such involvement is not limited to a virtuosic display of steps and physical energy. Fundamentally speaking, *duende* is a state of mind or emotion emanating from the subconcious, an imperceptible psychic communication or hypnotic energy which a performer shares with his or her audience. It is an intimate happening almost like communicating through prayer·or as one "possessed" and may be likened to a ritual manifesting itself through dance.

See *expresión, reposao, tic.*

ECHADO *(eh-CHA-doh)*
(Thrown, flung)

This movement is similar to a balletic *jeté*.

Beg pos   Feet—R foot raised and slightly be-
          hind L calf.
          Arms—4th L up.

  Ct &   Bending L knee slightly, extend R
          foot out to side and jump into air.
  Ct 1   Land on R foot, drawing in L foot to
          just behind R calf.

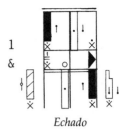
Echado

EMBOTADO   *(ehm-boh-TAH-doh)*
(Blunted, dulled, edgeless)
(Of two possible origins: from Spanish *embotar*, to step into one's boots; or
   from Hispanicized French (*emboité*, fitted together, boxed)[1]

Typical of the *seguidillas manchegas*, the undeniable origin of many classic and
folkloric Spanish dance forms, this ubiquitous step is performed in soft ballet
slippers (*zapatillas*) of the *escuela bolera* and in various heeled shoes, such as
zapatos and *botas*. It is interesting to note its close resemblance to steps in folk
dances of Russia and the Ukraine and in English and Irish hornpipes.

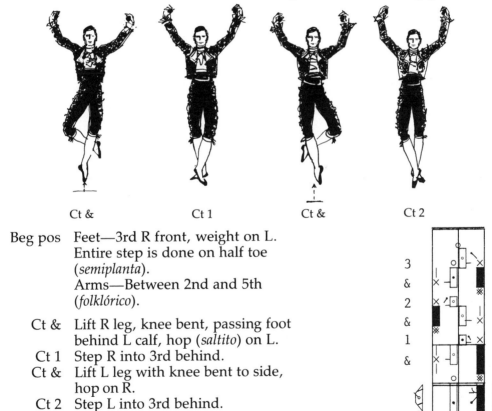

Ct &   Ct 1   Ct &   Ct 2

Beg pos   Feet—3rd R front, weight on L.
          Entire step is done on half toe
          (*semiplanta*).
          Arms—Between 2nd and 5th
          (*folklórico*).

  Ct &   Lift R leg, knee bent, passing foot
          behind L calf, hop (*saltito*) on L.
  Ct 1   Step R into 3rd behind.
  Ct &   Lift L leg with knee bent to side,
          hop on R.
  Ct 2   Step L into 3rd behind.
  Ct &   Lift R knee again, hop on L.
  Ct 3   Step R into 3rd behind.

Embotado

[1] The action of closely passing the feet, one directly down and behind the other, would fit either word.

Ct: &   1   &   2   &   3

EMBOTADO DE ESCUELA BOLERA *(em-boh-TAH-doh deh ehs-CWEH-lah boh-LEH-rah)*
(*Embotado* as performed in the *escuela bolera*)

The step is performed as illustrated under *embotado* but is preceded by three additional movements, a *punta y talón* and a *punta cruzada* (tip of right toe touches the floor over the instep of the left foot). This extended variation of *embotado* is also seen in the folk dances of various regions of Spain and is adapted to various rhythms, thereby keeping its own identity while assuming the character of the particular locale.

ENCAJES
See *lazos*.

EN CUADRO *(ehn CWAH-droh)*
(In a square, frame)

The basic set formation in folkloric and early social dances in which the dancers are arranged in a square.

See *baile de figuras, danza*.

EN DIAGONAL ANTERIOR DERECHO
See *direcciones básicas*.

EN DIAGONAL ANTERIOR IZQUIERDO
See *direcciones básicas*.

EN DIAGONAL POSTERIOR DERECHO
See *direcciones básicas*.

EN DIAGONAL POSTERIOR IZQUEIRDO
See *direcciones básicas*.

ENGAÑO *(ehn-GAH-nyoh)*
(Deception, trickery)
Also called *variedades*.

Surprising or misleading variations in movements executed with a partner. The term applies to an unexpected or sudden shift of weight, focus, change of direction, or variation in arm movement (*braceo*), usually by the male partner, which makes for an exciting or dramatic highlight in a dance. These *engaños* are displays of technical brilliance in virtuosic combinations.

EN JARRAS *(ehn HAH-rrahs)*
(In a juglike position)

A common arm position in folk dancing in which the elbows are bent and the hands rest on the hips. The Spanish term is derived from the shape of the handles of a jug *(jarra)*. In English the term is *akimbo*.

ENLACES *(ehn-LAH-thays)*
(Linkings, interlacings, connections)
Also called *lazos, encajes.*

Brilliant weaving or beating steps *(batidos)* such as those of the *escuela bolera.*

See *batidos, batuda, cuarta cuadrada, lazos, pistolea.*

EN PUNTAS *(ehn POON-tahs)*
(On point, on tiptoes, in toe shoes)

A term applied to eighteenth- and nineteenth-century *escuela bolera* dances which were adapted and performed in the theater by professionally trained ballet dancers *(bailarinas)*. The balletic movements of the popular *bolero* took many forms and invaded the ballroom as well. In solo *(liso)* dances these movements were particularly suitable to point shoes.

See *bolero.*

ENSAYO AL MEDIO *(ehn-SAH-yoh ahl MEH-dee-oh)*
(Practice in the center [of the studio])

With the exception of the *escuela bolera,* which is based on Italian and French ballet techniques that are practiced at the barre, Spanish dance is taught and practiced in the center *(al medio)* of the floor, often without a mirror. This practice *(ensayo)* should include all the preparatory bending and stretching exercises of the arms, legs, and torso; strengthening exercises for the feet; and rhythmic foot patterns *(zapateado)* and castanet playing. As in the established system of teaching ballet, the practice *(ensayo)* of these basic techniques is essential to a training curriculum in Spanish dance.

See *braceo, castañuela, movimientos de las manos* and *pies* (Basic Positions and Techniques), *zapateado.*

EN SITIO *(ehn SEE-tee-oh)*
(In place)

A term describing the movement of a given step that is performed in one place and does not travel.

ENTERADO *(ehn-teh-RAH-doh)* or Enterao *(ehn-teh-RAH-oh)*[1]
(Informed, knowledgeable)

A word which could also be translated as "initiated" or "learned." In the language of the flamenco, *enterao* refers to one who has a thorough knowledge of flamenco, dance *(baile)*, song *(cante)*, guitar playing *(toque)*, and all their rhythmic subtleties *(compases)*.

EN TONO ALEGRE *(ehn TOH-noh ah-LEH-greh)*
(In happy, wholesome tone)

A term used to describe a performer who is vivacious and animated. It is similar to *joie de vivre*.

See *chico*.

ENTRADA *(ehn-TRAH-dah)*
(Entrance)

This term has several applications. It can relate to a dancer, a choreographer, a singer, or a musician.

See *baile de presentación, introducción, salida* (definitions 1, 3, 4).

EN VUELTA *(ehn VWEHL-tah)*
(In a turn, while turning)

This is a modifying term applied to any step when it is performed turning. It is similar to the balletic *en tournant*.

EPILEPTICO *(eh-pee-LEHP-tee-coh)*
(Epileptic)

A term applied scornfully to "overachieving" flamenco dancers who perform, seemingly endlessly, at top speed with unleashed energy and convulsive movements in response to the encouragement of an undiscriminating audience.

ESCAPADA DOBLE Y TORDIN *(ehs-cah-PAH-dah DOH-bleh ee tohr-DEEN)*
(Double escape, or flight, and turn)

A step for a male dancer of the *escuela bolera*, probably the most unusual and most demanding, as it involves jumping onto both heels, a deep bending of the knees, then a spin in the air in rapid sequence.

---

[1]So pronounced by Flamencos. It is characteristic of Flamencos to drop the *d* sound.

Beg pos   Feet—3rd R front.
          Arms—Low 4th R front.

Ct 6   Preparation—bend knees (*plegado*).
Ct 1   Spring into wide 2nd on heels, knees straight.
Ct 2   Hold.
Ct 3   Spring into 5th R front, on balls of feet, knees almost completely bent (dancer very low).
Ct &   Jump into air, making one complete turn right; arms quickly change to low 4th L front.
Ct 4   Land in 5th L front with knees slightly bent.
Ct 5   Straighten knees.

       Repeat, reversed.

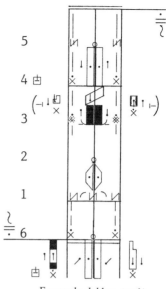

Escapada doble y tordín

ESCOBILLA (*ehs-coh-BEE-lyah*)
(Brush, brushlike step)

An extended flamenco dance sequence of heel-toe combinations (*zapateado*) performed to display the dancer's virtuosity during a specific portion of a dance. It is generally seen in *soleares* or *alegrías* and is a relatively recent development. Originally *escobillas* were small brushing steps with the ball of the foot which allowed women to display their beautiful arm and hand movements (*braceo* and *filigranas*) instead of the virtuosic display of footwork (*zapateado*) that is performed now.

See *alegrías, falseta, soleares*. See also Appendix: Basic Flamenco Rhythms.

ESCOBILLA DOBLADA (*ehs-coh-BEE-lyah doh-BLAH-dah*)
(Brushlike step doubled)

A pattern in rhythmic footwork (*zapateado*) in which the ball or tip of one shoe brushes the floor forward, then quickly brushes backward, ending with the ankle crossed (*cruzado*) in front of the ankle of the standing foot, making two delicate scraping sounds.[1] These soft, brushlike sounds are performed either during sections of subdued flourishings on the guitar or in silence.

See *cruzado, escobilla*.

ESCUELA BOLERA (*ehs-CWEH-lah boh-LEH-rah*)
(Bolero school, style)

A style of Spanish dance typical of the eighteenth and nineteenth centuries which was strongly influenced by the Italian and French ballet masters of that

[1]In a general way this double-brushing action can be compared to a "shuffle" in tap dance.

period. Bolero schools existed in such major cities as Madrid, Cádiz, Seville, Córdoba, and Murcia, as well as in many smaller towns. Its popularity (which almost reached the proportions of a mania) in ballrooms and theaters caused it to be considered the national dance for many years. Because jumps, beats, and leg extensions are characteristic of this style, the typical footwear is the soft ballet slipper (*zapatilla*).

The preservation of the *escuela bolera* dances is due largely to several generations of the Pericet family, founders of a school that has drawn thousands of students, teachers, and performing artists from many countries. It was Ángel Pericet Carmona (1877–1944) who organized the most characteristic steps and movements of his forefathers' dances into a graded curriculum of study, thus preserving their pristine character.

The entire repertoire of steps (*pasos*) and combinations of steps (*compuestos*) must be coordinated with the playing of castanets. Coordinating the playing of these instruments with the technically demanding beating movements in the air gives this style a special flavor and is one of the reasons why there are few *escuela bolera* dancers.

Although the *escuela bolera* was based on the principles of classical ballet (including the turn out of the legs), it was soon embued with the Iberian temperament, making it unique to Spain. The various styles of Spanish dance are often said to belong to four distinct "schools," but it is the *escuela bolera* which is most aptly named.

See *bolero, braceo de escuela bolera, compuesto, seguidilla, zapatillas.*

ESPAÑOLADO *(ehs-pah-nyoh-LAH-doh)*
(Spanishlike, Hispanicized)

A word describing a pseudo-Spanish dance or production that exaggerates the qualities and mannerisms that are often thought to be Spanish. It is the opposite of *castizo* (pure).

See *castizo.*

ESPARABARSE *(ehs-pah-rah-BAHR-seh)*
(Meaning unknown; from Caló, a Gypsy dialect)

An expression in Gypsy dialect meaning to go out of rhythm (*compás*).

See *compás, llevar el son.*

ESPLANTE *(es-PLAHN-teh)*
(Act of placing, setting down [the foot])

There are several lively folkloric versions of this step, depending on the region or the choreographer's choice. The step, which consists of three actions, can begin with any one of these movements. When it is performed in a slow, classical style, the arms move from fifth position in opposition; that is, the left arm makes a complete outward circle on counts 1–3 as the dancer steps to the right, and vice versa.

Beg pos   Feet—From any previous action.
          Arms—Throughout held between 5th
          and 2nd (*folklórico*); fingers are some-
          times snapped, or extended in front a
          little below hip level with palms up
          while playing castanets (see *palmas,
          pitos, y castañuelas*, Basic Positions and
          Techniques, *forma* 2).

Ct 1   Step in place or slightly sideways
          onto R, taking weight.[1]

Ct 2   Point L forward in 4th, taking partial
          weight on half toe (*semiplanta*), lifting
          R slightly.

Ct 3   Take weight on R in place (*en sitio*),
          where it was on ct. 1.

          Repeat above, reversed.

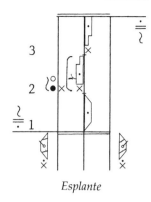

Esplante

See *esplante saltado*.

ESPLANTE CRUZADO
See *esplante*.

ESPLANTE SALTADO (*ehs-PLAHN-teh sahl-TAH-doh*)
(Act of placing, setting down [the foot] in a jumped manner)

This step is the same as *esplante* except that it is jumped or leaped (*saltado*),
especially by the male, who *never* minces his steps.[2]

Beg pos   Feet—From any previous action.
          Arms—Throughout held between 5th
          and 2nd (*folkórico*); fingers are some-
          times snapped, or extended in front a
          little below hip level with palms up
          while playing castanets (see *palmas,
          pitos, y castañuelas*, Basic Positions and
          Techniques, *forma* 2).

Ct &   Spring off floor lifting knees very
          high.

Ct 1   Step in place or slightly sideways
          onto R taking weight.

Ct 2   Set L heel down firmly forward in 4th
          taking weight, lifting R slightly.

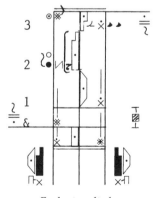

Esplante saltado

[1]When the step shown here moves sideways, it is called *esplante cruzado* or *paso de vasco*, a variant of the
balletic *pas de basque*, which is found in one form or another in folk dances all over the world. The accent is
on count 1.
[2]The step can travel forward or be performed in place (*en sitio*).

Ct 3   Take weight on R in place with a decided thud on ball of foot (*semipunta*).

Repeat above, reversed.

See *esplante, más saltadora, vistoso.*

ESTET *(es-TEHT)*
(Stay, hold)[1]

This simple ending is effective after partners have changed places, as in a final
pasada, thus finishing a musical phrase. It is typical of *seguidillas manchegas*, in
which each stanza (*copla*) ends almost unexpectedly with two chords,
abruptly followed by a silent beat during which partners remain posed on one
foot with the other knee raised in front.

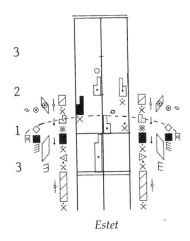

Beg pos   Feet—From any previous movement,
partners facing.
Arms—5th.

Ct 3   Step forward on L as arms pass
through 2nd to 5th low front (as
preparation).

Ct 1   Step forward on R.

Ct &   Lift L leg low forward, knee slightly
bent and spring into air as arms pass
through 1st to 5th.

Ct 2   Land on L with R leg raised front, hip
level, knee bent.

Ct 3   Hold pose (facing partner).

Estet

The accent is on ct 2.

In some *jotas*, the *estet* is with feet apart in an affirmative broad 2nd position
with knees slightly bent (*plegado*) and arms in a folkloric position between 2nd
and 5th positions.

See *bien parado, copla, parada, paso final, seguidilla, seguidillas manchegas.*

ESTILO *(ehs-TEE-loh)*
(Style, fashion)

A term referring to a dancer's individual interpretation or manner in performance or to the style (*estilo*) of the dance being presented. Spanish dance can
be generally categorized into several basic styles (*estilos*): *escuela bolera, an-*

---

[1] Very likely a word coined from the imperative case or command of Spanish or Italian dancing masters. The
Spanish imperative "esté," meaning "Stay," or "Remain," is similar to the Italian "State" meaning "Stop,"
"Stand still," "Hold." It is equivalent to an English-speaking dancing teacher saying, "Stop!" "Hold it!" or
"Freeze!" when a lively dance movement has ended.

daluz, de escuela, de palillos, flamenco, *folklórico, antiguo, contemporario, estilizado,* and *teatral,* each with characteristics and variations.

ESTOCADA *(ehs-toh-CAH-dah)*
(A lunge, tilt, thrust)

Throwing the weight of the body onto one foot with the knee well bent. It can be executed sideways (*de lado*), as in a *careo,* or forward (*delante*), as in a *caída.* The term is borrowed from the art of bullfighting (*tauromaquia*), and its action is similar to a balletic *tombé.*

See *caída, careo, tauromaquia.*

ESTRIBILLO
See *coletilla.*

EXPRESION *(ex-preh-see-OHN)*
(Expression, declaration, statement)

Drama is an integral part of flamenco dancing and is suggested by the dancer through changes in facial expressions, such as contractions of the eyebrows (*fruncimientos de entrecejos*) and through body gestures conveying the deepest emotions of the dancer (*bailaora*) or singer (*cantaor*). Since flamenco dance (*baile*) coexists with singing (*cante*), the dancer is inextricably involved with the lyrics (*letra*) and bares his emotions. Like the term *natya* in East Indian dance (considered by many to be the origin of flamenco), the term *expresión* is synonymous with both dance and drama.

See *duende, letra.*

FALSETA *(fahl-SEH-tah)*

A musical term used by dancers and guitarists to indicate an ornate melodic passage played on the guitar which acts as an important link in a flamenco dance. A *falseta* is a musical departure from the main or stated theme and can be a creative experience both choreographically and musically depending on the talent and experience of the performing artists. A possible origin of the word is *falsete* (falsetto voice), suggesting the manner in which the guitarist improvises his variations. Some *falsetas* are so unique that they have become associated with the guitarists who created them.

See *escobilla, silencio.* See also Appendix: Basic Flamenco Rhythms.

FANDANGO *(fahn-DAHN-goh)*
(Fandango dance; literally, "Go and dance")[1]

The *fandango* is thought by many authorities to be not only one of the oldest dances, possibly dating back to the Phoenicians of 1600 B.C., but also the most Spanish (*lo más español*) of Spanish dances. Its rhythm is intoxicating, and for years it was danced by rich and poor, young and old, on every occasion imaginable. An old Spanish proverb stated, "Este mundo es un fandango, y el que no baila es un tonto" ("This world is a fandango, and he who does not dance is a fool"). The *fandango* is performed by either an individual or a couple and, in one form or another, can be found in almost every region throughout the Iberian Peninsula. It is a dance in quick triple time (originally written in ⁶/₈ time, but some versions occur in ³/₈ or ¾) which appeared in Spain in the early eighteenth century. Because of its repetitious, intoxicating theme, which accelerates to a frenzied climax with the ceaseless sound of castanets, the *fandango* creates the sight and sound of merrymaking (*fiesta*) at its peak. In various cities of Andalusia it assumes local forms named for the cities of origin, such as *malagueña* (Málaga), *granadina* (Granada), *murciana* (Murcia), *rodeña* (Ronda), *fandango de huelva* (Huelva).

Once the Vatican threatened to ban the *fandango*. In its defense two dancers were chosen to perform the questionable steps before an assembly of high-ranking judges. To the relief of all Spain, the gaiety and grace of the dance so pleased the judges that the *fandango* was fully approved and restored to honorable standing.[2]

Although they are usually thought of as being flamenco, *fandangos* (like *boleros*, which we now call classical) were originally danced by the everyday folk on festive occasions in streets, at parties and cafes, in courts and salons, and even in churches. They were accompanied with castanets, tambourines, and violins. The dance is structured on verses and choruses which alternate. *Fandangos* are regional dances from Andalusia or classical derivations of these dances. Originally *fandangos* were couple dances of courtship, but more recently solo versions have emerged for concert performances in the theaters. Some *fandangos* are danced in heeled shoes and others in hemp-soled sandals (*alpargatas*). In the south the dance evinces Moorish influence in that it is danced as a trio, the man having two women as partners.

With the passage of time the *fandango* as a song took on a more and more serious character (*jondo grande*), giving it the present flamenco name *fandango grande*, which is never danced but is limited to singing (*cante*) and playing (*toque*). The *fandango grande* is not often heard today, but classical musical examples of it are faithfully preserved in the compositions of Padre Soler, Halffter, Mozart, Boccherini, and Rimsky-Korsakov.

---

[1] A possible but questionable origin given by the eighteenth-century Italian dancing master and scholar Carlo Blasis in *The Code of Terpsichore* (1728).

[2] "Their grace and vivacity soon drove the frowns from the brows of the Fathers, whose soules were stirred by lively emotion and a strange pleasure. One by one their Eminences began to beat time with hands and feet, till suddenly their hall became a ballroom; they sprang up dancing the steps imitating the gestures of the dancers. After this trial the *fandando* was fully pardoned and restored to honor." Gaston Vuillier, *La Danse* (Paris, 1983).

See *baile del candil, baile de plaza*. See also Appendix: Basic Flamenco Rhythms.

FANDANGO DE HUELVA
See *fandanguillo*.

FANDANGUILLO *(fahn-dahn-GHEE-lyoh)*
(Small fandango)
Also called *fandango de huelva*.

A variation of the *fandango* which combines Andalusian and Gypsy character-istics and is typical of the province of Huelva, in which each village has its own version. *Fandanguillos* are descendants of the *jota*. They are popular on all sorts of occasions, such as picnics, outings, religious processions, and any-time crowds assemble, sing, and dance. Originally, this dance was accom-panied by homemade instruments played in a carefree, natural, and im-provised manner. During the early 1920s it was a favorite woman's dance taught by the great dancing master José Otero, of Seville, to piano accompani-ment. This charming, though seldom seen, dance is today accompanied by a guitar.

See *fandango*. See also Appendix: Basic Flamenco Rhythms.

FARFULLEOS *(fahr-foo-LYEH-ohs)*
(Meaningless sounds, syllables)

Vocal passages, using sounds in place of words, by a flamenco singer (*cantaor*) to "feel" the rhythm (*compás*) and texture (*temple*) of the song he or she is about to sing. Typical examples are "Ti-ri-ti-tran," "Tran-tran," and "Le-le-le-le." The onomatopoetic expressions, such as "Riá-riá-pi-tá," used by many dancing teachers to indicate the sound of a *sevillana* rhythm by the castanets are also called *farfulleos*.

See *quejío, salida* (definition 4).

FARRUCA *(fah-RROO-cah)*
(Northerner from Asturias or Galicia; brave, courageous)[1]

A popular flamenco dance that has only a few flamenco or Andalusian roots. The *farruca* originated as an Asturian folk song, but when rendered in fla-menco style on the guitar, it closely resembles the rhythmic structure (*compás*) of a *tango*. El Faico of Triana, a late-nineteenth-century dancer, was one of its earliest innovators. For some time the *farruca* was treated with indifference and disdain by those who continued in the true tradition of the *cuadro fla-menco*, and its performers were given the appellation "*farruqueros*." Today, full of the essence and strength of traditional elements, it is danced on equal terms as *baile chico* with its inspiring parents, *tango* and *alegrías*. *Farruca* provides a strong (*macho*) vehicle for a male solo, with its abrupt stops (*paradas*) and sud-

---

[1] Authorities differ on the meaning. Some say that it is the name of a Galician song as well as the name for the bagpipe of that northwestern province.

den drops to the floor (*caídas*). When it is performed by a woman, the dancer usually wears a riding habit (*traje campero*) or men's high-waisted trousers (*pantalones ceñidos*). The music of the well-known "Miller's Dance" is a *farruca* adapted by Manuel de Falla in his ballet *The Three-Cornered Hat*. Unlike most other dances done in flamenco style, it can be performed without a singer.

See *caída, paseo de farruca, pica tacón* (Basic Positions and Techniques, music), *tiempo de farruca*. See also Appendix: Basic Flamenco Rhythms.

FIBRALTADA *(fee-brahl-TAH-dah)*
(Done with energy)

A vigorous hitch kick performed mostly by males and used in eighteenth- and nineteenth-century dances such as *boleros* and *seguidillas* and in Spanish regional and Basque dances. See *vuelta fibraltada*.

FIESTA *(fee-EHS-ta)*
(Festivity, merriment, entertainment)

A synonym for *jaleo*, which consists of rhythmic hand clapping (*palmas*), finger snapping (*pitos*), shouts of encouragement (*gritos*), and song (*cante*) as an accompaniment to flamenco and Andalusian dances. The term *fin de fiesta*, or grand finale, signifies the closing number of a program. The flamenco term *por fiesta* (festive) is the opposite of *jondo* (serious).

See *jaleo, juerga*.

FIESTAS
See *bulerías*.

FIGURA *(fee-GOO-rah)*
(Figure, model, look)

The outline presented by a dancer. In the arrangement of head, torso, feet, and arms, it is inimitably Spanish. As in painting, the term also refers to the line or general impression made by a group of dancers. The term is similar to the balletic term *ligne*. In the performing arts a prominent leading artist or star is referred to as a *figura*.

The various formations and floor patterns typical of the social dances (*danzas*) popular in eighteenth- and nineteenth-century ballrooms and in today's square dances are called *figuras*.

See *aire, camino, colocarse, compostura, figura plástica, mudanza*.

FIGURA PLASTICA *(fee-GOO-rah PLAHS-tee-cah)*
(Molded figure)

Beautiful momentary poses and attitudes which highlight a dance and leave a lasting impression. Mostly of the romantic era, they were often vividly described by the noted critics of that time. Many of these characteristic poses, such as Fanny Elssler's Cachucha, Anna Pavlova's Swan, and several of La Argentina, have been cast in marble, bronze, and porcelain. Each dancer has a unique and characteristic pose (*figura*) which is immediately identifiable.

See *figura*.

FILIGRANA *(fee-lee-GRAH-nah)*
(Filigree; ornamental, decorative detail)

A flamenco term which has three applications: (1) In dance, it refers to the *bailaora*'s flowing movements of the arms, wrists, and fingers, a form of choreographic filigree. (2) In music, it is a guitarist's variation in which he displays virtuosic fingering and melodic ornamentation before returning to the original theme. (3) The term also means the minutiae of fast footwork, the tricky, rhythmic patterns or fancy, delicate steps, such as *lazos, cuartas, batidos,* and *sacudidos.*

See *braceo* (note 2), *falseta, movimientos de las manos* (Basic Positions and Techniques).

FINAL
See *ida, paso final*

FINALES
See *paso final.*

FLAMENCO *(flah-MEHN-coh)*
(Literally, Flemish)[1]

This all-embracing term has many ramifications in dance (*baile*), singing (*cante*), music (*toque*), and rhythmic hand clapping (*jaleo*), each a major subject and field of endeavor. According to scholarly studies, Gypsies (Flamencos) first came to Spain about the middle of the fifteenth century from the Danube Valley by way of Catalonia. Some authorities believe that they originally came from Egypt, and others are convinced that they came from India. In Spain they have also been called *bohemios, hungáricos, albaneses,* and *gitanos* (Egyptians). Because of the varying esteem in which Gypsies have been held socially, flamenco, like our comparable "bohemian," generally meant to the Spaniard anything ranging from wild, unconventional, brilliant, dashing, and witty to shiftless and rather mad.

Ferocity and languor alternate in flamenco dancing, revealing its Eastern origins in that the arms, hands, and body muscles are given greater play than the legs. Instead of acquiring greater and greater mobility for arms in air design and covering much more floor space as in the European fashion, the flamenco dancer often seems to draw inward until he or she is all but standing still except for rapid action of the heels (*taconeo*), making the dancer a pillar of

---

[1]Speculations on the origins of this word are many. It is believed to have derived from the Arabic *felahmengu* (peasant in flight). Another theory is that the name is related to the boisterous behavior of the Flemish soldiers of occupation in the sixteenth century, when there were close commercial ties, under Charles I of Spain, between Seville and Antwerp. Still a third version comes from the word *flamante,* meaning "flaming," "bright," or "excessively ardent," attributes associated with Gypsies.

shimmering motion. Unlike couple and group dances of Spain, which follow a *copla* verse and chorus (*estribillo y copla*), flamenco dances are based on the individual's use and interpretation of the rhythmic structure (*compás*) of each dance.

A flamenco dance, like the Flamencos' general way of life, is a communal experience, so there is no division between "entertainer" and audience. It is traditionally a solo, usually introverted, dance even though it has been adapted otherwise for the theater and nightclub (*tablao flamenco*).

To quote Rafael Lafuente: "Flamenco is more than just an art; it is the way of looking at life, an integral form of feeling the cosmos and the small world of one's own personality." In every detail flamenco dance provides *tableaux vivants* of an ancient people. Clearly, its main influences are Arabic, Mozarabic, Jewish, Byzantine, and Moorish. So powerfully affecting is Gypsy art that it has colored to varying degrees not only the music of Andalusia but also that of the entire country.

See *compás, gitano*. See also Appendix: Basic Flamenco Rhythms.

FLAMENQUISMO *(flah-mehn-KEES-moh)*
(Deformation of *flamenco*)

Exaggerated and overused movements and clichés that stress only the obvious and spectacular elements of flamenco which both the purist and the discerning individual with good taste decry. *Flamenquismo* is the reverse of pure, or *castizo*, flamenco.

See *castizo, españolado*.

FLOJO *(FLOH-hoh)*
(Weak, lax, feeble)

A derogatory term applied to a dancer's movement, carriage, or style when it lacks energy (*fibra*) or affirmation (*afirmación*), which are principal characteristics of Spanish dance.

See *macho*.

FLOREO *(floh-REH-oh)*
(A flowering, flourish)

In this step, used mainly by women, the lifted leg causes the skirt to flounce or "flower"; hence the name.

Beg pos	Feet—3rd L front.
	Arms—4th L up, head turned slightly to right.
Ct 1	Lift R leg forward to hip level (*destaque*).
Ct 2	Draw back lower leg toward body as knee flicks up skirt.

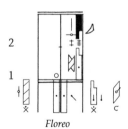

Floreo

The second count is the major accent.
The action can be performed in a slow
lyrical or sharp staccato manner.

FLOREO CON VUELTA *(floh-REH-oh cohn VWEHL-tah)*
(A flowering, flourish, while turning)

A lyrical step, usually done by women, consisting of a skirt movement made
with the knee, followed by a turn in place.

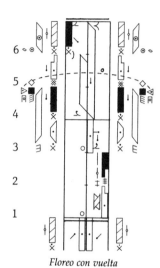

Beg Pos   Feet—3rd R front.
           Arms—5th.

    Ct 1   Lift R leg forward to hip height.
    Ct 2   Bend knee, drawing lower leg in to-
           ward body, lifting knee slightly, toss-
           ing skirt into air.
    Ct 3   Cross R tightly over L.
 Ct 4–6 Make one complete turn left on balls
           of feet, ending in 3rd, weight on R, L
           foot on ball *(vuelta normal* or *vuelta por
           delante).*

  Arms
 Ct 3–6 Circle out and down, passing through
           2nd to low 5th front, then up midline
           of body, returning to 5th.

Floreo con vuelta

FLORETA PASADA *(floh-REH-tah pah-SAH-dah)*
(Flowering, flourish, while moving)

Beg pos   Continues from previous action.

    Ct 1   Step L forward, arms move to 4th L
           up; turn head slightly to right.
    Ct 2   Lift R leg forward hip height.
    Ct 3   Bend R knee as lower leg comes in
           toward body *(retirada),* lifting knee
           slightly.
 Ct 4–5 Step R forward.
    Ct 6   Step L forward, or take weight next
           to R.[1]

           Repeat all, reversed. The step can
           travel in any chosen direction.

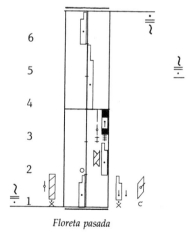

Floreta pasada

See *paseo.*

---

[1]If the step is repeated several times, as in a *paseo,* and greater distance must be covered, the last step is
taken forward, "passing by" *(pasada)* the other foot. If a shorter pattern is desired, the feet come together
side by side *(paralelo).*

FOLKLORE *(folk-LOH-reh)*
(Folklore; English word adopted by the Spaniards)[1]

The Spanish term is a contemporary one used generically to classify the folk or regional dances indigenous to particular provinces of Spain. However, many of those dances are now being presented as *danzas* in today's theaters in the repertoires of many professional *folklore* companies.

FRUNCIMIENTOS DE ENTRECEJOS *(froon-thee-mee-EHN-tohs deh enh-treh-THEH-hohs)*
(Frownings, knittings of the brow)

A natural reaction resulting from the complete emotional involvement of a true flamenco artist in his or her performance. When such facial expressions are artificially assumed (in the belief that they will "create" a flamenco appearance), the spirit of the dance is negated.

See *duende, expresión.*

GADITANA *(gah-dee-TAH-nah)*
(Woman of Cádiz)

The ancient name for Cádiz was Gadir. At one time Cádiz was the principal dance center, in which the finest female dancers, called *andaluces delicias* (delicious Andalusians), were recruited to entertain abroad as performing artists.

GAITA *(GAH-ee-tah)*
(Bagpipe)

This ancient instrument, indigenous to various provinces of northern Spain, especially Galicia, is often the principal accompaniment for the folk dances of those areas. Although many believe this bagpipe to be of Celtic origin, the *gaita* has only one drone, whereas the bagpipes of Ireland have two, and those of Scotland have three.

GARBO *(GAHR-boh)*
(Elegance, gentility)

"Con garbo" is the Spaniard's way of describing the qualities of elegance and gentility in a dance or in a performing artist's stage presence and demeanor.

---

[1] Note that the Spanish adjective form, *folklórico*, is used throughout this volume.

GARROTIN *(gah-roh-TEEN)*
(Literally, small club, garrote)

The *garrotín*, a Gypsy dance, has a marked, even rhythm like that of a *farruca* and falls in the rhythmic cycle (*compás*) of four or eight counts. The song which accompanies the dance is light in mood, joyful, and easygoing, with meaningless nonsensical syllables that often fill out an entire melodic line. In spite of its gracious South American overtones, it is not, as one would guess, from South America, and its origin is disputed among authorities. One theory is that the song which accompanies the dance is Asturian, from northwestern Spain; another credits the Gypsies of the *barrio* of Canaret, in Lerida, and of the city of Valls, a neighbor of Barcelona. The dance's light and carefree (*chico*) character and its music were welcomed with open arms throughout Andalusia, and slowly the Flamencos are adopting it into their repertoire.

The heyday of the *garrotín* has passed, but if one is ever fortunate enough to see a rare version of the old style (*estilo antiguo*) of the dance, one cannot help but be utterly captured by its charm.

See Appendix: Basic Flamenco Rhythms.

GESTO *(HEHS-toh)*
(Grimace, gesture)

Spontaneous expression or action caused by emotional involvement while dancing.

See *duende, expresión, fruncimientos de entrecejos.*

GIRADAS *(hee-RAH-dahs)*
(Gyrations, revolutions, turns)

Spins or turns on the ball of the foot in folkloric dances. The Catalonian term is *girats.*

GIRATS
See *giradas.*

GITANO *(hee-TAH-noh)*
(Gypsy)

The name given to Gypsies from the Sacromonte caves of Granada as opposed to those called Flamencos, from Triana, the outskirts of Seville. The vernacular name which all Gypsies recognize is Romne, Romano, or Rom. One theory of the origin of the Gitanos is that they migrated from Egypt; another is that the term is associated with the Sanskrit *gita* (song) of India, from which they are believed to have emigrated.

See flamenco.

GLISADA *(glee-SAH-dah)*
(Slide; Hispanicized French)

A dancing master's term of the eighteenth and nineteenth centuries for a motion similar to a balletic *glissade*. Sometimes called *glisés,* today these steps are also referred to as *lisadas* in the *escuela bolera.*

See *glisés, lisada por detrás de escuela bolera, lizada.*

GLISES *(glee-SEHS)*
(Glides; borrowed from the French *glissé*)

A term used by eighteenth- and nineteenth-century dancing masters in social dances of the court and ballroom. It includes those steps that display a gliding or sliding action, and each variation has its own name.

See *glisada, lizada.*

GOLPE *(GOHL-peh)*
(A strike, hit)

This term has three applications: (1) In dance, it is the short term for *golpe de pie,* a single stamp of the foot, one of the basic movements of *zapateado.* (2) In castanet playing, it is a single stroke on either or both castanets. (3) In guitar playing (*toque*), it is a knock or rap on a surface (*golpeador*) mounted on the instrument. In musical notation (*cifra*) a *golpe* is represented by a small square figure.

See *seco.*

GOLPECITO *(gohl-peh-THEE-toh)*
(Small strike, hit)

The term has two applications: (1) In dancing, it is a light stamp or tap with the ball of the foot, used more as an accent than as an audible sound. (2) In castanet playing, it is a gentle striking of both castanets together.

See *golpe, golpeo.*

GOLPE DE PIE
See *golpe.*

GOLPEO *(gohl-PEH-oh)*
(Repeated striking, knocking, beating)
Also called *martillo.*

The overemphasized, forceful beating of the left-hand castanet (*macho*). This loud, repetitive beating is prevalent in group folk and regional dances but is colorless and unmusical in concert dancing.

See *accentuación, crotalogía, golpeteo, macho, matiz.*

GOLPETEO *(gohl-peh-TEH-oh)*
(Continued, constant knocking, striking, hammering)

A beat derived from repetitious pounding on an anvil, used to maintain a basic rhythmic pattern *(compás)*. Singing *(cante)* was the only accompaniment to such flamenco items as *martinetes* (fatalistic songs of persecuted Gypsy blacksmiths). When the relentless repetition of *golpeteo* was added, it produced a powerful and dramatic background. These songs were never intended to be used for dancing *(para bailar)* until the renowned Antonio introduced this time-marking device in a theater piece. Today it is a unique feature in flamenco dance concerts.

See *golpeo, macho.*

GORGALLATA *(gohr-gah-LYAH-tah)*
(Whirlpool; from *gorga*)

An inside and an outside *rodazán* which travel to one side in the following sequence give the effect of small whirlpools. Step to the right followed by an inward *(por adentro) rodazán* with the left foot and a half turn of the body—then step on the left followed by an outward *(por afuera) rodazán* with the right foot and a half turn of the body completing the turn. Women in classic dance perform this step by lifting the *rodazanes* high and with much flourish, but men perform them very low. The action is like a balletic *gargouillade*.

See *rodazán.*

GORGALLATA DE ESCUELA BOLERA *(gohr-goh-LYAH-tah deh ehs-CWEH-*
    lah boh-LEH-rah)
(A *gargallata* done in the *escuela bolera* style)
Also called *rodazán afuera y adentro.*

The name of this step is derived from the "stirring" action of the lower limbs.

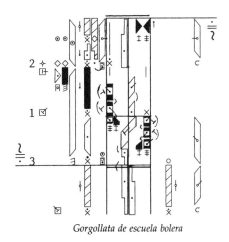

Beg pos	Feet—4th R front, facing downstage left. Arms—5th, head turned slightly to right.
Ct 3	Shift weight back onto L foot, R leg performing an outward *rodazán al aire* while turning body to face downstage right.
Ct 1	Make leap onto R *(echado)*, as L leg quickly performs inward *rodazán* while continuing to turn body to face stage right.
Ct 2	Make small leap onto L (R foot comes to pass back of left ankle very low on ct &); incline torso back and twist so

Gorgollata de escuela bolera

that shoulder blades face audience;
turn head left to full profile.

Ct 3   Step back on R to repeat to opposite
        side.

Arms   Make complete outward circle with L
        arm as follows:

Ct 3   Begin circling L arm out and down,
        passing through 2nd; turn head
        slightly to left.
Ct 1   Continue circling L arm to 5th low
        front.
Ct 2   Circle L arm up, passing up midline
        of body, returning to 5th.

See *rodazán*.

GRACIA *(GRAH-thee-ah)*
(Grace, charm, wit)

A woman dancer's personality, spontaneous movement, or mannerism that
has not been choreographed into a dance but is her personal expression. A
gracia should be original and, when not imitated or borrowed, should emerge
spontaneously.

See *pellizco*.

GRANDE *(GRAHN-deh)*
(Large, exceptional)

A flamenco classification of dance (*baile*), singing (*cante*), and music (*toque*)
which reflects the serious or tragic sentiments of life's endeavors. As its alternate name, *jondo* (deep, bottom), implies, it is the foundation on which all
other lighter, less serious forms are built.

GRAVES Y BREVES *(GRAH-vehs ee BREH-vehs)*
(Heavy, ponderous and short, concise [movements])

Musical terms applied by the dancing masters to steps of the seventeenth-
through nineteenth-century dances of the court and nobility. The first term,
grave, designated the style or manner in which the movement was to be performed, namely slowly and solemnly. The second, *breve*, was concerned with
the duration of a movement. At the time, it meant a note of the shortest duration. Today it is equivalent to two full notes. Contemporary ballroom dance
teachers use such terms as *quicks and slows* and *longs and shorts*.

See *bailes palaciegos, danza, pavana*.

GRITO *(GREE-toh)*
(Shout)

el fuego   the fire

Extemporaneous vocal expression of approval or encouragement for a performer which punctuates the general merry making atmosphere (*jaleo*) of a
party (*juerga*) or the more formal atmosphere of a concert-theater presentation. *Gritos* can range from a guttural sound of approval or single word such
as "¡Ole!" "¡Anda!" "¡Vamo!" or "¡Toma!" to a short phrase using the performer's name or "¡Viva tu madre!" "¡Así se baila!" or "¡Hija del fuego!" to a
longer phrase or whole sentence with philosophic or personal overtones. Although usually associated with Andalusian dancing, the term *grito* has its
equivalents throughout the Iberian Peninsula, such as *Alborbola* (Valencian),
Irrintzi (Basque), *Ixuxu* (Asturian), and *Aturuxo* (Galician).

See *irrintzi.*

GUAJIRA *(gwah-HEE-rah)*
(Rustic, peasant song; Cuban song)

The music of *guajira* is of sixteenth-century Cuban origin and has, when inter-
preted in a flamenco style, a sweet quality reflecting a warm atmosphere of
tropical palms. Its rhythm, like the rhythm of *peteneras,* is a broken one with
a gentle agitating quality, the first bar of ⁶⁄₈ meter followed by one bar in ¾,
and has no set choreographic form. This easygoing, almost lazy mood is a perfect vehicle for female dancers who employ lyrical fan movements (*abaniqueo*).
At the turn of the century, *guajira* was a popular school dance (*baile de escuela*)
arranged for piano accompaniment for Seville's great dancing master José
Otero.

See *abaniqueo.* See also Appendix: Basic Flamenco Rhythms.

GURPIL
See *pasos vascos básicos* (*grabiletia*).

HACER MUTIS
See *mutis.*

HECHO Y DESHECHO *(EH-choh ee dehs-EH-choh)*
(Done and undone)[1]

An unusual series of jumps with beating action of the *escuela bolera*.

Beg pos   Feet—5th L front.
          Arms—5th.

          Preparation—Jump into air.
Ct 1   Land in 2nd.
Ct &   Jump into air, beating R leg front, L
          leg back.
Ct 2   Land in 5th L front.
Ct &   Jump into air, beating R leg front, L
          leg back.
Ct 1   Land in 2nd.
Ct &–2–& Repeat, reversed.

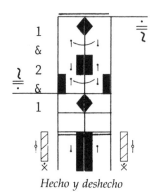

Hecho y deshecho

See *batidos, derechas, vistoso*.

HEMBRA *(EHM-brah)*
(Female)

The female aspect of Spanish dancing, in which the span of human emotions can be expressed dramatically. In contrast to her male (*macho*) counterpart, these qualities can range from a gentle expression of shyness and courtship in folkloric dances, with little movement of the arms and with the hands often resting on the hips (*en jarras*), to the flamenco style of Andalusia, in which the dancer's arms should be serpentine, entwining and insinuatingly sensual, ending in the fingers, which are held apart, curling, unfurling, and flowering in Moorish arabesques (*arabescos*). With the rise of "women's liberation," much of the *hembra* subtlety is being lost by the *bailaora's* retaliating gestures of strength toward her partner.

The term is also used to refer to the right-hand castanet, which is at least a third higher in pitch and is the *carretilla*, (rolling, trill-making) counterpart and companion to the left, the male (*macho*).

HILERA *(ee-LEH-rah)*
(Row, line, file)
Colloquially called *calles* (streets).

In regional dances, two or more lines of dancers that are parallel to each other. *Hilera* is the basic formation of contradances.

---

[1]The Spanish verb *deshacer* literally means to undo, untie, take apart; however, the early dancing masters used it as meaning to reverse the action, in this case the beating action.

Figure 1. Originally, flamenco and many Andalusian dances were performed as solos. Today, traditional steps and techniques choreographed for large corps de ballets accent organization and discipline. *Photo by Antonio de Benito, courtesy of the Royal Ballet Nacional de España.*

Figure 2. A favorite court dance of the Spanish, French, and English aristocracy was the *pavana*. Here cardinals of Narbonne and of Saint Séverin perform this *baile palaciego* for Louis XII at Milan in 1499. *New York Public Library Picture Collection.*

Figure 3. Children on a street in Seville improvise on rhythms that come naturally as a spontaneous ethnic expression. *Courtesy of Lydia Joel.*

Figure 4. Students of Irene Tungate are taught to assume a "Spanish look." *Courtesy of Lydia Joel.*

Figure 5. Dame Marina Keet, a founding member of the Spanish Dance Society of South Africa (an international network operating in twelve countries on five continents), with two of her students at the University of Cape Town Ballet School. Dame Marina presently teaches in Washington, D.C. *Courtesy M. Grut.*

Figure 6. Spain's beloved La Macarrona appears in a *bata de cola*, the ancestor of the dancing dress of the present-day *flamenca. Courtesy of José Udaeta.*

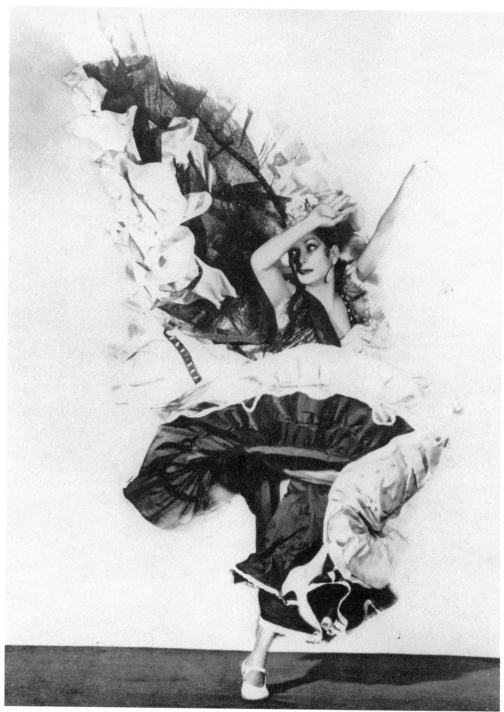

Figure 7. Carmen Amaya, pure-blooded Gypsy who overwhelmed audiences everywhere, seen performing her spectacular *coletazo en vuelta* (lashing of the tail while turning). *Reproduced from a souvenir program.*

Figure 8. The antecedent of the flamenco dancer as we know her today accompanied herself with finger snapping *(pitos)*. Until relatively recently a true *bailaora* (flamenco dancer) never used castanets. *Courtesy of José Udaeta.*

Figure 9. This photo of a female dancer wearing a man's outfit predates World War I, shattering the idea that this is a recent innovation. *Courtesy of José Udaeta.*

Figure 10. Manolo Vargas and Roberto Ximénez, co-creators in the early 1950s of such memorable dance-dramas as *La Peternera, La Monja Gitana, De Querer Amores,* and *Clavalina,* added a powerful creative force to the present-day Spanish theater dance. *Photo by Jack Mitchell.*

Figure 11. A view of the famous Sacromonte, outside Granada, dwelling place for thousands of Gypsies through the centuries and birthplace of many world-renowned *bailaoras* and *bailaores*. *Photo by Lydia Joel.*

Figure 12. Gypsies outside their hand-hewn cave dwelling at Sacromonte in 1890 danced spontaneously for their own amusement and the occasional sightseer. *Courtesy of* The Guitar Review.

Figure 13. María Heredia, "La Canastera," in her Sacromonte tourist cave during the mid-1950s, a period when nightly "flamenco entertainment" became a lucrative business divided between local hotels and the caves. *Photo by Lydia Joel.*

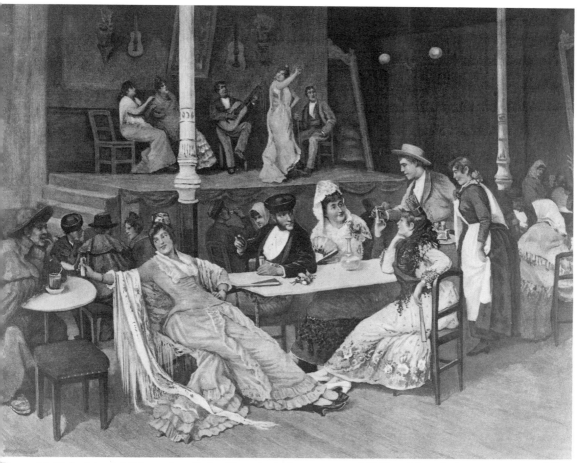

Figure 14. Colorful establishments called *cafés cantantes* began around 1842 and lasted almost a century. Offering as many as four flamenco performances nightly, they were the important link in transposing flamenco from the caves and barrios to the stage. *From Alarcón, New York Public Library Picture Collection.*

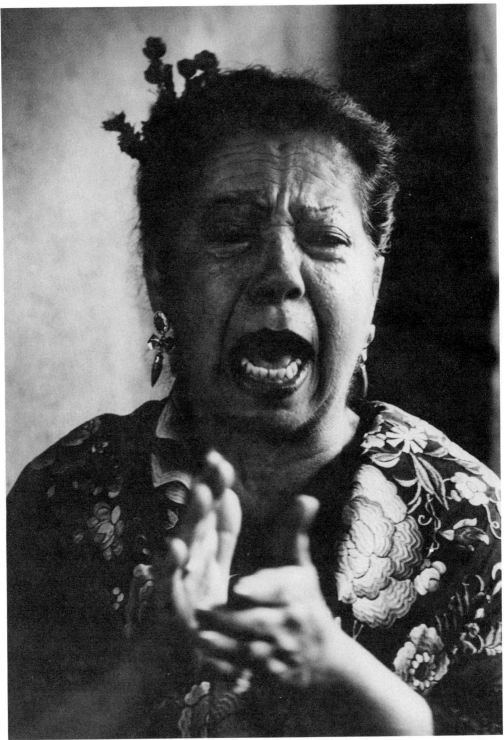

Figure 15. Fernanda de Utrera is one of this century's most important singers of *soleares*, melancholy, earthy songs with traditional lyrics that are embellished and improvised each time they are sung. *Photographed by José Arman-Pita for Vanity Fair/c. 1986 by the Condé Nast Publications, Inc.*

Figure 16. Joaquín Amador and La Farruquita (Rosario Montoya) performing *bulerías*, an improvised dance with difficult, constantly changing rhythms. *Photo by José Arman-Pita for Vanity Fair/c. 1986 by the Condé Nast Publications, Inc.*

Figure 17. Gypsy woman dancing on a table top, an early form of improvised stage. Pictured here is a dance for good luck in the presence of an anxious torero before a corrida. *New York Public Library Picture Collection.*

Figure 18 (above left). Teo Morca, one of America's outstanding dancers and teachers, caught in a *cigüeña* pose reminiscent of the characteristic stance of a stork, after which it is named. *Photo by Isabel Morca.*

Figure 19 (above right). La Meri performing a *panaderos en vuelta*, an example of counterline *(torcido)* of the upper torso, characteristic of most Andalusian dancing. *Photo by Dwight Godwin.*

Figure 20 (right). María Benítez, of American Indian and Puerto Rican descent, gives full dramatic expression with spontaneous shouts when moved by *duende*, the spirit within. *Courtesy of Harry Rubenstein Mgt.*

Figure 21. An unusual photograph of two of Spain's most revered turn-of-the-century maestros, José Otero (right) and his nephew, Manuel. In his definitive book, *Tratado de baile* (1921), José Otero strongly advocated the teaching of Andalusian dance by way of terminology. *Courtesy of Hortense d'Arblay.*

Figure 22. Dolores Serral (who taught her famous *cachucha* to Fanny Elssler) and León Camprubí dancing an eighteenth-century bolero. After taking on the polish and refinement of the royal Spanish court, the bolero became the rage and was presented by small groups, called *cuadros boleros,* much like today's *cuadros flamencos. Originally published by H. C. Maguire, London, in 1884.*

Figure 23. Eloy Pericet teaching an *escuela bolera* class in Barcelona. The Pericet family for four generations was largely responsible for the development and preservation of the classical nineteenth-century *escuela bolera* style. *Photo by Matteo.*

Figure 24. Puerto Rican Carlos de la Cámara caught in the airborne style of the eighteenth-century *escuela bolera*, which maintained its Spanish identity in the carriage of the arms *(braceo)* and castanets and the Italian dancing masters' balletic technique, which excels in spectacular *trenzados* (woven, plaited footwork). *Photo by John Lindquist.*

Figure 25. Matteo (center) with members of his EthnoAmerican Dance Theatre in a nineteenth-century Spanish sequence from "America Has Many Faces," celebrating America's bicentennial. *Photo by Susan Cook.*

IDA *(EE-dah)*
(Departure, a going out)
Also called *final.*

A specially arranged section in an *alegría* which ushers in the ending with a *bulería* rhythm. It usually consisted of two phrases (*compases*) of music, beginning characteristically with four stamps moving backward, and usually followed a particular well-known melody (*falseta*). It began the climax of the dance. The term is no longer in popular use.

IMPROVISACION *(eem-proh-vee-sah-thee-OHN)*
(Improvisation)

An aspect of a flamenco dance which allows the dancer artistic freedom to demonstrate his or her ability to improvise body movements and footwork (*zapateado*), but within the strict rules of rhythmic compliance (*compás*). Before they reached the theater, most flamenco solos were based largely on improvisation, that individual catalyst which induces true flamenco "magic" (*duende*).

See *a capricho, duende.*

INFUNDIDOS *(een-FOON-dee-dohs)*
(From *infundir:* to imbue, instill)

Visual body accentuations such as dipping and rising while making small running steps (*carrerillas*).

INTRODUCCION *(een-troh-dooc-thee-OHN)*
(Introduction, presentation)

The music played at the beginning of a dance. It may or may not be accompanied by movement. It is not to be confused with *salida.*

See *paseo de gracia, paseo de presentación.*

IRRINTZI *(ee-REEN-tzee)*
(Traditional shout, ululation; Basque)

A sound unique to the Basques and often heard during their dancing. The Basque will sing and shout when the spirit moves him, and on festive occasions he gives vent to the old war cry (*irrintzi*). Its uniqueness makes it difficult to describe accurately; it is both heroic and hideous, a shout of supreme joy but at the same time a warning challenging anything in its way. It is quite long and can begin as a derisive laugh that changes to a horse's shrill neigh to a wolf's howl and ends with the expiring notes of a jackass's bray. It is said that this foreboding shout was so hair-raising that Napoleon's soldiers, invading Spain, shuddered to hear it.

See *grito.*

ITALIANA *(ee-tah-lee-AH-nah)*
(Italian)
Also called *cuarta italiana.*

One of the virtuosic beaten steps (*batidos*) of the *escuela bolera* as taught in the Italian manner. This action closely resembles a *cuarta cuadrada.*

Beg pos	Feet—2nd, knees bent.
	Arms—Optional.
	Preparation—Jump into air, beating R leg in front of L, then beating L leg in front of R.
Ct 1	Land in 2nd, knees bent.

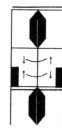

1

Italiana

JALEADOR *(hah-leh-ah-DOHR)*
(One who makes merry)
Also called *jaleista.*

Usually used in the plural, *jaleodores* are those in a *cuadro flamenco* who animate and encourage the dancer or dancers. This encouragement may include hand clapping, finger snapping, shouts, and singing (*palmas, pitos, gritos, cante*). To the onlooker it may appear to be spontaneous noise making, but one has to have a thorough knowledge and mastery of the many flamenco rhythms (*compases*) and counter-rhythms (*contra tiempos*) to be a true *jaleador.* Expert *jaleadores* are well known for their capabilities and are in great demand at concerts and parties (*juergas*).

See *contratiempo.*

JALEISTA
See *jaleador.*

JALEO *(hah-LEH-oh)*
(Rhythmic sound accompanying performers)

(1) An inclusive term referring to the general atmosphere of a dance performance, but usually pertaining to a *cuadro flamenco*. It can include any rhythmic sounds that urge on the dancers, who alternate with the singers, such as rhythmic hand clapping (*palmas*), finger snapping (*pitos*), shouts (*gritos*), song (*cante*), and tapping of wooden canes (*báculos*). Although generally thought of as a flamenco term, *jaleo* accompanies all types of Spanish dancing in which spectators take an active and helpful part. (2) A gay Andalusian dance in triple meter, usually performed as a female solo. For many aficionados of Spanish dance, *Jaleo* is the principal American publication dedicated to the propagation and advancement of authentic flamenco music, song, and dance.

See *fiesta, grito, juerga.*

JALEO DE MANOS
See *palmas.*

JEREZANA CON VUELTA *(heh-reh-THAH-nah cohn VWEHL-tah)*
(A step from Jerez with turn)

As stated under *paso de jerezana,* the woman kicks backward high enough to flounce the hem of her skirt. Men always perform this step very low unless they are dancing certain classic eighteenth- and nineteenth-century dances such as *boleros, seguidillas,* and other energetic regional dances.

Beg pos Feet—Weight on L.
        Arms—4th L up.

Ct 1 Touch ball of R diagonally forward, incline torso and head, and turn slightly toward R leg.

Ct 2 Hold.

Ct 3 Brush R toe backward describing small inward semicircle (*media luna*) and kick same foot backward and outward (as leg rotates slightly inward); turn torso slightly away from moving leg.

Ct 4–6 Cross R in front tightly over L, leading into one full turn left on balls of feet ending in 3rd L front (*vuelta normal*). Pass L arm through 2nd to low 4th behind; then change arms to low 4th L front, returning torso and head to normal. In *flamenco* dance, men often slap the side of the lifted shoe (*palmada*) just as the turn is started.

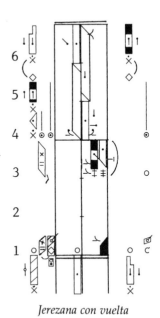

Jerezana con vuelta

See *paso de jerezana.*

JEREZANA SALTADA EN VUELTA *(heh-reh-THAH-nah sahl-TAH-dah ehn VWEHL-tah)*
(Step from Jerez, with a hop in a turn)

A showy (*vistoso*) ending to a musical phrase typical of *seguidillas*.

Beg pos   Ct &   Ct 6–1   Ct 2–3   Ct 4–5–6

Beg pos Feet—3rd or 5th R front.
         Arms—5th.

  Ct &   Extend L toe diagonally forward, both
         knees slightly bent, torso inclined to-
         ward L leg.
  Ct 6   Spring vertically, brushing L foot up
         in back of knee (*jerezana*).
  Ct 1   Land on R.
  Ct 2   Cross L tightly over R.
Ct 3–6   Make one full turn right on balls of
         feet, ending in 3rd or 5th R front, as
         in *vuelta normal.*

Arms
Ct 6–6   Make one full outward circle, the
         arms passing through 2nd, 5th low
         back, and 1st and returning to 5th.

         The woman's part is described above;
         the man does the opposite when they
         are turning away from each other. If
         partners turn toward each other (as
         pictured), the woman begins by ex-
         tending her R toe; then, following the
         spring, she turns to her left and the
         man to his right.

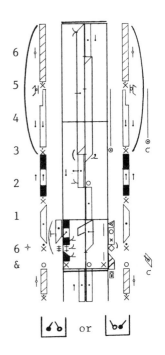

Jerezana saltada en vuelta

JONDO *(HOHN-doh)*
(Spanish; *hondo* deep, low, bottom)

A flamenco term which is applied to dance (*baile*), singing (*cante*), and guitar playing (*toque*), indicating a serious, profound, or tragic sentiment or mood.

JOTA *(JOH-tah)*
(Spanish dance and its music)[1]

The word *jota* not only is a choreographic term but also includes song (*cante*), both melody and the words that are sung before or during the dance. The words, like the dance, express a variety of emotions, such as feelings of love, bravery, and manliness. Since all *jotas* are based on social encounter and courtship, the steps are always performed face to face with a partner (*pasos enfrentados*). The *jota*, like many of the other principal dances of Spain, has many "brothers, sisters, and cousins," all of which are related yet highly individual. Indeed, one could witness an entire evening of *jotas* from various provinces of Spain, each with its own indigenous costume, character, style of movement, and music, and the array would be amazing. *Jotas* of Aragón (*jotas aragonesas*) are marvelously suited to the Aragonese—tenacious, stubborn, strongly built men and women. What they seem to lack in sophistication they more than compensate for in outspokenness and sincerity. Their dances, which are the ones most often seen in Spanish dance concerts, are very lively and exuberant and literally spring from the soil with challenging kicks, leaps, and turns. These steps, in spite of their almost acrobatic nature, are often performed on the tips of the dancers' hemp-soled canvas sandals (*alpargatas*).

A *jota* can vary in style and tempo depending on its geographical setting. The *jota* from the province of Valencia is slow and easy, not jumped, and women use heeled shoes. Some *jotas* are danced in parallel lines (*hileras*), others in a circle, and another in groups of two or three, but always face to face. In some dances the castanets are played on the thumb, in others on the middle finger. In some dances castanets are played by both men and women, in others only by the women, or, as in Basque versions, not at all. *Jotas* can be calm and sedate with dainty, footwork, never moving off the ground and the dancers only modestly looking at each other. In another version, the women

---

[1]From folkloric hearsay and scholarly research come several theories concerning the etymology of *jota*: (1) from *sotar* (to jump); (2) from Aben Jot, a twelfth-century Moorish poet and musician, the reputed inventor of the dance; (3) from Basque *jotu* (to play an instrument).

are lifted into the air by their partners. Still another is danced while the dancers plait the ribbons of a maypole.[1]

At the introduction of a *jota* a singer begins with a verse (*copla*); then the dance section breaks out in showy (*vistoso*) and strongly accented steps, all very robust, vigorous, and energetic—it is almost more an endurance contest than a dance. To the native there can be no *jota* without singing (*cante*). It is believed that the sung sections were introduced and alternated with the danced sections as rest periods (*descansos*). However, many times this is ignored when a *jota* is presented in the theater, and the sung sections are either choreographed or filled with mime (*mímica*). The basic position for almost all *jotas* is with the arms open wide at shoulder level or higher, sometimes almost squared off (*folklórico*). The chest is held high, and in *jotas* such as those of upper Aragón the weight of the body leans well back, with knees bent enough to give the torso a seated (*asentado*) appearance.

These ethnic characteristics are often overlooked. This is especially true in stage presentations, in which women wear tights and brief panties rather than the traditional white knee-length stockings and bloomers. The result is that some theatrical *jotas* give a very balletic or "graceful" look to an essentially earthy dance.

See *caballo folklórico; cabriola; cuna; más saltadora; palmas, paso de jota sencillo (variaciones en vuelta, despedida, tubo); pitos, y castañuelas; vuelta de rodilla* (Basic Positions and Techniques, *forma* 2).

JOTA EN VUELTA *(HO-tah ehn VWEHL-tah)*
(A *jota* step in a turn)

Beg pos   Same as *paso de jota sencillo o básico.*

 Ct &   Jump into air.
 Ct 1   Land firmly with feet apart in 2nd, knees bent (*cuadrada*).
 Ct 2   Pause.
 Ct 3   Spring onto L, raising R leg sideward, knee bent.
Ct 4–6   Make one complete right turn of three small running steps R, L, R in place (*en sitio*).

  Repeat all, reversed, finish facing audience if a solo or partner if a duet.

See *paso de jota sencillo.*

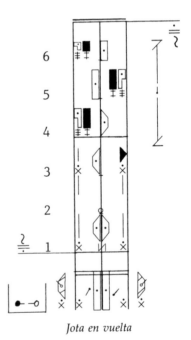

Jota en vuelta

JUERGA *(HWEHR-gah)*
(Merrymaking party, get-together, flamenco "jam session")

Generally speaking, a *juerga* consists of an evening get-together of flamenco dance, music, and song (*baile, guitarra, y cante*), during which participants enjoy each other's company, talents, food, and drink. For decades *juergas*, especially in the caves of Granada, have been scheduled and staged for tourists. With their superficial dances, prearranged noise making (*jaleo*), photo taking, and souvenir buying, there is little to recommend them. A true *juerga* evolves and is never the same. Such functions have been known to last several days and nights. Some Spaniards use the term *fiesta flamenca.*

Although the average dance enthusiast may not realize it, *juergas* are not confined to Spain. More than ever, individuals who have traveled and studied flamenco dance, guitar, or singing wish to share their talents and exchange experiences in an atmosphere of fun and camaraderie. *Juergas* are held periodically in the United States, especially in the West and Midwest. A bimonthly calendar of these events is published and available to all flamenco lovers (*aficionados*). Since theatrical performances are not comparable in impact to the spontaneous event, such *juergas* are the only way to re-create this intimate art form and make it available outside Spain.

See *aficionado, enterao, fiesta, jaleo.*

JUGUETILLOS
See *coletilla.*

LABERINTO *(lah-bah-REEN-toh)*
(Labyrinth, maze)

A term usually applied to eighteenth- and nineteenth-century dances of the *escuela bolera* in which the dancer moves in various directions while making a circuitous path and weaving delicate foot patterns (*filigranas de pie*) such as *lazos*. These movements are eye-catching and a pleasure to watch.

See *filigrana, lazos.*

LARGO
See *llarg.*

LAZOS *(LAH-thos)*
(Slipknots)
Also called *encajes.*

This step gives an effect of brilliance and fleetness. It is a virtuosic (*vistoso*) step usually performed in *zapatillas* (soft, heelless slippers) typical of the eighteenth and nineteenth centuries and is invariably an applause winner.

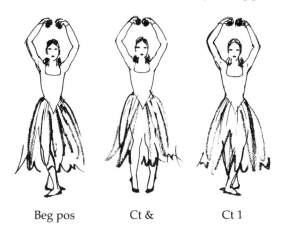

Beg pos   Ct &   Ct 1

Beg pos   Feet—5th R front.
          Arms—5th.

   Ct &   Turn heels outward (pigeon-toed) on
          each count &.

   Ct 1   Slip L foot into 5th front with thighs
          held closely as legs move easily from
          the hip sockets. *Lazos* are actually se-
          ries of 5th positions performed rap-
          idly on half toe, "skimming" the floor.
          They can be performed either forward
          (*adelante*) or backward (*detrás*).

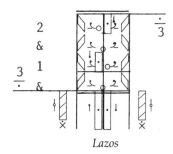

Lazos

See *enlaces*.

Ct: & 1 & 2 & 3 & 1 & 2 & 3 &

LETRA *(LEH-trah)*
(Text, words, lyrics)

The text or words of a song (*cante*) which is an inseparable part of many Spanish dances. *Letra* can express the complete panorama of life, its joys, sorrows, and various other experiences. *Letra* can be personal, metaphysical, sentimental, satirical, and even political. It establishes the mood of a selection, be it light (*chico*), somewhat serious (*intermedio*), or profound (*jondo, grande*).

See *copla*.

LISADA POR DETRAS DE ESCUELA BOLERA *(lee-SAH-dah por deh-TRAHS deh ehs-CWEH-lah boh-LEH-rah)*
(Gliding movement [finishing] in back in *escuela bolera* style)
Also called *glisada;* from French *glissade*.

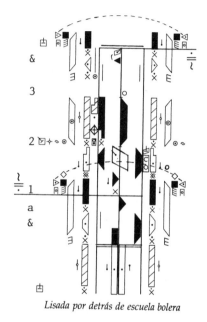

Beg pos Feet—5th L front.
Arms—5th.

Ct & Lift R leg low to side and spring into air.
Ct a Land on R, traveling right (*echado*).
Ct 1 Quickly step L across R (*paso cruzado*).
Ct & Leap into air, extending R leg low to side (*asamblé saltada*).
Ct 2 Land on R, traveling right, facing downstage left corner, swinging L leg to back, knee bent, torso inclined forward, head and chest turned slightly right.
Ct 3 Hold.
Ct & Repeat above counts starting L.

Arms
Ct & a 1 & 2 Circle arms out and down, passing through 2nd to 5th low front; rotate lower arms in, then pass up midline of body to 5th.
Ct 3 Hold.

Repeat all above, reversed.

Lisada por detrás de escuela bolera

LISO *(LEE-soh)*
(Unadorned, alone)

A term applied to a dance such as a classical *bolero* when it is performed as a solo. It is the opposite of *robado*, in which partners alternately present variations.

See *robado*

LIZADA *(lee-THAH-dah)*
(Slide; from French *glissade*)
Also called *glisada*.

In old manuscripts the term refers to gliding motions in social dances (*danzas*).

See *glisada, sease y contraseasé de escuela bolera*.

LLAMADA *(lyah-MAH-dah)*
(Call or signal to attract attention)
Also called *Llamada flamenca*.

A means by which a flamenco dancer notifies or cues the guitarist of a forthcoming change of rhythm or the next section of the dance being performed, such as *soleares, alegrías, romeras, mirabrás, caracoles,* and *cantinas,* all of which are played in a three-four rhythm *(compás)* in phrases of twelve counts.

The usual *llamada* consists of six quick, consecutive stamps *(golpes de pie)*, which utilize the first six counts of the phrase to be closed *(cierre)*. The remaining six counts usually consist of two stamps *(golpes)* on the left foot (ct 7), two on the right (ct 8), two more on the left (ct 9), and a final stamp on the right (ct 10). The last two counts (eleven and twelve) are held absolutely immobile *(parado)*, with much affirmation *(afirmación)* before the dancer continues on to the next tempo and musical theme *(tema)* or ends the dance entirely *(paso final)*.

A *llamada* can also signal a dancer's entrance *(salida)* or the closing *(cierre)* that is approaching. It is similar to a *break* in American terminology. Although it is simply referred to as *llamada*, correct usage of the term requires that it be followed by the name of the section or the music for which the signal is intended, e.g., *llamada por castellana, llamada por bulerías*.

See *aviso, desplante*. See also Appendix: Basic Flamenco Rhythms.

LLAMADA ANDALUZA *(lyah-MAH-dah ahn-dah-LOOTH-ah)*
(Motion or sign to call attention in Andalusian style)

The step is the same as the *sostenido* or the *escuela bolera*. This term was used in the school of José Otero, of Seville, Spain's famous teacher of Andalusian dance.

See *sostenido*.

LLAMADA EN VUELTA
See *sostenido en vuelta*.

LLARG *(lyahrg)*
(Long, extended, prolonged; Catalonian for *largo*)

The *llarg* is a typical step in a Catalonian *sardana*. It determines in which direction the circle moves.

Beg pos Feet—1st position (dancers standing in a circle).
Arms—Holding hands slightly above 2nd, elbows very slightly bent.

Ct 1 Point L toe forward on the ground (*punto en suelo*).
Ct 2 Step L to left.
Ct 3 Point R foot forward on ground.
Ct 4 Step R into 1st position.
Ct 5 Point L forward on ground.
Ct 6 Step L to left 2nd position.
Ct 7 Step R into 4th behind L.
Ct 8 Step L into 1st position.

The cts 6 and 7 cause the circle to move left in the clockwise version of Ampurdan. There are three slight rhythmic bounces of the arms on every two counts above as follows: 1 & 2, 3 & 4, 5 & 6, 7 & 8.

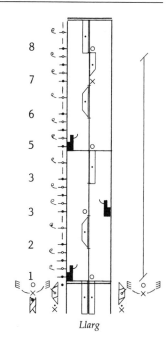

Llarg

See *ampurdanesa, curt, punt, sardana.*

LLARGS Y CURTS *(lyahrgs ee coorts)*
(Longs and shorts; Catalonian for *largos y cortos*)

The basic steps of the *sardana*, the "national" dance of Catalonia, consisting of two parts, the first, of shorter duration, generally of a sad and melancholy character, and the second, much longer, usually gay and festive. The steps called *curts* (shorts) are used in the first part, and those called *llargs* (longs) are used in the second. The steps of one part are actually no longer than those in the other, but in the "longs" twice as many steps are taken. The basic movements of the *sardana*, similar to those of the older *contrapás* and danced by the monks of Ariente, are simply a number of steps to the left followed by others to the right. It is when these steps are varied by alternately "pointing" the toes of each foot (*punts*) before they are taken that the many combinations (*tiradas*) require much concentration and memory for a dance which initially appears simple. The equivalent Spanish terms are *pasos largos* (longs) and *pasos cortos* (shorts).

See *llarg, punt, sardana, tirada.*

LLEVAR EL COMPAS
See *llevar el son.*

LLEVAR EL SON *(lyeh-VAHR ehl sohn)*
(To carry or convey the sound or meaning)
Also called *llevar el compás.*

An idiomatic flamenco expression which signifies the innate ability to maintain the perfect rhythms and interpret the moods of the singing (*cante*) and words (*letra*) of the songs which accompany most flamenco dancing.

See *duende, expresión.*

MACHO *(MAH-cho)*
(Masculine, robust, vigorous)

The Spanish dance is characterized by contrasts in male and female movements. With few exceptions, there are no steps which are only male or female. It is only in the degree and manner in which a step is performed that it differs in "gender." The male, however, has a broader range of more spectacular, eye-catching (*vistoso*) steps such as falls (*caídas*), knee turns (*vueltas de rodillas,* knee slides (*resbalados*), multiple spins (*vueltas de cigüeña*), and double *tour en l'aire* (*tordín*). In all styles of Spanish dance the male must, like a torero, hold his ground and dominate at all times and, as a soloist, occasionally employ only powerful and highly individualized, abstract, symbolic gestures of the arms (*gestos hiereticos*).

The term *macho* is also used to identify the left-hand castanet, which has a lower pitch (*suena bronca*) than that of the right-hand castanet and usually marks the steady basic beat that accompanies the delicate trills of the right hand (*hembra*) castanet.

See *afirmación, castañuela, decálogo, flojo, hembra, pulsación.*

MALAGUEÑA *(mah-lah-GEH-nyah)*
(From Málaga)

Malagueña is a popular dance of the people of Málaga, from which it is named. It is danced in ¾ or ⅜ rhythm and usually in three sections (*coplas*) similar to those of *sevillanas.* Each *copla* begins with four *paseos de malagueña*, establishing the characteristic *malagueña* motif (*tema*). This same theme acts as a bridge linking each subsequent *copla.* Castanets are played throughout.[1] *Malagueñas flamencas* are songs (*cantes*) sung in free style with an undetermined rhythm (*compás*) and are not danced.

The world-famous composition "Malagueña," by Cuban-born Ernesto Lecuona, was written as a concert piano solo. This musical departure, admired

---

[1]The typical castanet rhythm which accompanies these *paseos* is roll, roll, right, left.

by Spaniards and used in dance concerts to accompany a contemporary stylized Spanish dance (*baile estilizado*), utilizes the traditional folk rhythm and melody to achieve its Iberian flavor.

See *baile estilazado, malagueña en media vuelta, paseo de malagueña.*

MALAGUEÑA EN MEDIA VUELTA (*mah-lah-GEH-nyah ehn MEH-dee-ah VWEHL-tah*)
(*Malagueña* step done in a half turn)

This easygoing, ever-spiraling step allows the artist various nuances of timing in the arms and upper body and is associated more closely with classical than with regional dance. Here, the artistry of castanet playing should reflect the melodic subtleties of the music, imbuing the movement with an enigmatic quality.

The upper torso moves in opposition to the pelvis and feet (which move on each beat). Actually, the footwork resembles a basic *sevillanas* step, but instead of moving forward and back, it makes a gentle pivoting action to the right and left. The upper torso and arms are in constant motion, moving before, during, or after the movements of the feet, thus avoiding any static position.

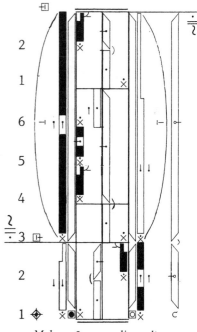

Malagueña en media vuelta

Beg pos	From any previous action, knees relaxed and slightly bent (*asentado*), head facing forward throughout.
Ct 1	Step L in place.
Ct 2	Touch ball of R foot forward.
Ct 3	Step R in place.
Ct 4	Touch ball of L foot forward (facing front).
Ct 5	Slightly lift L foot.
Ct 6	Step 5th L behind.
	Repeat all to opposite side.
Arms	
Ct 1–2	Turn upper torso to face right, moving arms into low 4th L front (lifted chest twists right against lower body).
Ct 3–6	Turn upper torso to face front, then slightly left, circling arms gently out into low 4th R front, (lifted chest continues to twist [*torcido*] to left against lower body).[1]

See *crotalogía, torcido.*

---

[1] The beauty of this Andalusian step, which is performed in one spot (*en sitio*).

MANERA *(mah-NEH-rah)*
(Manner, style, quality)

A performer's appearance or behavior while dancing.

See *aire, compostura, estilo.*

MARCAR *(mahr-CAHR)*
(To mark, stamp, impress)

Short for *marcar el compás,* to mark or beat time or to stamp the rhythm. In its strictest sense *marcar* is similar to the French ballet term *marquer,* meaning to accentuate a step. *Marcar* is also used synonymously with the American term *to mark,* which describes the action of a dancer who during rehearsals "walks through" or "sketches" the movements of a dance, expending only the minimum of energy, sometimes "marking" with his hands what his feet would be doing if he were actually dancing.

MARCAR EL COMPAS
See *marcar.*

MARCHAR *(mahr-CHAHR)*
(To walk, progress, go ahead, leave)

A term used in the old social set dances (*danzas*) such as *cotillones, lanceros,* and *contradanzas* in which the simple rhythmic walking steps (*pasos sencillos*) of partners and groups during their various maneuvers (*mudanzas*) maintained the steady, basic cadence of the music (a march, two-step, or gallop). It can be compared to a ballet *pas marché,* but performed in a less ostentatious manner.

See *camino, figura, mudanza, paseo, paso.*

MARIANAS
See *sa sa sa.*

MARTILLEO *(mahr-tee-LYEH-oh)*
(Hammering, clatter)

The repetitious, forceful, and authoritative pounding of one foot (*golpe de pie*) employed by a male singer (*cantaor*) to maintain the basic rhythm (*compás*) as he accompanies a dancer. The strong rapport or involvement between singer and dancer is evident from the tension and speed created by the counter-rhythms of the hand clapping (*palmas y contratiempos*) and stamping (*martilleo*). Invariably, when the singer is the sole rhythmic support, he expends as much energy as the dancer in maintaining this consistent, hammerlike leg action.

See *compás, golpe, golpeteo.*

MARTILLO *(mahr-TEE-lyoh)*
(Hammer)

A loud stamp of the dancer's foot (*golpe de pie*), usually repeated several times in a simple rhythmic phrase (desplante) with much force and animation. It occurs mostly in flamenco. The term also refers to the castanet stroke called *golpeo*.

See *desplante, golpeo, macho, remachos.*

MAS SALTADORA *(MAHS sahl-tah-DOH-rah)*
(Jumped or leaped higher)

Describing a style in folkloric dancing in which the jumping action is more pronounced in one style than in another; for example, the *jota* of Aragón is *más saltadora* than the *jota* of Valencia.

See *saltada.*

MATALARAÑA *(mah-tah-lah-RAH-nyah)*[1]
(Kills the spider)

As described below, this is a step of the *escuela bolera*. At a quick glance, it is similar to a low, broad ballet *pas de chat*. Several regional dances use the same step, inserting a tap of the foot (*golpe de pie*) on the right and a high lift of both knees before the second count. Dancing master Thoinot Arbeau, in his *Orchesography* (1588), used this analogy, "to kill a spider," in describing the action of the foot and possible origin of the term.

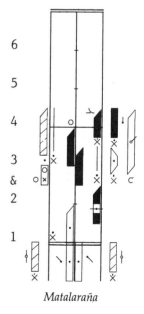

Beg pos   Feet—3rd L front.
          Arms—5th.
  Ct 1   Step L diagonally across R.
  Ct 2   Extend R leg diagonally forward and
          spring into air.
  Ct &   Land diagonally forward on R.
  Ct 3   Quickly step L diagonally across and
          beyond R.
  Ct 4   Touch ball or R foot to right diagonal,
          knees slightly bent.
  Ct 5–6 Hold pose.

Arms, torso, and head
Ct &–3–4   Circle R arm down, passing
           through 2nd to 5th front, inclining
           torso diagonally forward right, turn-
           ing head to right.

Matalaraña

---

[1] Also written *mata la raña.*

MATIZ *(mah-TEETH)*
(Shading, blending, tinting)

A sophisticated term identifying the special quality of sound provided by castanets played with unusual sensitivity to nuance and shading.

See *crotalogía*.

MAZURCA *(mah-THOOR-cah)*
(Dance from Masuria, Poland)

Short for *tiempo de mazurca*. The movement was the first step of *La Varsoviana* and *Polka Mazurca*, which were social dances (*danzas*) popular in late-nineteenth-century French and Spanish ballrooms, later used on the Spanish stage (*teatral*) for performance in musical dramas (*zarzuelas*).

See *baloné*.

MEDIA CORONA *(MEH-dee-ah coh-ROH-nah)*
(Half crown, halo)
Also called corona.

The fifth (*quinta*) arm position, in which the arms encircle the head, also known as *corona*. When the arms are held at that level but slightly apart, they are referred to as being *en media corona*.

See *corona*.

MEDIA LUNA *(MEH-dee-ah LOO-nah)*
(Half-moon)

A floor pattern (*camino*) in which the step makes the design of a half-moon. It can be performed as a solo or by couples, as in many folk dances in which partners facing each other move in a curve to the right and then the left, the curve describing a halfmoon. A small inward semicircle made on the floor with the foot is also referred to as a *media luna*.

See *jerezana con vuelta*.

MEDIA PLANTA *(MEH-dee-ah PLAHN-tah)*
(Half sole)
Also called *semiplanta*.

Any step in which one or both of the dancer's heels are off the floor.

See *sostenido en pies*.

MEDIA PUNTA *(MEH-dee-ah POON-tah)*
(Half toe)
Also called *semipunta*.

In this position the dancer has risen as high as possible on the ball of one or both feet, whether standing or moving. To move about on tiptoe is to do so *en puntas*.

See *en puntas, media planta, pies* (Basic Positions and Techniques), *sostenido en pies*.

MEDIA SEVILLANA *(MEH-dee-ah seh-vee-LYAH-nah)*
(Half a *paso de sevillana*)

This step is the first three counts of a basic *sevillana* step (*paso de sevillana*). It is used as a means of linking one step to another in three beats. When it is performed in a series (*corrida*), taking a longer step to the side on count 1 and a very small one on count 3, it slowly progresses to one side, making an effective exit (*mutis*), especially when the dancer accompanies herself with hand clapping (*palmas*).

See *paso de sevillanas, salida de bulería.*

MEDIA TIJERA *(MEH-dee-ah tee-HEH-rah)*
(Half scissor-kick)

This is a *tijera folklórica*, but performed lower and at a more rapid speed. Commonly seen in regional dances of central and northern Spain, it takes its name from the quick scissorlike action of the legs.

Beg pos	Feet—Optional.
	Arms—Between 2nd and 5th (*folklórico*).
Ct 1	Step in place on R.
Ct &	Lift L leg low in front.
Ct 2	Step in place on L.
Ct &	Lift R leg low in front.
	Repeat

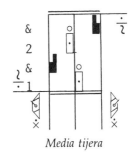

Media tijera

See *tijera folklórica.*

MEDIA TORTILLES
See *retortillés.*

MEDIA VUELTA *(MEH-dee-ah VWEHL-tah)*
(Half-turn)

An about-face or pivoting turn finishing in the opposite direction. It may be done as the first half of a *vuelta por detrás* or *vuelta por delante*. The action is similar to a balletic *demi-détourne*, but performed with knees relaxed.

See *detourné, vuelta por delante, vuelta por detrás*.

MEDIA VUELTA POR DETRAS
See *detourné*.

MEDIO *(MEH-dee-oh)*
(Half, partial, medium)
Also called *semi* or *demi*.

Used in combination with another word, it indicates that the step is to be partially performed, for example, in height, distance, tempo, completion, etc. (Such as *media corona* or *media sevillana*).

MENEO *(meh-NEH-oh)*
(A shaking, wriggling action)

A term in flamenco dancing describing the quivering, trembling movement of a female flamenco dancer (*bailaora*).

See *zarandeo*.

MENUDEO O REPIQUETEO *(meh-noo-DEH-oh oh reh-pee-keh-TEH-oh)*
(The act of repeating minutely or the sound of chopping, ringing)

This compound term refers to the manner in which sounds are executed in rhythmic footwork (*zapateado*) or in castanet playing. A series of subtle repetitive movements of the heels, close to the floor, giving a smooth rippling sound effect, or castanets played in an aesthetic and musical manner are examples.

MIMICA *(MEE-mee-cah)*
(Pantomime, mime)

That aspect of movement in dance which tells a story or delineates the character. *Mímica* is usually employed in a slow sung section, as in a *jota*. Such musical interludes are often used as "fillers" for silly, gauche, or overdone characterizations instead of movement that depicts the true character of the people and the music. *Mímica* plays a major part in Spanish ballets such as *The Three-Cornered Hat* and *El Amor Brujo*. *Mímicos* were public entertainers of the Visigoth era who performed with narrators. Because women were forbidden to perform in public, *mímicos* would take their parts, singing lewd songs and making gross gestures. They were also called *histriones* (actors, buffoons, jugglers).

MORISCA ANDALUZA *(moh-REES-cah ahn-dah-LOO-thah)*
(A Moorish movement in Andalusian style)

An action by a female dancer in which the lower spine gives the upper torso an undulated and slightly rippling effect as she executes a step.

See *ondulado.*

MORISCA CATALANA *(moh-REES-cah cah-tah-LAH-nah)*
(Moorish step in Catalonian style)

This step, common in Catalonian folk dance, is airborne and quickly covers much ground as the dancers travel in a circular direction.

Beg pos   Feet—Weight on L, legs parallel.
          Arms—Women's low to sides, hands
          holding skirt; men's optional.

Ct optional   While jumping forward into air,
          swiftly lift R knee, bending it so that
          foot touches back of thigh; imme-
          diately repeat same with L.
          Land on R.
          Quickly leap forward onto L.

          The action resembles a balletic *pas de chat* moving forward.

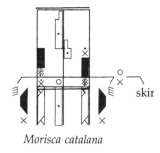

Morisca catalana

MOVIMIENTOS DE LAS MANOS
See Basic Positions and Techniques.

MUDANZA *(moo-DAHN-thah)*
(A change, move)

A change in the figure or floor pattern in social dances (*danzas*) of the court and early ballrooms. When used as a flamenco term, *mudanza* refers to the various movements of the feet without sound. These may vary from simple forward and backward steps to more elaborate crossings and recrossings of the feet, but they are used only to accompany the main focus of interest, namely, the arms, body, and head.

See *camino, figura*.

MUÑECAS *(moo-NYEH-cahs)*
(Wrists)

The gentle rotary motions of the wrists and fingers typical of flamenco dance. The term usually applies to the movements of a female dancer (*bailaora*).

See *decálogo* (definition 3), *filigrana, movimientos de las manos* (Basic Positions and Techniques).

MURISKA *(moor-JZEES-kah)*
(A beating step; Basque)
Also called *yauzika*.

A vertical jump followed by one or more crossings of the calves before the landing. Identical to an *entrechat*, the *muriska* was performed by male Basque dancers (*dantzaris*) in their traditional dances long before it was adopted into the art of ballet.

See *batidos, cuarta*.

MUTIS *(MOO-tees)*
(Exit)

A dance which does not end on stage but carries its ending off into the wings. *Hacer mutis* means to make an exit.

See *paso final, salida*.

NATURAL *(nah-too-RAHL)*
(Natural, plain, unaffected, usual)

A word describing an ordinary motion or action, such as a single step (*paso natural*). It is synonymous with the term *sencillo* and the balletic term *simple*.

See *básico, sencillo*.

OIDO *(oh-EE-doh)*
(Sense of hearing, listening)

Used mostly in flamenco to refer to that essential element which unifies song *(cante)*, music *(música)*, and dance *(baile)*. *Oído* is the ability or gift, either innate or acquired, to hear and interpret correctly the exactness of each rhythm *(compás)* and the intent or mood of the words *(letra)*. In English one says, "To have a good ear"; in Spanish, "Prestar oído" (to lend, adapt one's hearing).

See *llevar el son*.

OJAS
See *conchas*.

OJOS *(OH-hohs)*
(Eyes, perforations)

The two holes on each shell *(concha)* of castanets through which passes the cord that laces the shells together in pairs, one pair for each hand. Their size and angle, and the distance between them, is crucial. The projected areas at the outer sides of the *ojos* are referred to as the ears *(orejas)*.

See *castañuela*.

OLE *(OH-leh)*
(Bravo, hurray)

An expression of approval, the one most often heard almost anywhere in the world where exciting Spanish dance (especially flamenco) is being performed. It is variously pronounced *óle (oh-*leh), *olé* (oh-*leh), *ale (ah-*leh), *ala (ah-*lah), and, at the bullfight *(corrida)*, *oh-o-o-o-o-lé* (o-o-o-o-o-*leh)*. Unfortunately, at times its magical effect is diminished when well-meaning admirers become carried away and in their eagerness to communicate approval use it almost nonstop with little discretion. The *olé* of flamenco singing *(cante jondo)* reflects the *wa-Allah* (O God) with which the Arabs of Moorish Spain cheered every poetic recitation.

See *grito, jaleo*.

OLE EN VUELTA *(OH-leh ehn VWEHL-tah)*
(Fun, merriment while turning)

This step is the same as *paso de ole,* but is repeated several times in place as the dancer makes a complete turn right.

Ct 1–3 *Paso de ole* beginning R, turning right.
Ct 4–6 *Paso de ole* beginning L, continuing to turn right.

Repeat ct 1–6 finishing complete turn in place (*en sitio*).

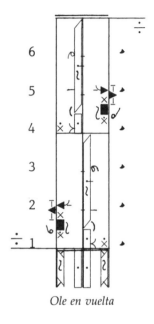

Ole en vuelta

See *paso de ole.*

ONDULADO *(ohn-doo-LAH-doh)*
(Undulated, wavelike)

Any movement performed in a liquid or soft-flowing manner, with or without the sound of footwork (*zapateado*). *Ondulado* is short for *paso ondulado* and is usually applied to women's dancing.

See *danza mora, morisca andaluza.*

OPOSICIONES *(oh-poh-see-thee-OH-nehs)*
(Competitions, oppositions)

Classical *boleros* danced by a two-person team in which the partners perform alternate solos (*robado*), vying with each other to present ever more spectacular (*vistoso*) variations. The same spirit of friendly competition exists in a *cuadro flamenco. Oposiciones* also refers to the placement or movement of the arms or legs in counterdirection to each other, giving an impression of poise (*figura*) and balance.

See *cuadro flamenco, figura, robado, torcido.*

PADEBURE
See *pas de buret natural*.

PALILLERA *(pah-lee-LYEH-rah)*
(Female castanet player)

The term is applied to one who plays *palillos* (castanets) in regional dances. In America the word "castanetist" is used in place of *palillera*. A virtuoso who appears in concert playing castanet solos is called a *castañetista*. A similar term was used in early Greek and Roman times when a player of castanets, which were then called *crótala*, was called a *crotalistra*.

See *castañetear, castañuela, crotalogía, palillos*.

PALILLOS *(pah-LEE-lyohs)*
(Little sticks)

An colloquial Andalusian term for castanets *(castañuelas)*.

See *castañuela, crotalogía, postiza, pulgaretes*.

PALMADA
See *palmas*.

PALMAS *(PAHL-mahs)*
(Palms of the hands; rhythmic hand clapping)
Also called *palmateo, palmadas* and *jaleo de manos*.

Hand clapping *(palmas)* is an inseparable rhythmic foundation for many ethnic dances the world over, but in Spain it has become an art form. *Palmas*, the basis for flamenco *jaleo*, maintain the basic pulsation and provide a rhythmic embroidery by keeping the rhythm *(compás)* and accenting certain beats louder than others. They can also provide a counterpoint *(contratiempo)* to the rhythm.

Basically, there are two types,[1] styles, or sounds of *palmas: sordas* (muffled; literally, deaf), performed with cupped or hollowed palms, and *secas* (dry), performed by clapping the three fingers of the right hand at a slight angle on

---

[1] Years ago in Seville I saw a third type which produced an extremely high-pitched, piercing sound that soared high above the din of the other *palmistas* in a flamenco ensemble *(cuadro flamenco)*. It is performed by stretching the fingers and palms wide open *(abiertamente)* and then clapping the entire surface of each palm directly against the other (not at an angle). There is only one word to describe this shrill sound: *ruidoso*.

the left palm, producing a sharp clack. The first style of clapping is used during singing (*cante*) or in delicate sections of a dance, and the second as needed. Slapping of one's boot, side of the shoe, or thigh is called a *palmada*.

See *contratiempo; jaleo; palmas, pitos y castañuelas* (Basic Positions and Techniques); *palmista; seco*.

PALMAS, PITOS, Y CASTAÑUELAS
See Basic Positions and Techniques.

PALMERO
See *palmista*.

PALMISTA *(pahl-MEES-tah)*
(One who is adept at rhythmic handclapping)
Also called *palmero*.

Technically speaking, the term for one who accompanies a flamenco dancer with hand clapping. Such a person is as much an artist in his or her right as the dancer. Not only the guitarist but also the other artists who accompany the dancer, namely, the singer (*cantaor*) and the rhythmic accompanists (*palmistas*), are vitally important to the presentation of a fine performance, as they help to "underscore" the effect the dancer wishes to give.

See *jaleador, palmas*.

PANADEROS *(pah-nah-DEH-rohs)*
(Bakers' dance)[1]

Los panaderos is a captivating dance performed as a duet in triple meter. It is believed to have originated in the city of Cádiz, in southwest Spain, and was a favorite in the eighteenth and nineteenth centuries among the populace; it was danced wherever there was a happy gathering. It was known then as *pa-*

---

[1]There are two theories about the origin of the term. Bread being the staff of life, every neighborhood had its own bakery. Vendors (*panaderos*) carrying sweet rolls hooked on long sticks for sale in the streets and public parks would express in song the deliciousness of their twisted dough pieces. Another interpretation of its meaning refers to the bakers' various arm movements while stretching the dough. A characteristic of *panaderos* steps is the twisting in the floor patterns (*caminos*) as the couples frequently exchange places and the twisting of the upper torso and arms as the couples pass by each other, giving the counterline typical of Andalusian dance. Whichever origin one wishes to accept, and even though there are many romanticized interpretations of the origins of regional steps, the actual movement reflects its name.

naderos de la tertulia (*panaderos* of the social gathering, street, or park). It was one of many dances, such as the *fandango* and *bolero*, which later had great success in the theater. Typical of the *escuela bolera* and performed in soft slippers (*zapatillas*), with strong influences of the classic Italian ballet, it remains today a favorite dance to perform and to watch as a theater piece.

See *baile de zapatillas, panaderos en vuelta, panaderos sencillo afrente, paseo de panaderos, paso de panaderos, torcido.*

PANADEROS EN VUELTA *(pah-nah-DEH-ros ehn VWEHL-tah)*
(*Panaderos* step while turning)

This step is a favorite of women. The motion is even and continuous, maintaining a spiraling effect as the skirt constantly swirls and unswirls.

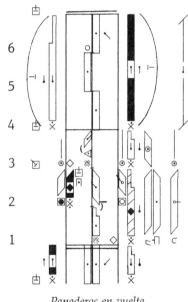

Beg pos   Feet—3rd R front.
          Arms—Low 4th R front.

Ct 1–2   Take a very small step forward on R, twisting upper body far to left against pelvis, which twists right; lift L leg across, knee bent, foot turned out; stretch R arm high forward (between 1st and 5th—elbow turned down); head remains facing audience over R arm.

Ct 3   Step very slightly back onto L, returning body and head to normal alignment and returning R arm to low 5th R front.

Ct 4–6   Take three steps in place (R, L, R), making one full turn to right, ending in 3rd R back (*vuelta en tres tiempos*), circling arms slightly out, changing to low 4th L front.

Panaderos en vuelta

Repeat all, reversed.

See *paseo de panaderos, torcido, vuelta en tres tiempos.*

PANADEROS SENCILLO AFRENTE *(pah-nah-DEH-rohs sehn-THEE-lyo ah-FREHN-teh)*
(Simple *panaderos* step facing front)

The floor pattern (*camino*) of this step is a curve or half-moon (*media luna*), the open end facing the audience.

Beg pos   Feet—3rd R front.
          Arms—R 5th, L 5th low back.

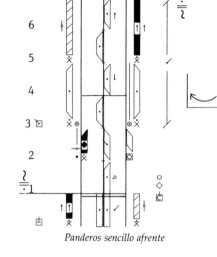

Ct 1   Step R diagonally forward.
Ct 2   Lift L leg, knee bent, diagonally
       across R; rise slightly, twisting torso
       left in opposite direction to raised
       L leg.
Ct 3   Step L, beginning curved path (*media
       luna*), moving to left (slight clockwise
       circling).
Ct 4   Step on R, going toward and crossing
       in front of L.
Ct 5   Step L to left, continuing curve.
Ct 6   Step onto R, crossing slightly
       behind L.

       Repeat ct 1–6, reversed.

Panderos sencillo afrente

Arms
Ct 3–6   Open arms slowly, passing through
         2nd, ending in reversed beginning
         position, i.e., L arm 5th and R 5th
         low back. During these counts un-
         twist torso to face front.

PANDERETA (*pahn-deh-REH-tah*)
(Tambourine)

A small, one-headed drum with metal discs or jingles (*cascabeles*) on the sides.
This folk instrument is played to accompany regional dances and songs. *Panderetas* come in sizes ranging from tiny drums with high-pitched jingles to the
very large type (*pandero*) carried on the shoulder, as in the old Moorish dance
called *zambra*. The Galicians have a square tambourine called a *pandeira* which
they play with both hands while holding it across the chest. The actual number of Spanish dances in which tambourines are used is very small and includes some dances of Valencia and Castile. Playing requires great skill, and
the performer (*panderetero*) is as important in folkloric dancing as the *jaleador*
is in flamenco dancing. The prevalent idea that holding a beribboned tambourine and occasionally whacking it is a Spanish characteristic (as in the ballet *pas de deux* of *Don Quixote*) is false. In Spain, unlike Italy, tambourines are
rarely played by the dancers themselves.

PARA BAILAR (*PAH-rah bah-ee-LAHR*)
(For dancing)

A term describing Spanish music written, sung, or played specifically as an
accompaniment for dancing. Many a novice or unaware teacher has met with
disappointment or frustration after purchasing music that was not identified
as *para bailar*. There are many recorded guitar and orchestral Spanish dances
which have been used to teach or accompany dances such as *sevillanas, far-*

rucas, and *jotas* and every flamenco item imaginable which are not *para bailar.* They are virtuosic pieces or arrangements for listening enjoyment. The same musician or singer performing the same piece would make several adjustments in the performance if its purpose were *para bailar.* For this reason it is virtually impossible to perform traditional flamenco dance to recorded music. Many flamenco pieces, such as *granainas, saetas, fandangos grandes,* and *calceleras,* are not *para bailar.*

The term is also applied to music by composers whose compositions were originally created for dancing. However, there are choreographers who radically edit, speed up, or slow down the music to accommodate it to their choreography. By no means is all music by Spanish composers written for dance.

PARADA *(pah-RAH-dah)*
(Stop, pause)

The instant when a dancer becomes immobile, which may occur at the end of a *copla,* dance, or phrase or at whatever moment in the music the dancer chooses to create a dramatic effect. *Parado* is also used to refer to a variety of Mallorcan folk dances that are slow, solemn, and majestic and during which the dancers at a given moment remain at a standstill (*parada*). In flamenco guitar playing (*toque*) the term refers to the muting of the strings by the fourth finger of the left hand; this muting is also called *apagado.*

See *bien parado, copla, paraditas, pausa.*

PARADITAS *(pah-rah-DEE-tahs)*
(Little stops, hesitations)

Small heel and toe movements which travel sidewards without the feet entirely leaving the floor. This step is seen in old Andalusian school dances. It is also seen in regional dances such as the *jota aragonesa.*

Beg pos   Feet—1st turned out.
               Arms—Optional; man lightly grasps edges of jacket (*chaquetilla*), elbows held away from torso.

    Ct 1   On heel of L and ball of R turn legs in (in pigeon-toed position).

    Ct 2   On ball of L and heel of R turn legs out (again in 1st position).

 Ct 3–4 Repeat ct 1–2 several times, traveling to right.
               Step can also move in clockwise circle, facing out. A *folklórico* variation can be performed with feet remaining throughout in parallel (*paralelo*) position. Weight is carried on balls of

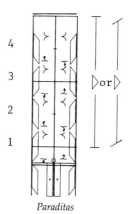

Paraditas

both feet as heels swing to right; then
weight is carried on heels, and toes
swing to right, thus continuing travel
in same direction.

See *pies* (*paralelo*, Basic Positions and Techniques), *retortillés*.

PARADITAS DE SEVILLANAS (*pah-rah-DEE-tahs deh seh-vee-LYAH-nahs*)
(Little stops, pauses, in *sevillanas*)

This step is traditionally the second in the first *copla* of the *sevillanas*. When it
is danced with a partner, it is performed four times, followed by a pass (*pasada
de sevillanas*). Since the fifth and sixth counts are held, or stopped, the Andalusian maestros referred to it as a "brief stop" (*paradita*).

Beg pos   Feet—Weight on R, L touching to one
          side.
          Arms—4th R up, head turned toward
          L foot.

    Ct 1   Step L, crossing behind.
    Ct 2   Step R.
    Ct 3   Step L, crossing in front.
    Ct 4   Touch ball of R foot to side, turning
           head toward R foot.
  Ct 5–6   Hold.

    Arms
    Ct 1   Travel to right; move arms through
           2nd, changing to 4th L up.
  Ct 5–6   Hold.

           Repeat to opposite side.

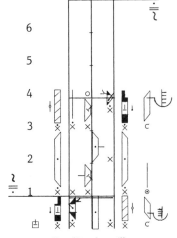

Paraditas de sevillanas

The above is a solo version facing front.
As this step was danced in the early 1900s, there was a decided sideward
bend *cimbrada* of the torso in the same direction and over the pointed toe.
In a modern version of *sevillanas populares* seen in the familiar settings of
festivals (*ferias*) and night clubs (*tablaos*), performers do not move from one
side to another in opposite directions but forward and backward in a U-shaped
floor pattern.

See *cimbrado, copla, sevillanas.*

PARONES (*pah-ROH-nehs*)
(Stops; of uncertain origin, probably from *parar*, to stop, hesitate)

Sudden, brief pauses in eighteenth- and nineteenth-century dances in which
dancers take one step toward each other, point the other toe forward on the

floor as the arms open wide, hesitate, then retreat from each other. They repeat the action several times, alternating feet. It is typical of many old dances such as the *panaderos*.

PASADA *(pah-SAH-dah)*
(Pass, passing, pace, step)

A movement during which dancers exchange places with each other. The transition can be made face to face *(enfrentado)* or back to back. It usually occurs at the end of a phrase, such as those in *sevillanas*, *seguidillas*, and many regional dances. Because of its possibilities for inventiveness, it is often used by choreographers to add excitement and variety to group numbers. It is not to be confused with the term *paseo*.

See *careo, paseo, pasos enfrentados*.

PASADA CON MEDIA VUELTA
See *pasada en cuatro tiempos*.

PASADA DE SEGUIDILLAS MANCHEGAS *(pah-SAH-dah deh seh-ghee-DEE-lyahs mahn-CHEH-gahs)*
(A passing [of partners] in the *seguidillas manchegas*)

Beg pos Feet—From previous action.
    Arms—5th, partners facing.

Ct 1 Step R in 5th behind.
Ct 2 Step L diagonally forward.
Ct 3 Tap ball of R foot diagonally crossed forward.
Ct 4 Step forward on R.
Ct & Step on ball of L in 5th behind.
Ct 5 Step forward on R.
Ct & Step on ball of L in 5th behind.
Ct 6 Step forward on R.

   On Ct 4–6 partners pass facing each other, curving ½ circle *(media luna)* to right and end facing each other *(enfrentado)*.

Ct & Extend L leg low to side and jump into the air.
Ct 1 Land in 5th L front.

   Last &–1 is usually a link or bridge to the next step of the *seguidillas manchegas*.

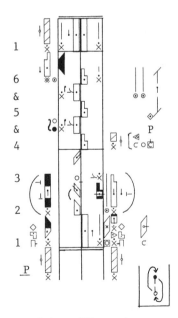

Pasada de seguidillas manchegas

Arms
  Ct 1   Circle arms down to right side while
         turning chest slightly to right; end R
         arm behind body while turning head
         to right.
  Ct 2   Swing arms out slightly while moving
         them to low 4th R front.
  Ct 3–6 Hold.
  Ct 1   Move L arm up midline of body to
         end in 5th.

See *pasada, pasos enfrentados.*

PASADA DE SEVILLANAS
See *panaderos, paso de panaderos.*

PASADA EN CUATRO TIEMPOS *(pah-SAH-dah en CWAH-troh tee-EHM-pohs)*
(A passing, crossing, in four counts)
Also called *pasada con media vuelta.*

An exchange of places with one's partner (*pasada*) in four counts. The movement may include three walking or running steps, concluding on the fourth
count, each dancer turning to face his or her partner. The step is seen in both
classical and regional dances.

See *pasada.*

PAS DE BURET NATURAL *(pahs deh boo-REHT nah-too-RAHL)*
(Simple bourrée step; Hispanicized French)
Also called *pas de buret sencillo* and *padeburé.*

A movement to either side in three counts. It can be performed slowly with
much ostentation and preciseness, as in eighteenth- and nineteenth-century
social dances (*danzas*) or performed quickly as a simple transition or link between steps.

Beg pos   Feet—1st.
          Arms—4th L up or low 4th R front,
          head turned slightly right.

Por detrás (pohr deh-TRAHS)
(By way of the back)

          Ct 1   Step L behind R, heel slightly off
                 floor.
          Ct 2   Step R to side, heel slightly off floor.
          Ct 3   Step L in front of R to 5th or 3rd.

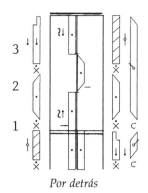

Por detrás

Pas de buret natural

Por delante (pohr deh-LAHN-teh)
(By way of the front)

> Ct 1 Step L in front of R, heel slightly off floor.
> Ct 2 Step R to side, heel slightly off floor.
> Ct 3 Step L behind into 5th or 3rd.

Arms (for both versions)

> From 4th L up, pass through 2nd to 4th R up, or from low 4th R front circle slightly out to low 4th L front, turning head slightly to left on Ct 1–3.

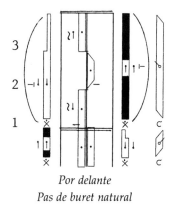

Por delante

Pas de buret natural

See *danza, vistos*.

PAS DE BURET SENCILLO
See *pas de buret natural*.

PASEILLO *(pah-seh-EE-lyoh)*
(A little walk, passing)
Also called *cruces*.

A colloquial Andalusian folkloric term used in various types of *sevillanas*. The term is comparable to *pasada*. In flamenco it is a simple walk or promenade (*paseo*) in a dance. Musically speaking, the *paseillo* is a rhythmic linking between variations.

See *paseo*.

PASEO *(pah-SEH-oh)*
(A walk, promenade)

A general term usually used in combination with another step which determines its movement or character, for example, *paseo de gracia*. The term is not to be confused with *paso* or *pasada*. Technically speaking, *paseo* refers to a movement which "travels" or is repeated in a straight path or in a circle and without necessarily returning to its starting point. It is not done in place (*en sitio*).

Paseo also refers to a section of an *alegrías* during which there is a minimum of footwork, thus emphasizing movements of the torso and the lyric, soft-flowing action of the arms (*braceo*). In music (*toque*), it refers to preluding on a guitar.

See *castellana, corrida, paseo de gracia, paso, paso sencillo*.

PASEO DE DESTAQUES *(pah-SEH-oh deh dehs-TAH-kehs)*
(From paseo, walk, promenade, and *destacar,* to detach, bring out, make
  conspicuous. A walk or promenade, of [lifted] steps)

This step suggests that of a balletic *battement;* however, the accent is always on
the lift upward. It is generally performed by women and is done in a series
with an appropriate floor pattern (*camino*).

Beg pos	Feet—From any previous action. Arms—5th or 4th L up.
Ct 1 (or 3)	Step forward onto L.
Ct 2–3 (or 1–2)	Lift R leg forward hip height, knee slightly bent.
	Repeat, reversed.

See *destaque, destaque en dos tiempos, vacío.*

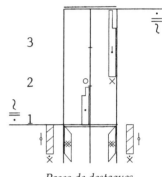

Paseo de destaques

PASEO DE EMPUJOS *(pah-SEH-oh deh em-POO-hohs)*
(Pushing steps)

A series of small pushing steps in which partners change places in a *seguidilla.*
The action is the same as several *sacados* performed in a straight line.

Beg pos	Feet—3rd R front. Arms—Low 4th R front.
Ct 1	Step R forward, relaxed knee, R taking weight.
Ct 2	Close L foot into 3rd back (*asamblé sencillo*) keeping knees easy and flex- ible throughout. Do not bounce.
	Repeat above three times during which partners change places and finish facing each other.

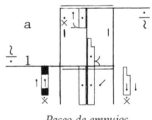

Paseo de empujos

See *sacado.*

PASEO DE FARRUCA *(pah-SEH-oh deh fah-ROO-cah)*
(Walk, promenade, in a *farruca*)

A simple time-marking step used in old Andalusian school (*escuela*) dances.

Beg pos   Feet—From any previous action, legs
          parallel.
          Arms—Female—5th; male—low 4th,
          R front, or simply grasp edges of
          jacket (*chaquetilla*).

  Ct 1   Step L forward.
  Ct 2   Touch ball of R foot beside L.
  Ct 3   Reach R back on ball of foot, taking
          weight momentarily.
  Ct 4   Stamp L taking weight, knee slightly
          bent.
  Ct 1   Reverse above beginning R and con-
          tinue as a series in a circular floor pat-
          tern (*camino*).
          Accent is on Ct 4.

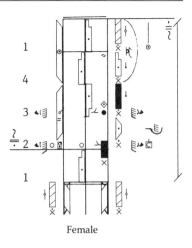

Female

Arms—female
  Ct 2–3 Circle R arm out and down, passing
          through 2nd to 5th low front, turning
          torso (and hips) slightly to right.
  Ct 4–1 Circle R arm up, passing through 1st,
          returning to 5th, turning torso back to
          normal.

          Turn head relating to right arm; snap
          fingers on ct 2–3.

Arms—male
  Ct 4–1 Change to low 4th, L front.

          Reverse all of above to opposite side.
          The step, as its name suggests, is re-
          peated several times, making a clock-
          wise circular pattern (*camino*) on the
          floor.

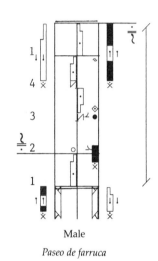

Male

Paseo de farruca

See *camino, farruca.*

PASEO DE GRACIA *(pah-SEH-oh deh GRAH-thee-ah)*
(Pleasing, light, charming promenade)

As an *entrada*, also called *paseo de presentación*.

A gracious walk which can be used either as an entrance (*entrada*) during a
dance or as an exit (*salida*). When used with artistry, it has an ingratiating and
irresistible effect on the audience. A true artist has only to circle the stage to
establish his or her authority. If exaggerated, such a *paseo* can be obvious,
overbeguiling, or flirtatious.

See *gracia, presentación.*

PASEO DE JEREZANAS *(pah-SEH-oh deh heh-reh-THAH-nahs)*
(Promenade of steps from Jerez)

This step, a favorite of women dancers, can be performed in a circle about the room, on a diagonal or directly upstage, the dancer looking back at the audience, first over one shoulder, then over the other.

Beg pos   Feet—Weight on L.
          Arms—4th L up.

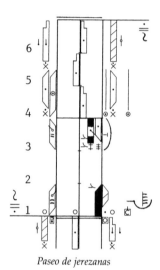

Ct 1   Touch ball of R foot diagonally forward, inclining torso and head and turning slightly toward R leg.

Ct 2   Hold.

Ct 3   Brush R toe backward, describing small inward semicircle (*media luna*), and kick lower leg backward and outward (rotating leg slightly inward), returning torso to normal.

Ct 4–6   Take three steps forward, R L R, passing arms through 2nd position, and change places (4th position R up).

Repeat above, reversed.

Paseo de jerezanas

See *paso de jerezana.*

PASEO DEL TREN *(pa-SEH-oh del TREHN)*
(Passing [sound] of a train)

A series of tiny, closely repeated shuffling or stamping steps (*golpes de pies*) imitating the sound of a passing train. It is often used as a novelty exit (*mutiz*) in *bulerías.*

See *bulerías, repiqueteo.*

PASEO DE MALAGUEÑA *(pah-SEH-oh deh mah-lah-GHEH-nyah)*
(Passing step in a *malagueña*)

Ct 1   Ct 2   Ct 3   Ct 4   Ct 5   Ct 6

Beg pos	Feet—From previous action (facing stage right). Arms—5th.
Ct 1–2	Step forward on R (ct 1); draw L foot forward along floor (ct 2).
Ct 3 & 4	Step forward L while pivoting full turn L (ct &), passing partner on left; step back R (ct 4).
Ct 5–6	Lift L knee, extending leg forward (*vacío*).

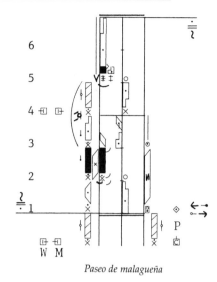

Arms

Ct 1–2	Circle L arm out and down, passing through 2nd to 5th low front, twisting torso (*torcido*) to right; keep head facing partner (*careo*).
Ct 3–6	Circle L arm up, passing through 1st, returning to 5th; untwist torso to normal (partners have now changed places and are facing each other).

Repeat, reversed.

This step can be performed as solo. When performed with partner, begin facing and maintain face-to-face (*careo*) contact during entire step by twisting to left while traveling on cts 3 & 4.

Paseo de malagueña

Andante

Ct: 1 2 3 & 4 5 6

PASEO DE PANADEROS *(pah-SEH-oh deh pah-nah-DEH-rohs)*
(Promenade of *panaderos* steps)

This step is a series of half-turns which follow a clockwise path (*camino*) and alternately face in and out of the circle.

Beg pos   Feet—3rd R front.
          Arms—Low 4th R front; back to center of circle.

Ct & 1   Step R to right side, twisting upper body far to left, lifting L leg toward R with knee bent, foot turned out, while

Ct 2   Reaching R arm high forward between 1st and 5th, elbow down. Keep head facing over right shoulder in line of circular floor pattern.

Ct 3   Step L across, returning body and head to normal alignment and returning R arm to low 4th R front.

Ct 4–6   Step R, L, beginning to make half-turn right; step R behind L, completing half-turn while circling arms out slightly, changing to low 4th L front (body is now facing into circle).

          Repeat, reversed, still traveling in circular clockwise floor pattern, twisting upper torso alternately in and out of circle, keeping head facing line of direction throughout.

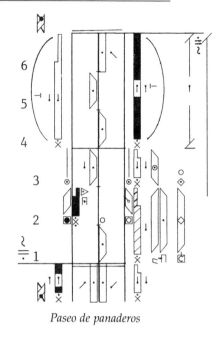

Paseo de panaderos

See *panaderos, paseo, torcido.*

PASEO DE PRESENTACION
See *paseo de gracia.*

PASEO DE SALIDA
See *salida.*

PASEO DE SEVILLANAS
See *paso de sevillanas.*

PASEO DE TANGO *(pah-SEH-oh deh TAHN-goh)*
(Promenade in a tango)

A promenade in a syncopated rhythm which links various steps of an Andalusian tango (*tango andaluz*).

Beg pos   Feet—3rd R front.
          Arms—Optional or low 4th L front,
          head turned slightly left.

Ct 1–2   Step R forward.
   Ct 3   Step forward onto L.
   Ct 4   Step R, cutting behind L with decided
          accent, extending L foot.

          A fancy version is accomplished by
          describing with left foot small half
          circle (*media luna*) inward on ground
          on cts 2–3.

          Repeat, reversed. This can be done in
          series in circular floor pattern (*rueda*).

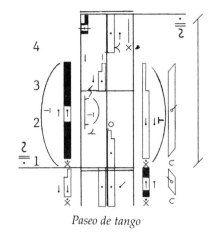

Paseo de tango

Arms
Ct 1–2   Begin to assume low 4th R front.
   Ct 3   Arrive in low R front.
   Ct 4   Hold.

See *tango*.

PASEO DE ZAMBRA *(pah-SEH-oh deh THAM-brah)*
(A sideways movement typical of a *zambra*)

In this step, of Moorish origin, there is only a gentle rise and fall. It can be
performed barefooted and accompanied by finger cymbals (*crótalos*), or with a
large tambourine (*pandero*) carried on the shoulder.

Beg pos   Feet—From previous action, facing
          audience.
          Arms—5th, head turned slightly
          right, eyes cast down, knees slightly
          bent throughout.

   Ct 1   Step L across R (in *paso cruzado*).
   Ct &   Step right on ball of R foot.

Paseo de zambra

          Repeat above several times, accenting
          ct 1 while slowly traveling to right.

See *vuelta de zambra*. See also Appendix: Basic Flamenco Rhythms.

PASEO DE ZAPATEADO *(pah-SEH-oh deh thah-pah-teh-AH-doh)*
(A walk making audible sounds with the toes and heels)

This term describes the use of delicate rhythmic heel-and-toe combinations
(*zapateados*) which travel on a course (*corrida*). The dancer moves in various
floor patterns, often without accompaniment. This is a relatively recent use of

zapateado, which originally referred to a dance performed in place (*en sitio*), often on a tabletop, in which the dancer exhibited rhythmic virtuosity.

See *vuelta zapateada, zapateado.*

PASO *(PAH-soh)*
(Step, movement)
Also called *paso sencillo* and *paso natural.*

A step in any direction (with or without upper body movement) which involves a transfer of weight. This term is often mistakenly used as a synonym for *paseo*, which means walk or promenade.

See *paseo, paso sencillo.*

PASO ALTO *(PAH-soh AHL-toh)*
(High step)

A step which is jumped or performed high off the ground.

See *más saltadora, saltada.*

PASO CIGUEÑA SINCOPADO *(PAH-soh thee-GWEH-nyah seen-coh-PAH-doh)*
(Syncopated stork step)

Tap the ball of one foot (*golpe*), immediately lifting the same foot to the side of the standing knee, then by lifting and dropping the standing heel, advance slightly with a series of short shifting or slipping steps on the standing foot.

See *caída.*

PASO CRUZADO *(PAH-soh croo-THA-doh)*
(Crossed step)

A transitional or connecting step in which one foot moves across the front or the back of the other and takes the weight. The foot can cross either diagonally forward, diagonally back, or directly to either side.

PASO DE CACHUCHA *(PAH-soh deh cah-CHOO-chah)*
(A step of the *cachucha*)

In this famous eighteenth- and nineteenth-century dance a specially designed little cap (*cachucha*) of flowers was worn by the *bailarina* and became associated with it. *Cachucha*, also a term of endearment, is applied to a particularly attractive or graceful person or object. The step shown here did not appear in the choreography of the often hailed "La Cachucha" made famous by Fanny Elssler in its premier performance in Paris in 1836. The version described below was taught by José Otero. It moves laterally from right to left, involves much leg and skirt action, and lies mostly in the domain of female dancers.[1]

Ct 5–6   Ct 1–2   Ct 3   Ct 4   Ct 5–6

Beg pos   Feet—3rd.
           Arms—5th.

Ct 5–6[2]   As preparation from previous measure, lift R knee almost hip high and make small outward circle of foot under knee (*rodazán*), pivoting on L to face stage right.

Ct 1–2   Step forward onto R.

Ct 3   Step forward onto L, bending knee slightly, inclining torso slightly back.

Ct 4   Step onto R behind L, returning torso to normal.

Ct 5–6   Repeat ct 5–6 above, reversed.

Arms
Ct 5–6   Circle L arm out and down, passing through 2nd to almost low 5th front, turning torso slightly to right, facing head over L shoulder.

Ct 1–2   Bring L arm to low 5th front and continue circling up through 1st.

Ct 3   Bring L arm to 5th.

Ct 4   Hold.

Ct 5   Repeat cts 5–6, reversed.

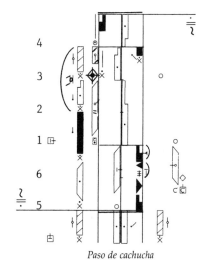

Paso de cachucha

[1] It can be displayed in various degrees of execution, from the modest to the flamboyant. When a male dancer encounters the step in some eighteenth- and nineteenth-century couples dances, he executes his *rodazanes* in a modified form, low and small (*bajos y pequeños*). In the old dances the step was often performed with a small, quick hop (*con saltito*) on the sixth count, and the upper body displayed an extreme twist (*torcido*); that is, if performed to the right, the L shoulder blade (or the back) was visible to the audience, and vice versa when performed to the left. This step is often called *rodazán*.

[2] This "pickup" or upbeat preparatory phrase is typical of many Spanish dance steps and may best be described as an *anacrusis* (a phrase before the main accent or downbeat).

A simpler form taught by Otero does not require the torso turn, and the left foot drags along the floor to take the weight on the third count. The entire step is done facing front (*a frente*).

See *cachucha*.

Ct: 5 6 1 2 3 4 5 6

PASO DE CADERAS (*PAH-soh deh cah-DEH-rahs*)
(A step with movements of the hips)

A feminine, easygoing manner of walking in which the hip slightly sways when taking the weight or in response to beating the foot. The effect can be frivolous or humorous as in *bulerías* or sensuous as in *baile jondo*.

See *biscas, continencia, zarandeo*.

PASO DE CAIDA (*PAH-soh deh cah-EE-dah*)
(A falling, dropping step)

This step is typical of a *farruca*. Because its timing is flexible, it can be used for punctuation within a dance by reversing the action—the fall comes first, followed by a sudden spring to a vertical position (on the balls of both feet), which is accented on the second count.

Ct 1   Ct 2

Beg pos   Feet—From any previous action.
          Arms—Low 4th R front.

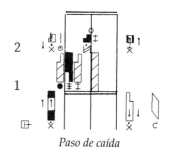

   Ct 1   Rise on R half toe as with weight
          thrust forward (L knee bent as high
          as possible), falling forward into a
          lunge.
   Ct 2   Land on L foot, R knee also taking
          weight, moving arms to low 4th L
          front or as illustrated.

Paso de caída

See *caída, paso final*.

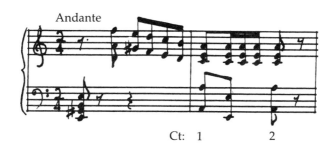

PASO DE CHOTIS *(PAH-soh deh CHOH-tees)*
(A schottische step)
Also called *paso de schotis*.

This charming dance, originally associated with Germany and Scandinavian
countries, evolved as a ballroom dance in Spain at the turn of the twentieth
century. Unlike the sprightly Scandinavian rendition, the Spanish version is
performed much more slowly and in an easygoing manner. *Chotis* selections
can still be heard in several *zarzuelas*.

Beg pos   Partners facing each other in standard
          closed ballroom position with male's
          R arm around female's waist. Female's
          head rests gently on male's R
          shoulder.

   Ct 1   Male: move 1 step forward R; female:
          step back on L.
   Ct &   Male (only): bend L knee, raising foot
          in back.
   Ct 2   Male: move 1 step forward L; female:
          step back on R.
   Ct &   Male (only): bend R knee, raising foot
          in back.

Ct 1–& Male: take 2 steps forward R L; fe-
        male: take 2 steps back.
   Ct 2 Male: take 1 step forward R; female:
        step back L.
        Female's right cheek may rest on
        man's shoulder throughout.

        Above counts are performed three
        times, followed by this typical *chotis*
        ending: Maintaining very close posi-
        tion, partners make full turn clock-
        wise in place (*en sitio*) as follows:

   Ct & Male: with feet parallel (*paralelo*) and
        knees straight, pivot ¼ turn on ball
        of R foot to right; female: pivot on L
        to left.
   Ct 1 Lower heels.
Ct & 2 & 3 & 4   Ct &-1 is performed three more
        times, completing circle. Feet skim
        floor with no rise and fall of body.

See *zarzuela*.

PASO DE CIERRE *(PAH-soh deh thee-EH-rreh)*
(A closing step)

In flamenco a step which closes or rounds off a phrase or section of a dance.
Not to be confused with *paso final*.

See *cierre, paso final*.

PASO DE EXALTACION
See *cambiamientos bajos y altos*.

PASO DE JEREZANA *(PAH-soh deh heh-reh-THAH-nah)*
(A step from Jerez)

A small, accented brushing action of the foot. The female version, high (*alta*),
can be seen in the following illustration.

Ct 1–2   Ct 3

Beg Pos Feet—weight on L.
         Arms—4th L up.
  Ct 1 Touch ball of R diagonally forward,
         incline torso and head and turn
         slightly toward R leg.
  Ct 2 Hold.
  Ct 3 Brush R toe backward indicating a
         very small inward semicircle (*media
         luna*), lifting the foot backward and
         outward as knee rotates slightly in-
         ward; return torso to normal.

         The male version, low (*bajo*), of this
         step is the same as the *alta* only more
         restrained. The arms are low 4th R
         front, or the hands grasp the edge of
         the jacket (*chaquetilla*). There is no
         torso movement; R foot is lifted low
         on ct 3. The dancer sometimes slaps
         the side of his raised shoe (*palmada*),
         followed by a quick turn (*vuelta*) to
         the opposite side.

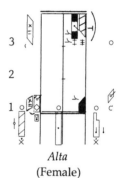

Alta
(Female)

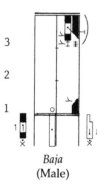

Baja
(Male)

Paso de jerezana

See *jerezana con vuelta, jerezana saltada en vuelta, paseo de jerezanas.*

Ct: 1 2 3

PASO DE JOTA *(Variación despedida)* *(PAH-soh deh HOH-tah vah-ree-ah-thee-OHN dehs-peh-DEE-dah)*
(A *jota* step, farewell variation)

The *jotas* of Spain are of many regional varieties, each with its local character and temperament. The colloquial name given to this variation means leavetaking or farewell. It is usually the last step (*paso final*) and is performed at an accelerated speed and higher into the air (*más saltada*) as if the dancer were "taking off."

Beg pos   Feet—From any previous action (facing partner).
          Arms—Between 2nd and 5th (*folklórico*).

   Ct 1   Spring to right onto R foot, knee bent, lifting L leg, knee bent, diagonally across; twist chest slightly to right and bend over to left.
   Ct 2   Step L to side, returning chest to upright.
   Ct &   Swing R leg up around to back, knee bent, while springing into air.
   Ct 3   Land on L.
   Ct 4   Step R, knee bent, crossing behind L.
   Ct 5   Step L to side.
   Ct &   Lift weight, sliding R foot inward.
   Ct 6   Catch weight on R foot behind L, knee bent.

   Ct 2–6 Travel on clockwise curve (*media luna*) toward left.

          Repeat all, reversed, still facing partner.

See *jota*.

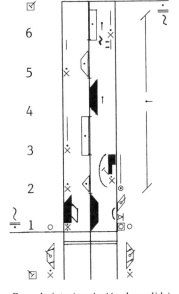

Paso de jota (variación despedida)

PASO DE JOTA *(Variación tubo)* *(PAH-soh deh HOH-tah vah-ree-ah-thee-OHN TOO-boh)*
(A *jota* step, tube variation)

The floor pattern (*camino*) of this step is straight and narrow like a pipe or tube (*tubo*). Similar to a performance on a tightrope, the dancer's actions suggest

balancing and dancing in first one direction and then the other along a pipe
or tube.

Beg pos   Feet—From any previous action.
           Arms—Between 2nd and 5th
           (*folklórico*)   12

    Ct 1   Step R forward, lifting L knee
           forward.   11
    Ct 2   Hop onto R, extending L leg forward.
    Ct 3   Step L forward.   10
  Ct 4–6   Repeat ct 1–3.

    Ct 1 7 Touch R heel diagonally forward,   9
           bending L knee.
    Ct 2 8 Take weight on R foot, lowering toe   8
    Ct 3 9 Touch L heel diagonally forward,
           bending R knee.
   Ct 4 10 Take weight on the L foot, lowering   7
           toe.
   Ct &–a Spring into air, turning ½ left, bend-   (6)
           ing knees, quickly bringing feet up to   3
           buttocks; land on R.
   Ct 5 11 Quickly step L beside R.   (5)
   Ct 6 12 Step R beside left.   2

    Arms   (4)
   Ct 1–6 Move L elbow near side of body   1
           slightly forward, palm up, keeping R
           in place.

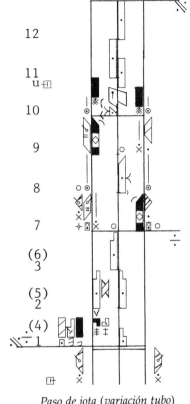

Paso de jota (variación tubo)

    Ct 1   Turn torso toward R leg and incline to
           right, bringing L arm up between 2nd
           and 5th (*folklórico*).
    Ct 2   Return torso to normal.
    Ct 3   Turn torso toward L leg, inclining to
           left.
  Ct 4–6   Return torso to normal.

See *jota*.

PASO DE JOTA SENCILLO *(PAH-soh deh HOH-tah sehn-THEE-lyo)*
(A simple or basic *jota* step)
Also called *paso básico de jota.*

This lively variation is typical of a *jota aragonesa.*

Beg pos Feet—3rd R front or 1st, facing audience or partner.
Arms—Between 2nd and 5th (*folk-lórico*).

Ct &   Jump into air.
Ct 1   Land firmly with feet apart in 2nd,
knees bent (*cuadrada*).
Ct 2   Pause.
Ct 3   Spring onto L, raising R leg sideward,
knee bent.
Ct 4–6 Make *pas de buret natural* to left, step
R back of L, L to 2nd, R to 1st.

Floor pattern can be on curve (*media luna*) to each side, either facing part-ner or facing front.

Ct 1 is strongly accented.

See *pas de buret natural*.

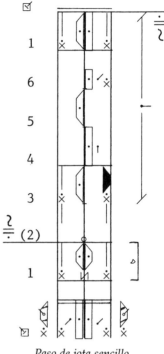

Paso de jota sencillo

PASO DE LADO (*PAH-soh deh LAH-doh*)
(A step to the side, lateral step)

A step in which one foot moves sidewise, taking the weight. Also called *paso lateral*.

See *direcciones básicas*.

PASO DEL DEMONIO (*PAH-soh dehl deh-MOH-nee-oh*)
(Step of the demon)

A step of the eighteenth and nineteenth centuries in the style of the *escuela bolera*, similar to an arabesque balanced on one foot with one arm strongly raised above the head. The stance suggests a menacing or diabolical figure. A humorous school of thought claims that the term refers to the most spec-tacular and difficult step of a classical *bolero*, which the dancer saves for the grand finish as a *paso de exaltación* and is "devilishly taxing."

See *bolero, cambiamientos bajos y altos, vistoso*.

PASO DE MULETA *(PAH-soh deh moo-LEH-tah)*
(Step performed with a bullfighter's *muleta,* a red cloth that covers and conceals the sword [*espada*])

A colloquial term used to describe the step in a charming woman's solo of the late 1800s called "El Vito," in the last movement of which a torero's cape and sword (*capa y muleta*) are used to imitate the movements of a bullfight (*corrida*).

See *tauromaquia.*

PASO DE OLE *(PAH-soh deh OH-leh)*
(A step of fun and rhythmic merriment)

All the movements of this step are audible. The accent is variable (usually on the first count), depending on the music and mood of the dancer (*a capricho*). The tempo is lively, as in *bulerías,* and the mood is one of lightness and fun (*por chufla*).

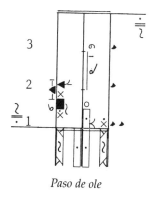

Beg pos	Feet—1st parallel.
	Arms—Optional, the female often grasping and brandishing her skirt from side to side or employing mimicry (*pellizcos*).
Ct 1	Step R in place with knee bent.
Ct 2	Jab ball of L foot to side, raising R heel slightly.
Ct 3	Stamp R foot, or drive down R heel (*tacón*).
	Repeat, reversed.

Paso de ole

See *chufla, ole en vuelta, pellizco.*

PASO DE PANADEROS *(PAH-soh deh pah-nah-DEH-rohs)*
(A *panaderos* step)

Often called *pasada de sevillanas.*

A basic step of the dance *los panaderos* in which partners pass back to back, exchanging places, usually four times between sequences. In *las sevillanas,* when partners pass each other only once as a link between steps, it is called a *pasada.* This step is shown below as a solo. If it is danced with a partner, he should face upstage (with back to reader).

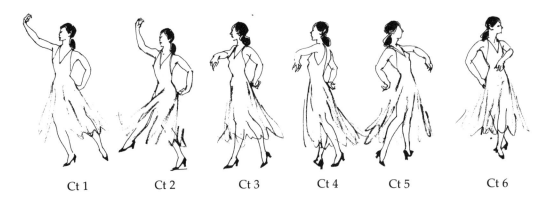

| Ct 1 | Ct 2 | Ct 3 | Ct 4 | Ct 5 | Ct 6 |

Beg pos Feet—3rd R front.
Arms—5th low back.

Ct 1 Step R to side, beginning to pass behind partner (dancer now has diagonal relationship to partner).

Ct 2 Lift L leg (knee bent) diagonally across, rising slightly on R foot.

Ct 3 Step L across R, making a ¼ turn right (dancer will now be passing R shoulders with partner).

Ct 4–6 Step R, L, R into 3rd back while continuing to make one-half turn right, passing partner to end facing him. Dancer and partner have exchanged places (*pasada*).

Arms

Ct 1 Begin to circle R arm to 5th, elbow curved and pointing down.

Ct 2 Complete R arm movement.

Ct 3 Move R arm to low 4th front.

Ct 4–6 Arms circle out slightly, moving to low 4th L front.

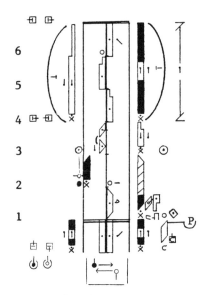

Paso de panaderos

See *media luna, panaderos, pasada, paso de sevillanas.*

Ct: 1   2   3   4   5   6

PASO DE SEGUIDILLA *(PAH-soh deh seh-ghee-DEE-lyah)*
(A step typical of a *seguidilla*)

This step reflects the typical lighthearted rhythm of a *seguidilla*.

Beg pos Feet—3rd L front, facing partner.
         Arms—5th.

Ct 1   Spring onto L, lifting R leg, ankle
       slightly flexed, heel touching behind,
       just above L ankle.

Ct 2   Hop on L as R leg moves out and
       around, ending with heel touching in
       front and just above ankle *(batimán)*.

Ct 3   Hop on L, moving R out and around,
       ending with heel touching behind
       and just above L.

Ct 4   Slide R to side *(desliz)*.

Ct 5   Move L into 3rd behind.

Ct 6   Move R to side.

       Entire step except ct 4 is done on half
       toe *(semiplanta)*.

Arms

Ct 1–2 Remain in 5th.

Ct 3–6 Make complete circle with R arm only
        as follows:

Ct 3   Circle R arm out and down, passing
       through 2nd, turning head slightly to
       right.

Ct 4   Move R arm through low 5th.

Ct 5   Move R arm through 1st, beginning
       to return head to front.

Ct 6   Return arm to 5th, facing head front.

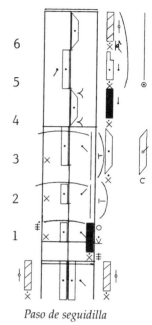

Paso de seguidilla

See *seguidilla*.

PASO DE SEGUIDILLA MANCHEGA *(PAH-soh deh seh-ghee-DEE-lyah mahn-CHEH-gah)*
(A turning step typical of a *seguidilla* of La Mancha)

Beg pos   Feet—5th R front, in diagonal rela-
          tionship to partner (R shoulders
          close).
          Arms—5th; look at partner through-
          out step.

Ct &   Preparation—Extend L leg low to side
          and spring slightly into air.
Ct 1   Land in 5th L front.
Ct &   Spring into air.
Ct 2   Land on R, extend L diagonally front
          low, knee slightly bent.
Ct &   Step on ball of L foot in 5th behind.
Ct 3   Step R to side.
Ct &   Tap ball of L foot in 5th front.
Ct 4   Step on L in 5th front (starting to turn
          left).
Ct &   Step on ball of R in 5th behind, taking
          partial weight.
Ct 5   Step on L in 5th front, continue turn-
          ing to left.
Ct &   Step on ball of R in 5th behind, taking
          partial weight.
Ct 6   Step on L in 5th front, facing front
          and finishing turn.

          Repeat, reversed.

          During ct 4–6 dancer can make either
          one complete turn (*vuelta empujada*),
          pivoting on left in place (as in some re-
          gional versions) or as above, three
          walking steps (*vuelta en tres tiempos*).

Arms
Ct &–1   Hold.
Ct &–2–&–3–&   Circle L arm out and down,
          passing through 2nd to 5th low front
          and up midline of body to return
          to 5th.
Ct 4–6   Repeat &–2–&–3–& with both arms.

          Repeat, reversed.

See *vuelta de zambra, vuelta en tres tiempos*.

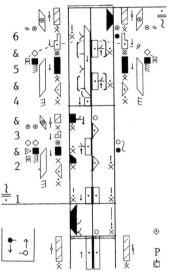

Paso de seguidilla manchega

PASO DE SEVILLANAS (*PAH-soh deh seh-vee-LYAH-nahs*)
(Step typical of *sevillanas*)
Also called *paseo de sevillanas*.

This step is probably the most popular and easily recognized step in all Spain. It is seen danced by many couples at fairs (*ferias*) and in solos on the concert stage.

| Beg pos | Ct 1 | Ct 2 | Ct 3 | Ct 4 | Ct 5 | Ct 6 |

Beg pos   Feet—3rd R front.
            Arms—5th.

Ct 1   Step R diagonally forward.
Ct 2   Touch L ball in 3rd behind.
Ct 3   L steps diagonally back.
Ct 4   Touch R ball in 3rd front.
Ct 5   Slightly lift R foot.
Ct 6   Set R foot down in 3rd back.

      Repeat ct 1–6 to other side.

Arms
Ct 1   With R arm begin to make complete outward circle.
Ct 2   Continue circle through 2nd.
Ct 3   Continue circle toward low 5th front.
Ct 4   Pass through low 5th front.
Ct 5   Continue circle upward through 1st.
Ct 6   Complete circle to 5th.

      Repeat ct 1–6 to other side.

The movement can also begin by stepping on L foot in place on ct 1 (instead of 6), then continuing with ct 2–6, leaving R foot slightly lifted. Each *paso de sevillanas* requires 6 beats (2 bars of ³⁄₈ music).

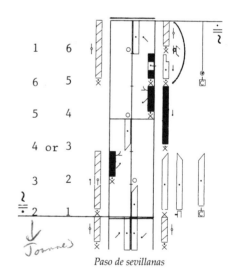

Paso de sevillanas

Ct: 1 2 3   4 5 6

PASO DE VACIO *(PAH-soh deh vah-THEE-oh)*
(flowing step)
Also called *bacío*.

This lyrical step resembles a balletic *développé* or *fondue*. Its action is one of developing, pouring forth, melting, or flowing, hence its name. It is danced primarily by women in a series as a *paseo*, where its lifting action gives the skirt a graceful, billowing, flowing movement.

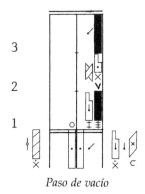

Beg pos	Feet—3rd R front. Arms—4th L up, head turned slightly right.
Ct 1	Lift R thigh, almost to hip level, with lower leg vertical.
Ct 2	Straighten leg by smoothly extending R foot forward to almost straight, but not locked, position.
Ct 3	Lower same leg to 3rd front.

3
2
1

Paso de vacío

PASO DE VASCO
See *esplante*.

PASO DOBLE *(PAH-soh DOH-bleh)*
(Two-step)

Choreographically speaking, *paso doble*, meaning two-step, is a misnomer. It is an ordinary walking or marching step called a one-step.

This term refers to the stirring marching music which is played as background at bullfights (*corridas*) and fiestas throughout Spain. It was used at times as the first (*entrada*) or last (*paso final*) movement in a medley of tunes for a promenade (*paseo de gracia*). *Paso doble* is a well-known term in Western ballroom dancing, but there is no traditional dance as such in Spain. However, in the 1920s and 1930s it was quite common for an artist to use the sprightly music of a two-step as a final number (*fin de fiesta*) in a dance concert. The catchy tunes provided the perfect vehicle for a serious *artista* (after an evening of classical dances) to become a little less formal by utilizing the movements of a torero (*tauromaquia*). Even the great La Argentina always ended her dance recitals with Joaquín Valverde's "La Corrida," invariably leaving her exhilarated audiences clamoring "Bis! Encore!" then leaving the theater humming the melody. Each *compás* consists of eight beats in ¾ rhythm, the first beat sometimes accented; but the evenness of the music lends itself to accentuation on any desired beat.

See *paseo de gracia, tauromaquia.*

PASO FINAL *(PAH-soh fee-NAHL)*
(Closing step)
Also called *finales.*

The term applies both to groups and solos, and the step can end either onstage or as an exit (*salida, mutis*).

See *cabriola, cierre, mutis, remate, salida.*

PASO LATERAL
See *paso de lado.*

PASO NATURAL
See *paso.*

PASO SALTADO
See *cambiamientos bajos y altos.*

PASO SENCILLO *(PAH-soh sehn-THEE-lyoh)*
(Simple, ordinary, unadorned step)
Also called *paso* and *paso natural.*

Technically speaking, the term indicates a single step in any direction, taking the weight from one foot to the other. The step is often simply called *paso*, and as a result it is often erroneously confused with *paseo*, a movement that travels. However, just as the word *step* is used to identify a series of movements, such as a "time step" in tap dancing, the Spanish term *paso* is used in a general sense to name a series of actions (or elements of movement) which make up what is called a "step."

See *compuesto, paseo, paso.*

PASO SENCILLO ATRAS
See *contrapaso.*

PASOS ENFRENTADOS *(PAH-sohs ehn-frehn-TAH-dohs)*
(Facing, opposing steps)

Steps or movements in which partners or lines of dancers encounter each other face to face (vis-à-vis) while dancing. The term is used in folkloric dances and old social *danzas* of the ballroom and court as well as in contemporary dances.

See *cadena, careo, hilera, pasada, sevillanas.*

PASOS VASCOS BASICOS *(PAH-sohs VAHS-cohs BAH-see-cohs)*
(Basic Basque steps)

Although they have an ethnic identity of their own, Basque dances often are part of a concert program of Iberian dances. The following steps are characteristic of these dances.

Posición normal

Puntapiyo

Grabiletia

POSICION NORMAL *(poh-see-thee-OHN nohr-MAHL)*
(Normal or beginning position)

The feet are in 1st parallel with arms hanging straight down at sides, chest lifted, back straight, chin level, eyes straight forward. This position of the body and arms is characteristic and is maintained throughout most Basque dances.

PUNTAPIYO *(poon-tah-PEE-yoh)*
(Literally, tip of the foot, kick)

A high kick, directly upward, while rising onto the half toe. The head remains level and the back straight. It is similar to the Spanish *puntapié*, but much more exaggerated and more often used.

GRABILETIA *(grah-bee-LEH-tee-ah)*
(Wheel)
Also called *burpil* and *gurpil*.

Beg pos　*Posición normal.*
　　　　Step L slightly forward on half-toe, preparing to make 1 turn (or more) left (swing R arm across front of body to help initiate turn). Simultaneously, with knees side by side, bend R knee (with toe pointing directly back) and with R foot make two or three small circles (*rodazanes*). The step is uniquely Basque and is done smoothly, with virility and grace.

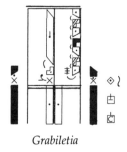

Grabiletia

According to Juan Urbelz, an authority on Basque dancing, circular foot movements resembling a *rodazán* should be made in an inward (*adentro*) direction when performed in the air (*en aire*) and in an outward (*afuera*) direction when performed on the ground (*al suelo*). Such a manner of executing these vigorous and often dangerous movements most likely evolved to prevent injury in performance.

PASO UNIDO *(PAH-soh oo-NEE-doh)*
(Step joined, connected, brought together)

A step which brings the feet together into first, third, or fifth positions.

See *asamblé batuda, asamblé hacia atrás, asamblé hacia delante, asamblé natural o sencillo.*

PATACOJA *(pah-tah-COH-hah)*
(Lame foot; Basque)

A time-marking step in Basque dancing in which the dancer makes a slight springing action on one foot while extending the other foot forward close to the ground. The dancer alternates the action from one foot to the other, keeping time to the music.

PATEO *(pah-TEH-oh)*
(A kicking, stamping of feet)

A term used in folkloric and occasionally in flamenco dances for referring to the action of legs and feet.

See *golpe, puntapié.*

PAUSA *(PAH-oo-sah)*
(A pause, rest, stop)

A very brief interval of stillness in a movement or in castanet playing which can, when used judiciously, give relief to incessant and possibly monotonous motion or sound. *Pausas* tend to create a slow, deliberate, calm effect for both the eye and the ear.

See *parada.*

PAVANA *(pah-VAH-nah)*
(From *pavo*, peacock, or *paduana*, suggesting Padua, Italy, a possible place of origin)[1]

An impressive sixteenth- and seventeenth-century dance of great ceremony and display which played an important role in the Spanish court as a *baile palaciego*. The *pavana* is basically simple and dignified, danced in a four-to-a-bar rhythm. Its steps have a swaying, graceful lilt that makes them peculiarly suitable for processional dances. The *Dictionnaire de Trevour* of 1721 described the dance: "The queens and princesses and great ladies accompanied the king, princes, and lords, with the long trains of their dresses let down and trailing behind them." Thoinot Arbeau, in his *Orchesography* (1588) tells us: "A cav-

---

[1]The exact origin of the word is uncertain.

alier may dance the *pavana* wearing his cloak and sword, and others dressed in long gowns, can walk with decorum and measured gravity. On solemn feast days, the *pavana* is employed by kings, princes and great noblemen to display themselves in their fine mantles and ceremonial robes." The English and French had their own versions of this dance, and Queen Elizabeth I, who was particularly fond of *pavanas*, commanded English composers to write them for her.

See *bailes palaciegos, danza, graves y breves, pavonear.*

PAVONEAR *(pah-voh-neh-AHR)*
(To strut, swagger, show off)

A term often used to describe the ceremonious or pompous character of the courtly *pavana* and used in either a complimentary or derogatory sense. The term refers either to an ostentatious action in a dance or to the obvious attitude of the performer.

See *aire, contoneo, pavana.*

PELLIZCO *(peh-LYEETH-coh)*
(A pinch, nip, small bit)

A small, spontaneous gesture, mimicry, or whimsy employed by a female flamenco dancer (*bailaora*) to heighten the effect of her dance, just as a cook adds a "pinch" of salt to food to accentuate flavor. As seen in *bulerías*, these subtle, unexpected or surprising movements tend to be light and humorous (*chicas*) and are meant to titillate and excite the audience.

See *gracia, chufla, salero.*

PETENERA *(peh-teh-NEH-rah)*
(Andalusian song and dance, origin uncertain)[1]

Petenera is a *baile intermedio* and, unlike other flamenco dances, such as *alegrías, soleares,* and *siguiriyas,* it has no set choreographic form, thus allowing much freedom. Although the rhythm is in a steady twelve counts, the dominant characteristic is that the bars of music in its rhythmic cycle (*ccmpás*) alternate between ¾ and ⅜ meters. Its origin is Cádiz. In 1887, Maestro José Otero of Seville choreographed *peteneras* to piano accompaniment as school dances (*bailes de escuela*) and taught them at his famous *academia* well into the twentieth century to countless students. *Peteneras,* accompanied by one or more guitars, have been used in the repertoire of many Spanish dance companies. Their repetitive broken rhythm creates an incessantly driving, fateful, yet sensuous atmosphere for creative dance dramas.

See *baile estilizado.* See also Appendix: Basic Flamenco Rhythms.

---

[1] Of the many romantic stories relating to the origin of this name, the favorite is that of La Petenera, a beautiful but sinister femme fatale with a sordid background whose wiles entrapped men, leading them to their doom.

PICA *(PEE-cah)*

See *pica tacón* (Basic Positions and Techniques), *redoble andaluz* (Basic Positions and Techniques).

PICADAS *(pee-CAH-dahs)*
(Punctured)

A descriptive term applied to the woman's delicate steps in folk dances such as *jotas*, performed in hemp-soled shoes (*alpargatas*), in which the tips of the toes are alternately and rhythmically set on the ground while the dancer remains in place or moves around her partner.

See *cuna, picante de pies.*

PICADITOS *(pee-cah-DEE-tohs)*
(Punctured)

Minute, rapid movements used while performing audible footwork (*zapateado*) in which the tip (*pico*), not the ball or sole, of the shoe is used to make delicately punctuated rhythmic accents, in contrast to the more forceful stamps (*golpes*) and heel work (*taconeo*). They can be done in motion (*corrida*) or in place (*en sitio*). Also called *picados.*

PICADOS
See *picaditos*

PICANTE DE PIES *(pee-CAHN-teh deh pee-EHS)*
(Piquancy of the feet)

A term describing quick, minute pointing and darting foot movements which exemplified the brilliance and charm of the eighteenth- and nineteenth-century *escuela bolera*. Originally, these dainty steps were performed on half-toes (*en media puntas*) in soft slippers (*zapatillas*). Later, in the theater, they were adapted to toe shoes by professional ballet dancers (*bailarinas*) and performed in a sharp, staccato manner similar in quality to balletic *piqué, batterie,* and *taqueterie.*

See *echado, en puntas, lazos, sacudida, sostenidos.*

PICA TACON   *punta tacon*
See Basic Positions and Techniques.

PICO *(PEE-coh)*
(Peak, top, bird's beak)

The very tip of a castanet shell (*concha*) or leaf (*oja*) (the part farthest from the cord on which the shells are strung) where it strikes against the other shell, thus producing the sound.

See *castañuela.*

PIES
See Basic Positions and Techniques.

PIFLAC ANDALUZ *(pee-FLAHK ahn-dah-LOOTH)*
(meaning uncertain, probably of onomatopoeic origin)
Also called *piflax.*

A leap to the side with a turn in the air, similar to a balletic *saute de basque.*

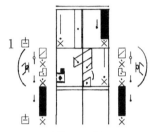

Beg pos   Feet—From any previous action.
          Arms—Low 5th front.

          Preparation—Step R diagonally for-
          ward, beginning to turn right, ex-
          tending L leg forward while lifting
          arms to 1st.
          Leap into air to complete one full turn
          right, lifting arms to 5th.
Ct 1   Land on L, R leg bent, foot in front at
          lower shin level.

Piflac andaluz

See *cruzado.*

PIFLAC DE ESCUELA BOLERA *(pee-FLAHK deh ehs-CWEH-lah boh-LEH-rah)*
(Meaning uncertain, probably of onomatopoeic origin)

This step, similar to a balletic *jeté,* is a small movement used in connection
with other steps to form a combination (*compuesto*) of the *escuela bolera.*

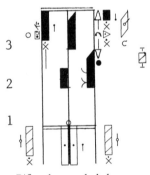

Beg pos   Feet—5th L front.
          Arms—5th.

Ct 1   Hold.
Ct 2   Brush R leg low diagonally forward
          right and leap high into air.
Ct 3   Land diagonally forward on R, knee
          bent (*echado*), circling R arm down,
          passing through 2nd to 5th low front,
          curving torso over diagonally right
          and turning head to right, L foot be-
          hind R calf.

Piflac de escuela bolera

PIFLAX
See *piflac andaluz.*

PISTOLEA *(pee-stoh-LEH-ah)*
(Pistolet, pocket pistol)[1]
Also called *pistolet*.

This difficult *escuela bolera* step, which resembles a balletic *jeté battu derrière*, was popular in eighteenth-century *seguidillas boleras*.

Ct &   Ct   1   2   3

Beg pos	Feet—3rd R foot front. Arms—Between 2nd and 5th (*folklórico*).
Ct &	Extend L leg diagonally left back, springing into air and beating R foot in front of L.
Ct 1	Land on R foot (keeping L leg extended diagonally left back).
C2	Hold.
Ct 3	Slide on ball of R foot slightly to right, knee bent, L toe extended low to side.[2]
Ct 4–6	Follow above step with three small steps (*pas de buret natural*) to right.
	Reverse all above to left.

See *batido, pas de buret natural*.

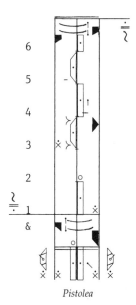

Pistolea

---

[1] *Pistolea* is an eighteenth-century Italo-Hispanic term. As an analogy in teaching, one uses the expression to "shoot" the foot to one side then the other.

[2] See figures in period costumes, each moving to his or her right. Ct 1–3 depicted above demonstrate the woman's action, which also moves to the right. Virtuosic dancers sometimes add an extra beat in back (see Ct &) before landing.

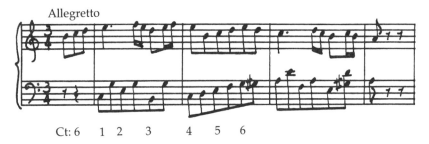

Ct: 6   1   2   3   4   5   6

PISTOLET
See *pistolea.*

PITOS *(PEE-tohs)*
(Woodpeckers)

One of several ways of making rhythmic sounds. *Pitos* are finger snaps made by the dancer while dancing and occasionally by a singer (*cantaor*) accompanying the dancer. *Pitos* are by no means inconsequential sounds. There are flamenco dancers, both male and female, who can make single, double, and triple sounds which resemble gunshots. They are often interspersed with rhythmic hand claps (*palmas*). The term is also the name for very small and rarely seen castanets of Aragon, which, although strung like ordinary castanets, are not strummed with the fingers but are worn on the thumb and played by snapping the middle finger directly onto them. Because of their miniature size, they are called *pitos*, which also means fleas or ticks.

See *chasquar los dedos; palmas, pitos, y castañuelas* (Basic Positions and Techniques).

PLANTA *(PLAHN-tah)*
(Sole of the foot; planted, steadfast)

The entire surface of the foot, which takes all or part of the weight in an action or a pose. The term is often used with a prefix, such as *semi* or *media.*

In the most typical foot position in Spanish dancing, the fourth position (*cuarta*), which is also called *planta natural,* only the ball of the forward foot is on the ground (*media planta*). The name is carried over from the old-style stance, in which both feet were parallel and the forward foot was planted (*plantada*), not as it has evolved, exposing the lifted heel with the foot turned out. The term is also used in rhythmic footwork (*zapateado*) when a stamp (*golpe*) is made.

See *pies* (Basic Positions and Techniques).

PLATILLOS
See *chinchines.*

PLEGADOR *(pleh-gah-DOHR)*
(Folder or doubler; a ballet barre)

Practice at the barre, an introductory warmup before an *escuela bolera* class.

POR DETRAS *(pohr deh-TRAHS)*
(Toward or by way of the back)

A term describing a movement, usually a turn *(vuelta)*, which is begun by placing one foot in back of the other. *Por delante* describes the opposite—that the foot initiates the same action, first being placed in front of the other.

POSTICEO *(pohs-tee-THEH-oh)*
(From *postiza*, castanet)
Also called *chapateo* in Seville.

The action of striking castanets *(postizas)* against each other.

See *choqueteo, golpe, postizas.*

POSTITO
See *postiza.*

POSTIZA *(pohs-TEE-tha)*
(Not natural, artificial, imitation)
Also spelled *postito.*

A Valencian term for castanets.

POSTURA *(pohs-TOO-rah)*
(Posture, position)
Also called *postura del cuerpo.*

A static pose, the unique identity or character of which is one of pride *(orgullo)*. It is short for *postura del cuerpo,* a term of the old dancing masters, who considered the carriage of the torso and the bearing of the head and limbs as important as the actual steps.

See *aire, bien parado, danza, figura.*

POSTURA DEL CUERPO
See *postura.*

PRESENTACION *(preh-sehn-tah-thee-OHN)*
(Presentation, personal introduction)

The first movements or *paseo* which bring the dancer into view during the entrance *(entrada)* of a dance.

See *baile de presentación, entrada, paseo.*

PROVOCATIVO *(pro-voh-cah-TEE-voh)*
(Action which provokes, excites, tempts, arouses)

Any step or motion which will stimulate an audience. *Provocativos* can range from a subtle, sophisticated lift of a shoulder to such obvious routine actions as knee slides and removal of a jacket, scarf, or shawl to brandish it at an actual or imagined partner or at the audience itself. *Provocativos* can cause opposite reactions in the same audience, bringing many *aficionados* to their feet with *oles* of approval or, on the other hand, leaving the more conservative shaking their heads with disapproval and disappointment. An overindulgence in *provocativos* can change the profile of Spanish dancing, giving an exaggerated picture of the truthful image. A classic example of how *provocativos* made dance history was the early-nineteenth-century "La Cachucha" as danced by Fanny Elssler. As a dance it did not have much substance, but Elssler's natural (or meticulously planned) use of *provocativos* earned her thousands of admirers.

See *cachucha, epiléptico, españolado, gracia, ole, pellizco, salero.*

PULGARETES *(pool-gah-REH-tehs)*
(Little fleas—Aragonese term for castanets)

The word *pulgar* means thumb, thus implying that one of the styles in which castanets are played is that of tying them to the thumbs and strumming them with the fingers. The Aragoneses, however, prefer to attach them to the middle finger (*al dedo medio*) and fling them against the palm.

See *palmas, pitos, y castañuelas* (Basic Positions and Techniques, *forma* 2).

PULSACION *(pool-sah-thee-OHN)*
(A pulsation, beating, throbbing)

The gentle accented and unaccented rhythmic patterns produced by the left-hand (*macho*) castanet. It implies a subtle technique that is not easily acquired, demanding a sensitive musical ear and very supple wrist. To quote castanet virtuosa Carola Goya, "Unlike a thing attached, the castanets should appear as part of the hand, as if born with the hand." The exaggerated flinging action of the wrists is characteristic of most folk and regional group dances, but is visually distracting and produces a sound that is tedious to the ear in classical dances.

See *crotalogía, golpe, golpeo, macho, matiz.*

PUNT *(POONT)*
(Step; Catalonian)

Punt, similar to Spanish *paso,* is usually thought of in connection with *sardanas.* But the term is often combined with the specific names of Catalonian steps and dances, as in *punt de bolangera, punt de sardana, punt y taló.*

See *llargs y curts, sardana, tirada.*

PUNTA CRUZADA *(POON-tah croo-THAH-dah)*
(Crossed point or tip [of foot])

A movement in which one leg is crossed over the other with the knee straight and the toe resting on the floor. As a static position, the dancer stands on one foot, the opposite knee is bent and turned out, the ankles are crossed, and the tip of the shoe touches the floor, its sole facing outward. The tip of the toe can rest on the floor either in front of or behind the standing foot.

See *embotado de escuela bolera, figura plástica.*

PUNTA EN SUELO *(POON-tah ehn SWEH-loh)*
(Tip or point of the foot on the floor)
Also called *puntera.*

A term indicating that one leg is extended to any open position, the foot pointed, and the heel raised so that only the tip of the large toe rests on the floor. The movement does not involve a transfer of weight but can be used to pass from one position to another. The term is to some extent synonymous with *punto, puntera,* and *puntilla,* just as the balletic terms *pointe tendue, piqué à terre,* and *dégagé* overlap.

See *pies* (Basic Positions and Techniques), *puntera en vuelta, puntilla.*

PUNTAPIE *(poon-tah-pee-EH)*
(Literally, tip of the foot; kick)
Also called *putapieyo;* Basque.

A folkloric term indicating a simple kick high above the head. It can be used for striking a tambourine (*pandereta*) with the toe or as a kick while hitting the tambourine with the knuckles under the raised leg. It was called *voleo* in the eighteenth and nineteenth centuries, when it was used as a classical term, similar to a balletic *grand battement.* It is a typical step in Basque men's dancing.

See *pasos vascos básicos.*

PUNTA TACON
See *pica tacón* (Basic Positions and Techniques).

PUNTA Y TACON CRUZADO *(POON-tah ee tah-COHN croo-THAH-doh)*
(Tip of the toe and heel crossed)

A term for a step in which the dancer hops on one foot, the other foot touches the heel in front, then the toe crosses over the hopping foot touching the tip on the ground. The step is typical of regional dances.

See *punta y talón, tacón.*

PUNTA Y TALON *(POON-tah ee tah-LOHN)*
(Point and heel)

Ct 1–2   Ct 3

Beg pos   Feet—Weight on L, knee slightly bent
          throughout.
          Arms—4th L up, chest inclines
          slightly over R leg, head turned to-
          ward R foot.
Ct 1   Hop[1] on L, turn R knee in, and touch
          R toe to floor to side (women allow
          hips to twist, causing skirt to swish;
          men are more restrained).
Ct 2   Pause.
Ct 3   Hop onto L and place edge of R heel
          (*de filo el talón*) on floor with knee
          turned outward.

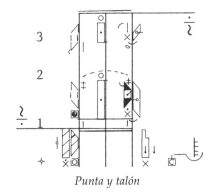

Punta y talón

See *talón*.

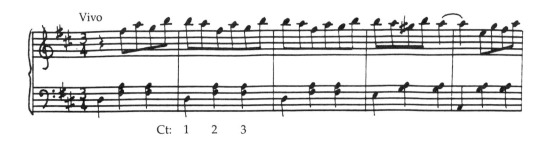

Ct: 1   2   3

---

[1]The hop is typical of the *jota aragonesa* and other regional dances. It is sometimes eliminated (*sin salto*) in
the *escuela bolera* and sometimes in the Andalusian style pictured above.

PUNTA Y TALON EN VUELTA *(POON-tah ee tah-LOHN ehn VWEHL-tah)*
(Point and heel while turning)

In this step a turn is made (while repeating the action of the *punta y talón*) in the direction of the pivoting foot.

See *Punta y talón, tacón.*

PUNT DE BOLANGERA *(poont deh boh-lahn-JEH-rah)*
(Catalonian, from French *boulangère,* which means baker, baker's wife or dance.)

The action, all on half-toe, closely resembles that of a polka step and is seen in many Catalonian dances.

Beg pos   Feet—Half-toe (*semiplanta*), weight on L.

Arms—Low at sides, woman's holding skirt, man's optional.

Ct &   Give hop (*saltito*) on L.
Ct 1   Step R forward.
Ct &   Step L into 3rd back.
Ct 2   Step R forward.

Repeat all, reversed.

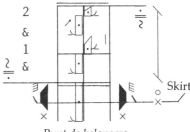

Punt de bolangera

See *salto.*

PUNT DE PERDIU *(poont deh pehr-DYOO)*
(Step of a partridge; Catalonian)

One of a series of easy-flowing steps done on high half-toe (*semipunta*) which seem to skim delicately along the surface of the ground. This step in Catalonian dancing, performed in three-quarter rhythm, is sometimes danced with two steps on half-toe and the third on the flat foot. The name comes from the characteristic movement of the indigenous partridge (*perdiz*) which inhabits the forests.

PUNTEADO *(poon-teh-AH-doh)*
(Playing on the guitar)

This term has two applications which refer to style or action. In flamenco dance it refers to the action in which the feet move softly while advancing, retreating, and crossing as the arm movements (*braceos*), torso, and head carry the focus of attention. In guitar playing (*toque*) it describes the technique which the *guitarrista* employs, one of plucking the strings with each finger separately (*punteado*) to achieve the free-flowing sections (*falsetas*) which accompany the actions of the dance.

See *toque.*

PUNTERA
See *punta en suelo, puntera en vuelta.*

PUNTERA EN VUELTA *(poon-TEH-rah ehn VWEHL-tah)*
(Tip of shoe in a turn)

A step typical of the eighteenth- and nineteenth-century *escuela bolera* as well as various folkloric dances, including those of Mallorca, in which the dancer pivots on the ball of one foot, knee bent, while stretching out the toe of the other foot and lightly touching the floor four times, making the circumference of a circle. *Puntera* means a pointer or the hand of a clock. Thus the tip of the shoe depicts a compass action.

PUNTILLA *(poon-TEE-lyah)*
(Small point, tip, tip of toe)

This term refers to a position of the foot in regional dances, usually when flat slippers or low-heeled shoes are worn. This foot position is frequently encountered in the *escuela bolera.*

See *pies* (Basic Positions and Techniques), *sostenido en vuelta.*

PUNTO *(POON-toh)*
(Point, tip)

The tip of the large toe when the foot is stretched out.

See *pies* (Basic Positions and Techniques), *en puntas, punta en suelo.*

PUNTOS SALTADOS *(POON-tohs sahl-TAH-dohs)*
(Jumped, hopped steps on tiptoe)

In *sardanas,* some steps are slightly hopped (*saltados*) when, toward the climax of the dance, the music of the traditional *sardana* orchestra (*cobla*) becomes more animated.

See *cobla.*

PUNT Y TALO *(POONT ee tah-LOH)*
(Toe and heel; Catalonian)

The Catalonian counterpart of the Spanish *punta y talón.* It is essentially the same step except that the toe and heel alternately touch the floor in the same spot, diagonally front, with only an ankle action. In dances in other parts of Spain the toe and heel touch the floor to the side, the knee facing outward when the heel touches and inward when the toe touches the same spot. The second variation, which involves a pivoting action of the same hip, is often seen in the *jota aragonesa. Punt y taló* is usually performed with a small hop (*saltillo*).

See *punta y talón.*

Figure 26. The graceful movements of a *baile de plaza* ("dance in the town square") are enhanced by the dancer's song, which says, "This dance is enjoyed by young and old in nature's environment of the open sky, green fields, fruit-bearing trees, and pure air perfumed by the fragrance of plants and trees." *From a nineteenth-century etching by P. Ribera.*

Figure 27. Basque dances have intricate patterns requiring intense vitality and physical energy that are animated by ululating cries *(irrintzi)* made by the dancers, cheering each other into greater effort like the high kicking action, *puntapieyo. Courtesy Albert Morini.*

Figure 28. Manuel de Falla's *El Amor Brujo*, first performed in 1915, is an early example of a dance-drama *(baile teatral)*. This version, choreographed by La Meri, was presented at Jacob's Pillow in 1953 with Ted Shawn as the spectre and Carola Goya as Lucía. *Photo by Jack B. Mitchell.*

Figure 29. The psychological approach to *Don Quixote* is a contemporary creation of Luisillo, a unique dancer-choreographer who since the early fifties has staged several major works in this vein. *Photo by antonio de benito, courtesy of Royal Ballet Nacional de España.*

Figure 30. Carola Goya and Matteo in *Perfidia* ("Treachery"), an early experimental work *(baile teatral)* performed without music and accompanied only by a dull thudding with the balls of the feet and the sound of castanets. The high-pitched castanets of the female dancer conveyed the hissing sound of a serpent (treachery), while the male's deep, hollow-toned castanets expressed the fear and desperation of a haunted victim. *Photo by John Van Lund at Jacob's Pillow Dance Festival, 1955.*

Figure 31. Scene from a cinematic dance-drama version of Garcia Lorca's play, *Blood Wedding*. This production, a skillful blending of modern dance, ballet, mime, and traditional flamenco, was a collaboration of Antonio Gades and film director Carlos Saura. *Photo by Libra Films, courtesy of ALMI Pictures, Inc.*

Figure 32. Scenes such as the above, called *un baile del candil* (a dance by candlelight), were frequent in Andalusian patios and inns, and were lighted by burning wicks *(candiles)*. Such *de candil* dances are being preserved through the technique and style of *escuela bolera. From a painting by Llovera.*

Figure 33. The *duende,* or spirit, of the dance moves a child as she improvises steps which come naturally as her doting grandmother sings the tune and claps the rhythm *(compás). Suevia Films photo, courtesy of Lydia Joel.*

Figure 34. In many folk dances of the north such as *quita y pon* from Monte Hermoso, dancers play intricate rhythms with their castanets fastened to their middle finger *(al dedo medio)* instead of their thumb, as in other parts of Spain. *Courtesy of M. Garcia Matos*, Danzas populares de España.

Figure 35. A pass *(pasada)* in the *fandango* of Comares. *Courtesy of M. Garcia Matos, Danzas popu-*lares de España.

Figure 36. The *jota fogueda* from Tarragona requires exceptional energy and takes its name (meaning "flare" or "outburst") from small rockets hidden in the mens' sashes that they light and let loose to snake along the ground and scare the women. *Courtesy of Sección Feminina de F. E. de las J. O. N. S.*

Figure 37. The *parado* or *bolero viejo* (Valldemosa). The boleros of Majorca are quite different from those of Spain. This folkloric version from Valldemosa, accompanied by violins, guitars, castanets, and a peculiar triangle *(tríangulo)*, has a lordly and distinguished air. It is a slow version of the *seguidilla*, and its name, *parado* (stop, halt), refers to the sudden ending *(paso final)*, which contrasts with the easy-going smoothness of its rhythm. *Courtesy of Sección Feminina de F. E. de las J. O. N. S.*

Figure 38. It is grape-harvesting time, a happy occasion in Ciudad Real, and this version of the *jota* is accompanied by improvised instruments such as a mortar, caldron, ladle and frying pan, and tambourine. *Courtesy of Sección Feminina de F.E. de las J.O.N.S.*

Figure 39. Well-known *jota* specialist *(jotero)*, Jorge Sánchez Arnas, demonstrates the vigorous, *a lo alto* sequences of the *jota de albalate*. *Jotas*, many of which are slow and sedate, are identified by their local names such as Andora, Alcañiz, Caspe, Epila, and Fuendejalou. *Photo by José Borastero.*

Figure 40. Matteo in *Bolero Goyesco*. Photo by John Lindquist.

Figure 41. The final note of music, and there is loud cheering and applause as the dancers remain motionless in difficult and graceful positions like the rarely seen variations of *balanceado a tierra*. Such an occasion is shown in a drawing by the nineteenth-century painter Gustav Doré. *New York Public Library Picture Collection.*

Figure 42. Each subsequent movement shown here is a subtle variation or development of the same step, using a knee action called *rodillazo*. Originally associated with flamenco dancing and the guitar music of a *tablao* (nightclub), the *bata de cola* (train dress) can be used dramatically to interpret the music of such composers as Albéniz, Falla, Granados, Turina, and Halffter. When done with varying degrees of energy, the visual effect is heightened by the weight, texture, and style of the dress. When handled with the expertise of a fine artist, it becomes an instrument for conveying a multitude of moods and nuances. *Photos of Carola Goya by Jack B. Mitchell.*

Figure 43. Catalans dance *sardanas* in Barcelona Cathedral Square as an expression of patriotism. Tourists often join the seemingly simple impromptu dance, the Catalans showing beginners how to follow the tricky sequences of *llargs* and *curts* (longs and shorts). The *sardana* is, in the words of Eric Morera, more than a dance: it is "a hymn, a song; it is Catalunya." *Photo by Franke Keating.*

Figure 44. The *moixiganga* is a choreographic arrangement of a series of episodes depicting the Passion of Jesus. Distinctly theatrical since the fifteenth century, they were used to both instruct and entertain the masses of preliterate people. This production by the Esbart Dansaire de Rubí was choreographed by Manuel Cubelas and inspired by reproductions found in the archives of the city of Lledia. *Photo by Pau Barceló.*

Figure 45. Originally a dance of the people, the *bolero* became a mania in the ballrooms of Spain. Here, Núria Majó and Joan Fosas, principal dancers of Esbart Dansaire de Rubí, perform a Valencian version choreographed by José de Udaeta. *Photo by Jaume Font, courtesy of Esbart Dansaire de Rubí.*

Figure 46. Maintaining traditional Catalonian steps and a carnival atmosphere, choreographer Albert Sans of the Esbart Dansaire de Rubí has created "El Carnestoltes," a theater spectacle to symphonic music composed by Maestro Joaquím Serra. *Photo by Jaume Font, courtesy of Esbart Dansaire de Rubí.*

Figure 47. The effervescent quality of Albert Sans's choreography is seen above as his vital, fun-loving dancers portray a group of Catalonian Gypsies from Valles arriving at a town to perform at weddings, a fair, or whatever celebrations may take place. *Photo by Jaume Font, courtesy of Esbart Dansaire de Rubí.*

Figure 48. Manuela Vargas dances in *Medea*, a powerful classic work choreographed by José Granero, which delves deeply into the Spanish psyche. Still retaining its Iberian roots, ethnic style, and strength, Spanish dance finds new expression in a modern idiom. *Photo by antonio de benito, courtesy of the Royal Ballet Nacional de España.*

Figure 49. One of the few action photographs of the legendary La Argentina (1880–1936), universally considered to be the greatest Spanish dancer of her era. As an innovator of the neo-classic style, it was she who made the greatest impact in the world of concert Spanish dancing. She is shown here in one of her most popular numbers, *La Corrida*, with which she invariably ended her programs. *Photo by Monique Paravicini.*

QUEBRADA *(keh-BRAH-dah)*
(A break, doubling, bending)

A deep bending action of the middle or lower spine (usually a complete circle) performed during a turn *(vuelta)*. Classical ballet has a similar term, *cambré*.

See *vuelta quebrada*.

QUEBRADITA *(keh-brah-DEE-tah)*
(Little break, doubling, bending)

A small bend of the waist or upper spine in a pose or during a movement, usually a turn *(vuelta)*.

See *vuelta quebradita*.

QUEJIO *(keh-HEE-oh)*
(Moan)

An extended passage of "Ay!" intoned by a flamenco singer *(cantaor)* to create an atmosphere *(temple)* at the start *(salida)* or conclusion *(remate)* of a song.

See *farfulleos, salida* (definition 4).

QUIEBROS *(kee-EH-brohs)*
(Movements of inclination, dodging of the body)
Also called *suertes*.

The term is related to the powerful yet graceful maneuvers of the bullfighter that are imitated or adapted by Andalusian dance.

See *estocada, paso de muleta, tauromaquia, vuelta torera*.

RANGUEO
See *rastreado*.

RASGUEADO *(rahs-gheh-AH-doh)*
(Making of flourishes)

A guitarist's term for various ways of strumming the guitar and producing strong rhythmic patterns and flourishes. These sounds, characteristic of the flamenco guitarist (*tocaor*), emphasize the dancer's movements and add drama to the singing (*cante*).

See *cifra*. See also Appendix: Basic Flamenco Rhythms.

RASTREADO *(rahs-treh-AH-doh)*
(Dragged, traced)
Also called *rangueo* in Mallorcan dances.

A term describing the ball or tip of one foot dragged along the floor to join the other, which has already stepped to the side or backward. For many years in America this step was called "Spanish draw" by dance teachers.

REDOBLE *(reh-DOH-bleh)*
(A doubling, a clinching, a drum roll)
Also called *remate*.

A unit of rhythmic footwork unique to Andalusian and flamenco dancing. It is composed of four consecutive sounds, a triplet and a single beat.[1] A *redoble* is performed in an affirmative and decisive manner, often ending a phrase, when it is called a *redoble final*. It also, rarely, refers to a roll performed with the four fingers on a castanet.

See *redoble andaluz* (Basic Positions and Techniques), *redoble flamenco* (Basic Positions and Techniques), *remate*.

REDOBLE ANDALUZ
See Basic Positions and Techniques.

---

[1] The *redoble escudero* is performed with one added stamp (*golpe*), making a group of five sounds instead of the usual four.

REDOBLE CRUZADO *(ray-DOH-bleh croo-THAH-doh)*
(Crossed *redoble*)

A *redoble flamenco* performed in an unusual manner.

Beg pos   Feet—1st parallel.
            Arms—Optional.

    Ct 1   Preparation—Left R foot backward
            from knee.
    Ct &   Stamp R foot beside L, taking weight.
            Strike edge of L heel slightly forward,
            crossed diagonal right. Stamp L foot
            directly down, in same crossed posi-
            tion, taking weight. (These 3 sounds
            combine to make musical triplet.)
    Ct 2   Follow immediately with stamp on
            R foot, taking weight where it was.
            Accent is on ct 2.

            Repeat reversed.

            When performed in a series *(corrida)*,
            they are done in place *(en sitio)* and
            the preparatory ct 1 may be elimi-
            nated, using only ct &–2 as the
            redoble.

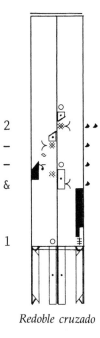

Redoble cruzado

See *redoble, redoble flamenco* (Basic Positions and Techniques), *remate.*

REDOBLE ESCUDERO
See *redoble* (note).

REDOBLE FINAL
See *redoble.*

REDOBLE FLAMENCO
See Basic Positions and Techniques.

REDONDO
See *rueda.*

REMACHOS *(reh-MAH-chohs)*
(Riveting, flattening movements or sounds)

This typical rhythmic pattern is performed in a *farruca* and usually occurs toward the end of the dance. Its name comes from the hammering action of the
lower leg, as though it were pounding a nail down firmly.

Beg pos Feet—3rd L front, facing audience, or
         1st parallel facing stage right, knees
         slightly bent.
         Arms—Low 4th L front, head facing
         audience.

Ct a Make a very small, audible hop on
      L foot, lifting lower R leg back from
      knee.
Ct 1 Stamp R foot loudly (with the action
      in the lower leg only) (*martillo*) in 3rd
      back (or 1st parallel).
Ct a–2 Repeat above ct a–1.
Ct a–3 Repeat above ct a–1.
Ct 4 Hold.

The entire pattern above is done three
times in quick succession, all movements are audible, accenting ct 3.
Step is done in place (*en sitio*) with
head remaining level.

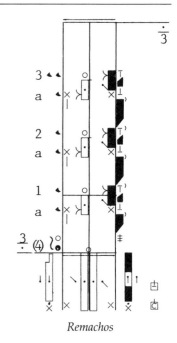

Remachos

See *farruca, golpeteo, martillo.*

REMATE *(reh-MAH-teh)*
(End, finish, conclusion)

An audible, abrupt, and decisive ending of a musical phrase made with the
feet in flamenco dance. The term is also used synonymously with *redoble*
when it terminates a phrase.

See *redoble.*

REMATE FLAMENCO
See *redoble flamenco* (Basic Positions and Techniques).

REPIQUE *(reh-PEE-keh)*
(A ringing, chopping sound)

The rhythmic, clear sound applied to castanet playing (*castañuelas*), heel work
(*taconeo*), hand clapping (*palmas*), and finger snapping (*pitos*), producing a
crisp, unmuffled tone when accompanying dancing.

See *matiz, seco.*

REPIQUETEO *(reh-pee-keh-TEH-oh)*
(Chopping, ringing sound)

The rapid, repeated staccato rhythm accounts for the name of this step, which skims the floor.

Beg pos Feet—1st parallel, knees slightly bent, weight on L.
Arms—Optional.

Ct 1 Stamp R foot (*golpe*) slightly forward, taking weight.
Ct & Jab L heel beside R foot.
Ct 2 Stamp L foot slightly forward, taking weight.
Ct & Jab R heel beside L foot.

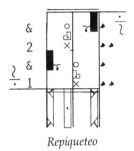

Repiqueteo

The stamps on ct 1 and ct 2 are sightly accented. The step is repeated rapidly many times as it travels in a forward direction.

See *seco, matiz.*

REPOSADO
See *reposao.*

REPOSAO *(reh-poh-SAH-oh)*[1]
(Quiet, in repose)

One of the two basic styles of flamenco dance from which all others appear to be derived. It is a more classical approach to movement in which the body carriage from the waist up, the head, arms, hands, and general demeanor are more stylized, with molded poses (*figuras plásticas*), giving a cool impression, almost one of aloofness. The style is replete with subtle nuances and, in the opinion of many flamenco authorities, has more *duende*. The *reposao* style is seldom seen among male dancers today and lends itself to taller female dancers, who tend to approach movement in a more lyrical manner. It is the opposite of the style known as *agitanado.*

See *agitanado, duende.*

REPRESA *(reh-PREH-sah)*
(A holding back, stopping)

A slow, stately receding step reminiscent of early court dances.

---

[1]From *reposado,* so pronounced by Flamencos. It is characteristic of Flamencos to drop the *d* sound.

Beg pos   Feet—3rd L front.
          Arms—Low at sides, elbows slightly
          lifted—old style (*estilo antiguo*).

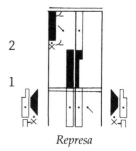

Ct 1   Step back into 4th, slightly bending
         both knees, torso erect. In old social
         or court dances (*danzas*), bending is
         deeper.
Ct 2   Straighten R knee, drawing ball of
         L foot into 3rd front.

Represa

See *contrapaso, retroceder.*

RETIRADO *(reh-tee-RAH-doh)*
(Drawn back)

A term describing the lower leg having been drawn back after it has been lifted forward; similar to *retiré* or *raccourci* in ballet.

See *destaque adelante retirada.*

RETORTILLES *(reh-tohr-tee-LYEHS)*
(Twistings, wrigglings, writhings; Hispanicized French)

A term for a step performed in three ways:
    1. A step executed in ballet slippers in which the dancer jumps into fifth position, turns both heels outward (leaving the feet pigeon-toed), and then turns the toes outward. Each action takes one count. The jump is repeated with the other foot in front. The step resembles *paraditas,* but with the feet moving away from each other. It is one small portion of a combination of movements (*compuesto*) of the *escuela bolera.*
    2. The step as danced in a *malagueña,* in which the torso is twisted from front to side, following the action of the feet.
    3. A step performed exactly like a *bordoneo* but called *media tortillés* (halfway or partial twists) because it is not so pronounced.

See *bordoneo* (step 3 above), *malagueña in media vuelta* (step 2 above), *paraditas* (step 1 above), *torcido.*

RETROCEDER *(reh-tro-theh-DEHR)*
(To move, draw, turn in a backward direction)

To move back in a solo or group dance.

See *contrapaso, represa.*

REVERENCIA AL SUELO *(reh-veh-REHN-thee-ah ahl SWEH-loh)*
(Bow to the floor)

Rarely used except in a few court and period dances as a final gesture.

Beg pos Feet—3rd R front.
Arms—Low 5th front.

Preparation—move arms to low forward, releasing R foot.

Feet—Move R foot slowly backward, lowering R knee to floor, then extending L forward on floor (woman only).
Arms—Woman: Open to low 2nd, palms up, inclining torso forward, head facing down. Man: kneel on R knee facing woman, taking her R hand in his R hand, L arm hanging loosely at side, inclining torso toward her.
  Ct Optional.

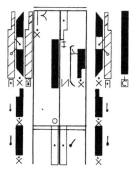

Reverencia al suelo

See *paso final, reverencia sencilla, saludo.*

REVERENCIA BAJA *(reh-veh-REHN-thee-ah BAH-hah)*
(Low, shallow, humble bow)

Performed by partners facing each other during a court dance (*baile palaciego*) or as a gesture of respect facing the royal attendants after the conclusion of a particular dance.

Beg pos Feet—3rd R front.
Arms—Low 5th front.

Preparation—Move arms to low forward, releasing R foot.

Feet—Move R foot back, bending knee deeply, inclining torso slightly forward, casting eyes down.
  Ct Optional.

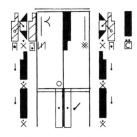

Reverencia baja

See *baile palaciego, paso final, reverencia sencilla, saludo.*

REVERENCIA SENCILLA *(reh-veh-REHN-thee-ah sen-THEE-lyah)*
(Simple bow without adornment)
Also called *cortesía sencilla.*

The bow described below is one of the three basic bows used in many eighteenth- and nineteenth-century social dances or figure dances (*danzas de figuras*) and in some folk dances. The other two, *reverencia al suelo* and *reverencia baja,* are more exaggerated. It must be remembered that the bow reveals the degree to which a person or group shows respect. It varied from one class of society to another, in location, purpose, and period in history. Likewise it can vary from the unadorned bow (*cortesía sencilla*) to the most elaborate bow in manner, timing, purpose, and affectation. Because of the great influence of France and Italy on Spain's dance and social behavior, many practice sessions were devoted to the proper way of bowing.

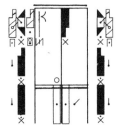

Beg pos   Feet—3rd R front.
          Arms—Low 5th front.

          Preparation—Move arms to low for-
          ward, releasing R foot.

Feet—Move R foot slightly back, bending knee,
          keeping L foot touching in front.
Arms—Open to low 2nd, palms up, inclining
          torso slightly forward.

Reverencia sencilla

      Ct   Optional

See *reverencia al suelo, reverencia baja, saludo, zalema.*

RINCONCILLO *(reen-cohn-THEE-lyoh)*
(Little corner, nook, lurking place)

A derogatory expression indicating a misinformed or highly personal point of view in evaluating dance, music, and theater, usually based on limited or second-hand knowledge—as a Spaniard would say, "Oír campanas y no saber dónde" ("to have been told incorrectly about a fact").

RISTO *(REES-toh)*
(A turn; Catalonian)
Also called *ristol.*

A turn (*vuelta*) which begins with the female's right hand held in her partner's right hand. With three small steps, holding her skirt with the free hand, she makes a turn under his raised arm. The step is sometimes used by a couple entering or leaving a dance, at which time the man shouts "¡Risto!" as a signal. This simple folkloric step and shouting animates the dancers and invariably creates a scene of joy in them and the onlookers.

RISTOL
See *risto.*

RITMO *(REET-moh)*
(Rhythm)

The rhythm within a phrase (*compás*) that identifies the type of music and/or dance, such as *ritmo de bulerías. Ritmo* is often mistakenly used synonymously with *compás* and *tiempo.*

See *compás.*

ROBADO *(roh-BAH-doh)*
(Stolen, robbed)
Also called *a medio paso*.

Usually applied to the classical *bolero*, in which partners carry on a friendly competition, alternating with each other in solo variations. Each succeeding variation is a bit more difficult and spectacular (*vistoso*) than the last, the soloist having "stolen" (*robado*) the limelight and applause. Likewise, the tempo is also altered to accommodate each successive variation. The term is equivalent to Italian *rubato*.

See *cambiamientos bajos y altos, paso del demonio, vistoso*.

RODAZAN *(roh-dah-THAN)*
(An encircling, surrounding, encompassing movement)
Also called *salerito*.

This step, used mostly by women, resembles a balletic *rond de jambe* except that the lower leg never extends so far that the knee is straightened. It can circle either outward (*afuera*) or inward (*adentro*) and either in the air (*al aire*), as described below, or while touching the floor (*al suelo*).

Beg pos	Feet—R knee raised diagonally right forward almost hip height, lower leg hanging down, L knee easy, not rigid. Arms—4th L up, head turned slightly right.	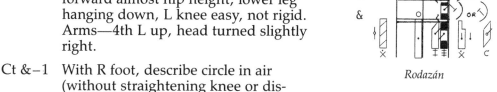
Ct &–1	With R foot, describe circle in air (without straightening knee or disturbing thigh).	*Rodazán*

See *adentro, afuera, al aire, al suelo, paso de cachucha*.

RODAZAN AFUERA Y ADENTRO
See *gorgallada, gorgallada de escuela bolera, salero*.

RODAZAN AL SUELO *(roh-dah-THAN al SWEH-loh)*
(Circular movement on the floor)

A *rodazán* in which the ball of the moving foot touches the floor (*suelo*) and the torso is slightly inclined over the working leg. With the arms usually held in fourth position, this gracious step is typical of the old school dances (*bailes de escuela*).

See *al suelo, rodazán*.

RODAZAN DE ESCUELA BOLERA HACIA ADENTRO *(roh-dah-THAHN deh ehs-CWEH-lah boh-LEH-rah AH-thee-ah ah-DEHN-troh)*
(A circling movement of the lower leg toward the inside in *escuela bolera* style)

This term indicates a circular movement of the lower limb in a particular combination (*compuesto*) unique to the *escuela bolera*.

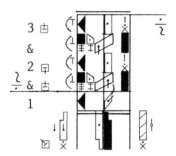

Beg pos	Feet—4th R front facing downstage, R knee bent, weight evenly distributed on both feet. Arms—4th R up.
Ct 1	Shifting weight onto R foot, lift L leg sideward, low.
Ct &	Spring into air, making half turn right to face upstage while circling L lower leg clockwise below knee (*rodazán*).
Ct 2	Land on R with L leg extended low to side (now facing upstage).
Ct & 3	Repeat ct & 2, completing circle, facing front.
	Repeat ct 2 & 3.

Rodazán de escuela bolera hacia adentro

RODAZAN DE ESCUELA BOLERA HACIA AFUERA *(roh-dah-THAN deh ehs-CWEH-lah boh-LEH-rah AH-thee-ah ah-foo-EH-rah)*
(A circling movement of the lower leg toward the outside in *escuela bolera* style)

This step, which remotely resembles a balletic *fouetté,* is often used as a last step (*paso final*) in a classical *bolero.*

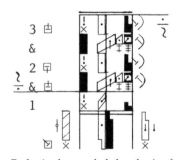

Beg Pos	Feet—4th R front facing downstage left, R knee bent, weight evenly distributed. Arms—4th L up.
Ct 1	Shift weight onto L foot.
Ct &	Spring into air, making a turn right to face upstage while circling R lower leg clockwise below knee (*rodazán*).
Ct 2	Land on L with R leg extended low forward (now facing upstage).
Ct & 3	Repeat ct & 2, completing circle, facing front.
	Repeat ct & 2 & 3.
	Because the step is usually taught in triple meter, the facings, upstage and downstage, will fall on different counts when executed in a series.

Rodazán de escuela bolera hacia afuera

RODILLAS DOBLADAS
See *biscas*.

RODILLAZO *(roh-dee-LYAH-thoh)*
(A push, or blow with the knee)

A single percussive movement which can be used repeatedly with the same knee or with alternating knees while advancing forward. In regional dances a man strikes his tambourine (*pandereta*) with his knee in a rhythmic variation. In flamenco dance the male movement walking from one knee to the other, dragging the foot, is *de rodillas*.

Beg pos   Feet—1st parallel, knees slightly bent.
          Arms—Optional or 5th.

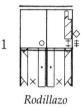

   Ct 1   Sharply lift bent R knee forward high
           above hip level causing skirt ruffles to
           billow vertically.

Rodillazo

See *caída*, figure 42.

RODILLAZO RESBALADO *(roh-dee-LYAH-thoh rehs-bah-LAH-doh)*
(Sliding knee step)
Also referred to as *de rodillas*.

A male flamenco walking movement from one knee to the other in which the *bailaor* lowers his right knee on the floor with the ball of the left foot close to it. The weight of the body is shifted forward, lowering the left knee to the floor as the right leg slides over the floor dragging the toe until the right knee, in turn, is drawn up with the weight resting on the ball of the right foot. He continues advancing forward by repeating the action on the other knee.

RODO
See *rueda*.

ROMPIDO *(rohm-PEE-doh)*
(Breaking off, falling out)

A premature interruption of a step or rhythm. For example, if a movement, step, or audible rhythm of the feet or castanets normally takes six counts and its action or sound is stopped arbitrarily on count four, allowing the remaining two counts to pass motionless and in silence, the pause makes a break (*rompido*) in the anticipated rhythmic cycle.

See *parada*.

RONDEÑAS
See *verdiales*.

RUEDA *(roo-EH-dah)*
(Wheel, turn, circle of people)
Also called *redondo.*

A circle formation in regional folk dances, or a curved path (*camino*) in which a step moves. The Catalonian term is *rodo,* which also refers to a dance done in a circle, not unlike a central European *kolo* (circle dance). It may be compared with the French folk dance *ronde.*

RUMBA GITANA *(ROOM-bah hee-TAH-nah)*
(Gypsy rumba, a solo dance; not to be confused with the social dance called rumba)

When this contagious rhythm of Cuba invaded every ballroom of the world, Spain was no exception. Adopted by Gypsies, it not only maintained its innate ethnic charm but was also imbued with that special ingredient of sex appeal (*salero*) that is unique to Andalusian women. In short, it is flamenco's sexiest dance in the most lighthearted (*chico*) sense. Its basic rhythm (*compás*) is very catchy, especially when slapping techniques on the guitar, typical of Latin America, are interpolated. It is an example of acculturation of the music and dance of two different cultures, making a hybrid that is thoroughly entertaining. The rhythmic cycle (*compás*) is in four or eight counts. It is often used to end other dances of the same rhythm, such as *tientos,* in the same way that a *bulerías* is used to end an *alegrías* because it is a faster and more exciting use of the *compás.* As a happy ending to an otherwise serious (*jondo*) program, the dance, with its infectious accentuation and mood, leaves an audience empathetically tapping toes or clapping in time.

See *chico, salero.* See also Appendix: Basic Flamenco Rhythms.

SACADO *(sah-CAH-doh)*
(Drawn out, presented)

This step resembles the sliding action of a balletic *chassé.*

Beg pos   Feet—3rd R front.
         Arms—Optional, usually 4th L up.

   Ct &   Preparation—Release R foot.
   Ct 1   Slide R foot diagonally R forward,
         bending knee, R taking weight,
         inclining chest slightly in same
         direction.
   Ct &   Close L foot into 3rd back (*asamblé*
         sencillo), keeping knees easy and flex-
         ible throughout.

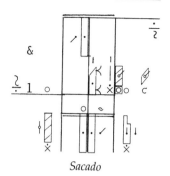

Sacado

SACUDIDA *(sah-coo-DEE-dah)*
(Little shaking, jerking, flapping movement)

These dainty, vibrating actions, like rapid *petits battements,* are little flourishes
used in combination with other steps. Seen mostly in classical eighteenth- and
nineteenth-century Spanish dances, they are also seen in the Spanish variations in ballets by Auguste Bournonville, who studied avidly in Spain.

Beg pos   Feet—R leg lifted low diagonal front,
         knee bent, toe pointing downward.
         Arms—4th L up, chest inclined to-
         ward R knee, head turned slightly
         right.

     Ct   Optional
         Without disturbing R thigh, make
         very short, rapid movements with R
         foot toward and away from L leg.

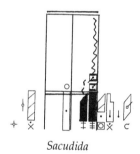

Sacudida

SALERITO
See *rodazán.*

SALERO *(sah-LEH-roh)*
(Charm, cleverness; literally, salt cellar)

A complimentary term for a female dancer or singer having a winning combination of wit, humor, grace, and sex appeal. Cyril Rice described *salero* as
"the form of savor or antiseptic wit which the Spaniards admire in women,
and which they believe to be especially the prerogative of the Andalusian.
They explain this trait by the accident of a celestial banquet, in the course of
which God upset a salt cellar which emptied its contents over Andalusia."

See *gracia.*

SALIDA *(sah-LEE-dah)*
(A going out [onto the stage], departure, exit)
Also called *paseo de salidas.*

This term is used by dancer, musician, and singer and has several meanings:
(1) the entrance *(entrada)* or preparatory steps or music of a dance; (2) the
movement or accompaniment for an exit from the stage *(mutis)*; (3) in many
folkloric dances, a marking time in place, allowing the music to set the pace
and mood; (4) the first section of a dance—a promenade of the village square
to choose partners for the dance; (5) a brief interval in which a singer *(cantaor)*
warms up or "places" the voice by intoning such syllables as "Ay" "La, la, la,"
or "Tarata tran," thus creating the mood.[1]

See *entrada, farfulleos, mutis.*

SALIDA DE BULERIAS *(sah-LEE-dah deh boo-leh-REE-ah)*
(Exit or entrance of a *bulería*)

A traveling step often used to enter onto the stage *(entrada)*, or to leave the
stage *(salida)*.

Beg pos   Feet—From any previous action.
          Arms—Hands clapping *(palmas)* over
          L shoulder , head turned to right.

   Ct 1   Stamp R to side.
   Ct 2   Touch L toe across to right.
   Ct 3   Stamp L slightly to left.

          Ct 1 is accented.

          The step is repeated several times
          (corrida) and travels to the right.

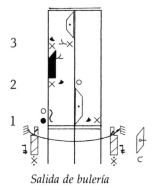

Salida de bulería

See *bulerías, mutis, palmas, salida.* See also Appendix: Basic Flamenco
   Rhythms.

SALTADO *(sahl-TAH-doh)*
(Hopped, jumped)

A term describing one of the basic movements in dancing, a particular step or
movement which is performed jumping or hopping, as in *campanela saltada.*
The term is similar to the balletic *sauté.*

---

[1]It is not unlike the *alap* (opening, blossoming) in East Indian music and singing, which many believe contributed greatly to the song *(cante)* of flamenco.

SALTILLO
See *salto.*

SALTITO
See *salto.*

SALTO *(SAHL-toh)*
(A hop, jump, leap, skip)
Also called *brinco.*

This action is seen in all styles of Spanish dance, especially in *escuela bolera* and *folklórico*. A *saltillo* or *saltito* is a little rhythmic hop or spring on one foot, barely clearing the floor and usually performed on the off beat. It is similar to a balletic *temps levé.*

See *más saltadora, saltado.*

SALTO DE SARDANA *(SAHL-toh deh sahr-DAH-nah)*
(Sardana skipping step)

A typical high-skipping step used in Catalonian folk dancing, with emphasis on elevation and lifted knees. It is often performed side by side with a partner. Because of its high springing action, it is classified as *más saltadora*. This step is not, as one might expect from its name, seen in a *sardana*, which is danced smoothly and close to the ground (*a lo llano*).

See *más saltadora.*

SALTO TONGO
See *tordín*

SALTO Y CAMPANELA
See *campanela folklórica.*

SALUDO *(sah-LOO-doh)*
(Bow, greeting, salutation)

A simple body gesture or a gracious curtsy made by the dancer at the beginning or end of a dance. *Saludos* are typical in the old social *danzas* of the court and drawing rooms, as well as in folk dancing. In Spanish dance, as in ballet, a *reverencia* or gesture of acknowledgment (*saludo*) should be part of class training in preparation for eventual public appearances. Most Asian dance curricula include a bow or salutation, both at the beginning and at the end of each class.

See *reverencia sencilla*.

SARDANA *(sahr-DAH-nah)*
(Circle dance of the Ceretani, inhabitants of the Pyrenees, in northern Catalonia; originally called *cerdaña*)

The *sardana* is of ancient Greek origin and is believed to have originated as a sun-worship ceremony. Catalonians claim it as their national dance. Performed in open squares, before cathedrals, and in public parks, this easygoing communal dance has an almost mystical effect, with trancelike overtones of a ceremony of worship, as in the performance of a rite.

In the dance, alternating men and women join hands in a circle, with arms usually held at shoulder level. The body remains quiet as the feet move sidewise with small interlocking steps close to the ground. The first part is slow and grave as the feet perform steps called shorts (*curts*), each of which takes four beats, followed by eight longs (*llargs*), of eight beats each (some experts claim that there are about four hundred combinations of *llargs* and *curts*). Other parts of the *sardana* include an *entrada* and a *repartícia y caijuda o final*. Jumped steps (*pasos saltados*) are introduced toward the climax of the dance.

Sardanas can vary in length and direction. Those of the *ampurdanesa* style move to the left (clockwise), while those in the *selvata* style move to the right (counterclockwise).

The orchestra that accompanies a *sardana* is called a *cobla* and has its own unique sound.

Throughout the warm weather *sardanas* can be seen any Sunday after mass in front of the cathedrals of Catalonia. New circles called *rodos* form constantly, sometimes concentrically, and bystanders are welcome to join in the deceptively easy *tiradas*. The *sardana* is the one dance that visitors the world over claim to have joined in, or at least tried. Although of ancient origin, the *sardana* as we now see it danced out of doors has undergone changes. Its music and choreography were created in later times. We owe today's larger orchestra and *sardana* music to Josep ("Pep") Ventura (1817–75) and its present choreographic form to Miguel Pardas (1818–72), who in 1850 published his *Método por aprende a ballar sardanas llargas*.

See *cobla, llargas y curts, pasos saltados, rueda, tirada*.

SA SA SA *(sah sah sah)*
(A meaningless vocal expression uttered by the dancer)
Also called *marianas*.

The dancer, usually a female, shouts these sounds on the counts of the step, which introduces the final section of a *tango andaluz*.

Beg pos   Feet—1st parallel, knees slightly
           bent.
           Arms—Optional, female lifts skirt
           slightly in front, elbows out, torso
           slightly inclined forward.

Ct 1   Jump to the right, "Sa!"
Ct 2   Jump to the left, "Sa!"
Ct 3   Jump to the back, "Sa!"
Ct 4   Hold.

        ct 3 is accented.[1]

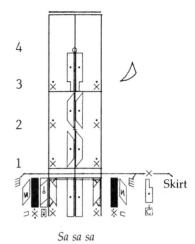

Sa sa sa

See *grito, tango.*

SEASE[2] DE ESCUELA BOLERA *(seh-ah-SEH deh ehs-CWEH-lah boh-LEH-rah)*
(Origin uncertain; see *Seasé y contrasease de escuela bolera,* note 2)

This step, as described below, is from the *escuela bolera.* It resembles a balletic gliding (*glissé*) and is a small unit of a more elaborate combination (*compuesto*).

Beg pos   Feet—5th R front, facing audience.
           Arms—Optional.

Ct &   Rise on L toe pivoting slightly to
        right; bend R knee, lifting R foot in
        front of L ankle.
Ct 1   Slide R foot toward stage right, taking
        weight, keeping L leg extended
        behind.

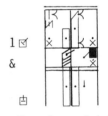

Sease de escuela bolera

See *ceasé y contraceasé andaluz, seasé y contrasease de escuela bolera.*

SEASE Y CONTRASEASE[3] DE ESCUELA BOLERA *(seh-ah-SEH ee con-tra-*
   seh-ah-SEH deh es-CWEH-lah bo-LEH-rah)
(Origin uncertain)[4]

---

[1]Some early Andalusian maestros added a fourth direction, i.e., right, left, front, back.
[2]Appears in eighteenth- and nineteenth-century texts as both *cease* and *sease*.
[3]Also appears in nineteenth-century texts as *ceasé y contraceasé.*
[4]The name, still in current use, is an ambiguous one. Some believe it to be a corruption of the French *chassé.* Another unconfirmed origin is the Spanish word *cea* (thighbone). Just like the early French *temps de cuisse* (*cuisse,* thigh), this Spanish step also involves a crossing and recrossing of the thighs. Since the spelling and accents are inconsistent, it may have simply derived from the comment, "¡Se hace!" ("It is done!" or "Like this!"), given by the dancing master. Different versions are taught by various teachers.

Beg pos   Feet—5th R front, facing audience.
          Arms—5th.

   Ct &   Rise on L, turning slightly to right;
          bend R knee, lifting R leg in front of
          L ankle; incline chest toward R leg,
          turning head slightly right.
   Ct 1   Slide R foot toward stage right, taking
          weight; keep L leg extended behind.
   Ct 2   Step L on ball of foot behind R.
   Ct 3   Step R on ball of foot toward stage
          right.

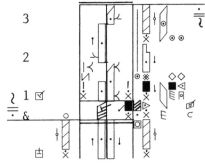

Seasé y contraseasé de escuela bolera

   Arms
Ct &–1–2–3   Circle R arm out and down, pass-
             ing through 2nd to low 5th front, then
             up midline of body, returning to 5th,
             as in *braceo de escuela bolera*.

             Repeat ct &–1–2–3, reversed.

See *braceo de escuela bolera, ceasé y contraceasé andaluz, seasé de escuela bolera*.

SECO *(SEH-coh)*
(Dry, abrupt, plain)

A word describing the ideal quality of sound for rhythmic footwork (*zapateado*)
or hand clapping (*palmas*). Just as a singer will "feel" the acoustics from various areas of the stage of a large concert hall to determine the ideal spot for the
carrying power and quality of her voice, so Spanish dance artists test various
sections of the stage surface to find which will yield the best *seco* sound, especially for delicate *escobilla* sections in which crescendo and diminuendo of the
heels are the highlight of the solo being performed.

   The new types of nonslip floorings, which are a must for ballet and modern-
dance companies, are self-defeating for the flamenco dancer since, though
being safer for dancing, they eat up the sound of rhythmic footwork (*zapateado*),
forcing the performer to double and even triple the amount of energy necessary to render a desired result. The technique for making rhythmic foot
sounds evolved from the various surfaces upon which they were performed,
from the old dry boards (*tablas*) of theater stages to tile patios and tabletops,
favorite improvised on-the-spot stages.

   "¡Seco!" is often used as a vocal command (*grito*) by a flamenco instructor
teaching *zapateado* and expecting the student to make a clear, sharp, unmuffled
"dry" sound.

See *repique, repiqueteo, zapateado*.

SEGUIDA *(seh-GHEE-dah)*
(Succession, continuation, series)

An action or rhythmic phrase which is repeated several times without an interruption or break (*rompido*). Continuous rolls on the castanets (*carretillas*) performed smoothly without heavy accentuation over several bars of music are called *carretillas seguidas*. Steps such as *careos*, which are done four times in *las sevillanas*, are typical repetitions referred to as *seguidas*.

SEGUIDILLA *(seh-gee-DEE-lyah)*
(The diminutive of *seguida*—small continuation, following, coda)

The *seguidilla* is a joyous, bucolic dance with a gay, bouncing, breathless rhythm which seems almost nonstop. In fact the word *seguidillas* (small successions) implies an ongoing, seemingly endless series of sung or played refrains, each corresponding step or variation following or continuing at an energetic tempo. The music, in either ¾ or ⅜ time, is played in an easygoing allegretto in its home, Castile, and is more lively in Andalusia. The *seguidilla* was the matrix from which other dances such as the *sevillanas* and the *bolero* took their choreographic form. Both begin with a musical introduction, during which the dancers walk graciously around the room to their places or prepare or rest (*descanso*) for the coming *coplas*. Another characteristic aspect of the music and dances is the sudden, abrupt stop which ends each *copla*, traditionally known as *bien parado* (well stopped). The general sequence of the *seguidilla* would be *introducción, salida, estribillo, copla, estribillo, copla, estribillo, copla, bien parado*. Castanets are played with a typical rhythmic phrase, "ta tarará tarará ta", which constantly repeats throughout each *copla* until all the dancers suddenly stop on the last count.

There are many kinds of *seguidillas*, each with its own character, steps, and choreographic formation, but the musical form is basically the same. The dance is performed by couples, usually in lines which advance toward and retreat from each other, at times changing places. They are also seen arranged in groups of four or in single and double circles.

For many years the *seguidilla* was used by dancing masters to teach precise footwork in preparation for other dances. It is one of the most pleasant and exciting dances to perform and to watch and has been used many times with great success in dance concerts. Well-known compositions of Nikolai Rimsky-Korsakov, Isaac Albéniz, and Mikhail Glinka, as well as a scene in George Bizet's *Carmen*, have been inspired by the lilting rhythm of the *seguidilla*, known since Miguel Cervantes's time as a symbol of joy.

See *atabalillos, bien parado, embotado, estet, lazos, pasada de seguidillas manchegas, paso de seguidilla, paso de seguidillas manchegas, pistolea, vuelta y figura*.

SELVATA
See *ampurdanesa; sardana*.

SEMI
See *medio*.

SEMIPLANTA
See *media planta*.

SEMIPUNTA
See *media planta, media punta.*

SENCILLO *(sehn-THEE-lyoh)*
(Simple, easy, plain)

A word describing the simple, basic, uncomplicated manner in which a step or movement can be executed. When used in performance, such understated movements and uninvolved rhythmic variations often require more command and artistry than a display of technical virtuosity.

See *básicos, compostura, gracia, natural.*

SEVILLANAS *(seh-vee-LYAH-nahs)*
(Dances and songs of Seville—Andalusia)

Sevillanas, often called the "mother" dances of many Spanish dances, are not only the most typical but also the most ubiquitous couple dances in Andalusia. They are the most widely taught Spanish dances in the world. *Sevillanas* are an integral part of fiestas, week-long fairs (*ferias*) of fun and dancing just following *Semana Santa* (Holy Week). They are derived from the *seguidillas manchegas* and, in spite of their apparent simplicity, are very difficult to perform accurately. These Andalusian dance-songs are arranged in the form of stanzas (*coplas*).

Of the seven original *coplas,* only four or five at most are danced today. Each *copla* is divided into three parts, each of these consisting of twelve bars of music.[1] The first, *copla primera,* begins with four *pasos de sevillana* followed by a *pasada de sevillana,* then four *pas de buret y punto en suelo* followed by another *pasada de sevillana,* then four *paseos de panaderos* and ending with a turn and stop (*vuelta y bien parado*). *Sevillanas* is short for *seguidillas sevillanas* and, as in the *seguidilla* from which it comes, the accompaniment was originally the voice, guitar, and castanets, with which the dancers played a constant rhythmic background.[2]

There are various types of *sevillanas,* such as that from Huelva called *sevillanas bíblicas,* with words inspired by the Old Testament, which are danced to flute and drum (*tambor*) accompaniment. The *sevillanas boleras* are of another variety, which exhibits many jumps (*brincos*) and beaten steps (*batidos*).

Because each successive *copla* gains momentum as the various steps become more elaborate (*vistoso*), ending with a sudden halt (*bien parado*), *sevillanas* have become favorite closing dances (*fin de fiesta*).

Sevillanas populares have always been and are still popular with Andalu-

---

[1] As with any *folklórico* dance, *sevillanas* are subject to gesture and execution, but the musical framework is invariable. Unlike many flamenco dances, which can be lengthened or shortened at various points, *sevillanas* can be danced only to the above musical form, which is unalterable and unquestionably the reason for its survival as a popular dance.
[2] The traditional castanet rhythm for *sevillanas* is played as follows: *riá riá pi tá* (roll, roll, right, left).

sians. Even in modern times one can occasionally encounter an old, hand-turned barrel organ merrily playing the jaunty *coplas* of *las sevillanas*. The music is cheerful, festive, easy to sing, and filled with charm, wit, and variety. It is easy to count, and, unlike flamenco singing, each syllable of every word takes one beat of music. In recent years many singing groups have enjoyed great success in popularizing these songs for dancing (*para bailar*), receiving critical acclaim for writing new music, lyrics, and special vocal arrangements. Over 100 *sevillanas* "clubs" are known to exist in Bilbao, the heart of the Basque country. Another 150 are reported in Barcelona, the center of Catalonia, and hundreds more from Madrid to Galicia, from Asturia to Cádiz.

Unlike flamenco dances, which were originally solo dances, *sevillanas* are couple dances and are not considered truly flamenco. Nevertheless, since they have been totally accepted by the Andalusians and are performed in many of their concerts and nightclub (*tablao*) presentations, it is only a question of time until they are accepted as flamenco.

See *bien parado, careo, copla, panaderos, paraditas de sevillanas, pas de buret natural, paseo de panaderos, paso de sevillanas, punta en suelo, seguidilla.*

SIGUIRIYAS *(see-ghee-REE-ahs)*
(Corruption of *seguidilla*)[1]
Also called *seguiriyas gitanas* and *seguidillas gitanas.*

Siguiriyas are the expression of the Gypsies in their most negative emotional state, telling of *dolores*, the sorrows which haunt the Spanish imagination in so many guises—violent jealousies, impossible loves, reproaches, loneliness and death, apparitions of tormented ghosts. Like much of Gypsy music, of which *siguiriyas* are considered the most serious (*jondo*), they mockingly refer to a Gypsy's four lodging places: the hospital, the prison, the church, and the grave. The music of their ancestral Hindu tribes as they left India filled the air with moaning incantations. Today in Andalusia their singing (*cante*) and movements of the dance are like a ritual born in the midst of their tribes as they once evoked their pagan rites in remote dances to the sun and moon. The dance as we now see it, is relatively modern. Vicente Escudero is credited for first presenting it in a theatrical setting, in 1944.

See *seguidilla*. See also Appendix: Basic Flamenco Rhythms.

SIGUIRIYAS GITANAS
See *siguiriyas.*

---

[1] One theory of the origin of the *seguiriya* is that the *seguidilla* of La Mancha spread throughout Spain and eventually to the Andalusian Gypsies, who in time transformed it into a liturgical, profound lamentation of sadness and deep sorrow. Hence the *siguiriyas* became the Gypsy counterpart of the *seguidillas sevillanas*, a non-Gypsy dance in lively triple meter. However, there are many, including most flamenco dancers, who think *seguiriyas* have no connection whatever with the *seguidillas* of Castile.

SILENCIO *(see-LEHN-thee-oh)*
(Silence, stillness, quiet)

A section of an *alegrías* played by the guitarist, sometimes in a minor key and, in contrast to the previous dance section, characterized by the *bailaora's* "dance of the arms" *(baile de braceo)*, a minimum of footwork, and a graceful promenade *(paseo)* to highlight lyric movements of the torso. When danced by a male, these movements are very restricted and understated. *Silencio* may also be applied to that part of a contemporary theatrical choreographic production *(baile teatral)* in which all instrumental accompaniment ceases, while the dramatic action continues to unfold. Such intervals of silence *(silencio)* in music can be powerful, as exemplified in José Granero's dance-drama version of *Medea*. This term is similar to the musical term *tacit*.

See *decálogo, falseta, hembra, paseo.* See also Appendix: Basic Flamenco Rhythms.

SOBRESALTO *(soh-breh-SAHL-toh)*
(Sudden attack or surprise; in folk dance, a high spring or sudden jump into
    the air)

This step resembles a balletic *soubresaut*.

Beg pos	Feet—3rd R front, knees bent. Arms—5th low front.
Ct	Optional.
	Jump into air, passing arms through 1st, land in 3rd R front, ending with arms in 5th (may be performed traveling forward).

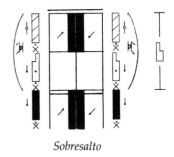

Sobresalto

SOBRESUT *(soh-breh-SOOT)*
(A sudden springing, bounding action; Hispanicized French)

The action resembles a balletic *pas de chat*. The version below is of the *escuela bolera*. It is not to be confused with *sobresalto*.

Beg pos	Feet—3rd R back, knees slightly bent. Arms—4th L up, head facing right.
Ct &	Spring into air, moving right while lifting both knees and almost touching buttocks alternately with R then with L foot.
Ct a	Land on R foot.
Ct 1	Close L foot front into 5th or 4th.

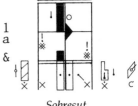

Sobresut

SOLEÁ
See *soleares*.

SOLEARES *(soh-leh-AH-rehs)*[1]
(Loneliness, solitude, homesickness)
Also called *soleá;* Gypsy abbreviation.

Soleares are dances for women and are usually performed in a ruffled-train dress (*bata de cola*). They are a perfect vehicle for feminine beauty and can portray a figure (*figura*) that is noble yet sensuous, restrained yet passionate. They are the quintessence of introspective dancing, which commands the constant attention of the viewer. Although traditionally performed as solos, *soleares* arranged (*estilizado*) for couples have been most successful as dramatic pieces for the theater. In recent years it has become the practice of some dancers to end *soleares* with the lively rhythms of *bulerías*, which, although adding variety to a serious (*jondo*) type of dance and song, is considered in poor taste by purists. Such *soleares* are referred to as *soleares por bulerías*.

Like many other flamenco rhythms, *soleares* have a basic twelve-beat rhythmic cycle (*compás*); it is usually accented on the third, sixth, eighth, tenth, and/or twelfth beats. The main accent is on the twelfth beat, which is used as a starting point for each step except in the *escobilla* section, when the steps usually start on count 1, giving it its typical rhythm. Because of its influence in begetting other flamenco musical forms, the *soleá* is often referred to as the "mother" of flamenco song (*cante*).

See *alegrías*. See also Appendix: Basic Flamenco Rhythms.

SOLEARES POR BULERIAS
See *soleares*.

SOLO DE PIES *(SOH-loh deh pee-EHS)*
(Only with the feet)

A short section of rhythmic footwork (*zapateado*) performed with only hand clapping (*palmas*) maintaining the basic rhythm (*compás*). The hand clapping can be provided by the dancer or by an assisting *palmista*.

See *a palo seco, palmista, zapateado*.

---

[1]From *soledades,* so pronounced by Flamencos. It is characteristic of Flamencos to drop the sound of *d.*

SOSTENIDO *(sohs-teh-NEE-doh)*
(Sustained, held)
Also called *llamada andaluza,* as shown in period dance below.

| Beg pos | Ct 1–2 | Ct 3 | *Llamada andaluza* |

Beg pos   Feet—3rd R front.
           Arms—4th L up, torso inclined from
           waist over R thigh.

   Ct 1 Touch ball of R foot diagonally for-
          ward, keeping knees slightly bent
          (accent is on extension).
   Ct 2 Hold.
   Ct 3 Touch ball of R foot close to L arch.

          Repeat several times.

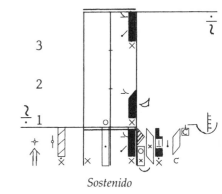

Sostenido

See *llamada andaluza.*

SOSTENIDO EN PIES *(sohs-teh-NEE-doh ehn pee-EHS)*
(Sustained on the feet)

A phrase describing one of the various levels to which the heels are raised off
the floor to maintain balance in preparation for, during, or at the conclusion of

a movement. *Sostenido en pies* can designate any level from a flat foot (*planta*) to tiptoes (*en puntos*), and on either or both feet. It is comparable to the balletic term *relevé*.

See *pies, sostenido.*

SOSTENIDO EN VUELTA *(sohs-teh-NEE-doh ehn VWEHL-tah)*
(Sustained or held while turning)
Also called *llamada en vuelta.*

A phrase describing a step reminiscent of the Andalusian school dances at the turn of the century. The step is performed the same way as *sostenido*, but the dancer simultaneously pivots on the ball of one foot. The turn progresses in a forward direction.

See *sostenido.*

SOUSOU *(soo-SOO)*
(Under-over; Hispanicized French)

A series of small steps on half toe (*semiplanta*) which begin and end in third position. They can travel to the right, left, front, or back. Such steps are usually associated with *escuela bolera.*

SUERTES
See *quiebros.*

TABALEO *(tah-bah-LEH-oh)*
(Drumming with the fingers)

The action by which a flamenco singer (*cantaor*) rhythmically accompanies himself with his finger tips and knuckles when seated at a table. Vicente Escudero improvised *tabaleo* to the point of featured theatrics, for which he became internationally associated, by tapping out various rhythms on the floor or the legs of a stool while intermittently "playing" his fingernails like miniature castanets and clicking his tongue with countrapuntal effects.

TABLAO *(tah-BLAH-oh)*[1]
(Board, platform, stage)

A stage on which flamenco dance is performed. Just as the English phrase "on the boards" originated with the use of improvised elevated planks set up outdoors to serve as a stage, the Spanish term *tablado* traces its origin to the use of *tablas* (boards) as a stage on which to perform. On such a small stage flamenco dancers appear as a *cuadro flamenco*. A *tablao flamenco* is a nightclub where *flamenco* is performed.

See *cuadro flamenco*.

TACON *(tah-COHN)*
(Heel of a shoe)

In Spanish dance, the sharp, audible floor contact in rhythmic footwork (*zapateado*) done with the heel of a shoe or boot. *Tacón* is sometimes used synonymously with *talón*, which describes a flexed foot extended to the front or side with the edge of the heel touching the floor and the toe facing upward. Unlike *talón*, however, *tacón* refers to an action done with a hard heel, usually in Andalusian and flamenco dance; hence, the word for rhythm made with the heels (*taconeo*). To further distinguish between the two terms, *tacón* is a step to be heard, whereas *talón* is usually a step of placement to be seen.

See *pica tacón* (page 7), *pies, taconeo, tacón raspado, talón*.

TACONEADO *(tah-coh-neh-AH-doh)*
(Sound made by the heels)

After the aristocracy and the ordinary people of the eighteenth and nineteenth centuries began to incorporate rhythmic heel beats and stamping into many of their dances, the terms *taconeado* or *zapateado* were added to the names of these dances as well as to the titles of the music for them.

See *golpecito, tacón, taconeo, zapateado*.

TACONEO *(tah-coh-NEH-oh)*
(Sound made with the heels)

Although used synonymously with the term *zapateado*, technically *taconeo* refers to rhythmic patterns made only with the heels (*tacones*).

See *tacón*.

TACON RASPADO *(tah-COHN rahs-PAH-doh)*
(A rasping or scraping of the heel)

An action in rhythmic footwork (*zapateado*) in which the heel of the shoe

---

[1]From *tablado*. So pronounced by Flamencos. It is characteristic of Flamencos to drop the *d* sound.

is struck or "scraped" against the floor with a forward-and-upward action, making a single sound. It is similar to the heel action and sound called *dig* in tap dance.

TALON *(tah-LOHN)*
(Heel of the foot)
Also called *de filo de talón* (edge of the heel).

A position extending the heel, either to the front or to the side, touching the floor with the ankle flexed and the toe facing upward. This term is often used synonymously with *tacón* (heel of a shoe). Technically speaking, *talón* is a classical term applied mostly to regional dances performed in soft slippers (*zapatillas*) or hemp-soled sandals (*alpargatas*), when the foot is fully flexed at the ankle with the toes facing up. *Talón* is a step to be seen, as opposed to *tacón*, one that is to be heard.

See *pies, punta y talón, tacón, zapateado.*

TANGO *(TAHN-goh)*
(Dance rhythm of South American or African origin)[1]
Also called *tango andaluz.*

This dance is not to be confused with the well-known ballroom dance of the same name. In the early part of the twentieth century the *tango andaluz* was a very popular woman's solo taught by Seville's great teacher José Otero. Transcribed for the piano by his pianist and partner of many years, it was one of the favorite school dances in his teaching repertoire. The phrasing (*compás*) of a tango is a steady, even rhythm consisting of eight beats that can be counted in twos, fours, or eights, which an experienced dancer can expand with additional phrases, thereby adding interest and variety. Its unique recurring *paseo de tango,* with its syncopated beat done in a large circular pattern (*rueda*) and the section in ⁶⁄₈ meter for heelwork (*zapateado*), along with its many special movements with a broad-brimmed hat (*sombrero cordobés*), made a charming vehicle for a dancer to win her audience in a naïve or subtle manner if she so chose. Even as a school dance (*baile de escuela*), *tango andaluz* was danced with considerable success in Spanish dance recitals by many well-known artists from the late 1920s into the early 1940s. One of La Argentinita's most memorable dances was a tango. Although the tango became a favorite solo dance among women, Faico of Triana and Joaquín (El Feo) of Madrid, respected turn-of-the-century male dancers, are credited with its initial success.

See *paseo de tango, tiempo de tango.*

TANGO ANDALUZ
See *tango.*

---

[1] The origin of the word is much disputed. Some scholars believe it comes from the old Spanish word *taño* (from *tañer,* to play an instrument)

TANGUILLO *(tahn-GEE-lyoh)*
(Little tango)

The happy atmosphere of its birthplace, Cádiz, called the "Queen of Gracia," best exemplifies the mood of the flamenco dance the *tanguillo*. It developed from the *tango flamenco*, better known as the *tiento canastero*, a dance of the Gypsy *canasteros* (basket weavers) of Cádiz, who are famous for their light-hearted antics, mischievous spirit, and joie de vivre. *Tanguillos*, although part of the accepted flamenco repertoire, are considered by many to be more Andalusian folklore than true flamenco.

See Appendix: Basic Flamenco Rhythms.

TARANTO *(tah-RAHN-toh)*
(Meaning uncertain)

A flamenco dance (*baile grande*) with a definite pulsating, earthy rhythm (*compás*) similar to the steady beat of the old *danza mora* or *zambra*. It is not to be confused with *taranta*, a sad flamenco "song of the mines" (*cante*) with no set rhythm and filled with hopelessness, despair, and resignation. Although *tarantos* are derived from music of the nineteenth century, their dance form emerged only in 1952, when Pilar López, sister of the great Argentinita, used it for choreographic purposes on the concert stage.

See *zambra*. See also Appendix: Basic Flamenco Rhythms.

TAUROMAQUIA *(tah-oo-roh-MAH-kee-ah)*
(The art of bullfighting)

Dance technique inspired by Spain's national sport. For centuries the bullfighter (*torero*) has been under as much scrutiny as any performing artist and has been reviewed by audiences and critics alike. His training to achieve perfect timing and the most aesthetic body line while performing the many required maneuvers (*suertes*) is as long and arduous as that of any classical dancer. The demands made on him are similar to those imposed by the ancient Greeks on their bullfighters. The bullfighter's art (*tauromaquia*), judged by its gracefulness and efficiency of movement (*toreando*), has been effectively imitated by many dancers and choreographers.

See *careo, estocada, paso de muleta, paso doble, quiebros, toreando, vuelta torera.*

TEJIDA
See *batuda*.

TEMBLAR LOS HOMBROS *(tehm-BLAHR deh OHM-brohs)*
(To tremble, shake, quiver the shoulders)
Also called *zalamería de hombros*.

Quivering shoulder movements for the most part are made by female dancers (*bailaoras*). They are evidence of Moorish and other Eastern influences in Spanish dance.

See *zambra*, *zarandeo*.

TEMBLAR LAS MANOS *(tehm-BLAHR lahs MAH-nohs)*
(To tremble, shake, quiver the hands)

Seldom seen in today's dances, this movement at one time gave a dramatic character to such dances as the *garrotín* (a dance with Parisian apache overtones), the *zambra gitana*, and other old-school dances based on Gypsylike themes.

See *garrotín*, *paseo de zambra*.

TEMPS DE CUI *(tahn deh CWEE)*
(Thigh movement; Hispanicized French, *temps*, time; *cuisse*, thigh)

The step has a "pawing action" that resembles a balletic *pas de cheval*. The version below is of the *escuela bolera*.

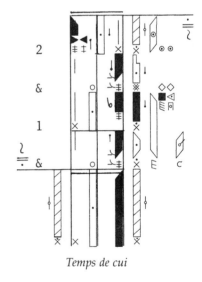

Beg pos	Feet—Weight on L, R leg slightly lifted diagonally right. Arms—5th.	
Ct &	From knee, brush R toe inward so that foot crosses behind L ankle, simultaneously springing into air, turning head to right.	
Ct 1	Land on L (hop).	
Ct &	Brush R toe inward again from knee so that foot crosses in front of L ankle, simultaneously springing into air.	
Ct 2	Land on R, passing L behind R ankle.	
Arms	With R arm make complete circle outward, passing through 2nd, 5th low front, 1st, and returning up body midline to 5th.	
	Repeat all, reversed.	

Temps de cui

TIC *(teec)*
(A colloquial Gypsy term, possibly from their language, *Caló*)
Also called *duende*.

The spirit, force, or energy which manifests itself during a dance.

See *duende*.

TIEMPO DE *(tee-EHM-poh deh)*
(Time or count of)

A convenient term used in combination with the names of various steps, such as *tiempo de tango, tiempo de farruca, tiempo de bulerías.* The step may be a fancy or a simple time-marking one consisting of a relatively easy movement which maintains the basic rhythm (*tiempo*) between sections or choruses (*coplas*) of a dance. It often employs a few repetitive bars of music as a link to connect the more virtuosic steps (*pasos vistosos*) of a dance.[1] It is not to be confused with the balletic *temps de,* which has a different meaning.

See *patacoja, tiempo de bulería, tiempo de farruca.*

TIEMPO DE BULERIA *(tee-EHM-poh deh boo-leh-REE-ah)*
(Time marked to a *bulería* rhythm)

The simple version below is usually used as a time-marking step or "vamp" between more complicated variations.

Beg pos Feet—1st parallel.
         Arms—In low 4th L front.

Ct 6 Touch ball of R foot beside the L foot.
Ct 1 Step on R beside L foot.
Ct 2 Extend L leg slightly forward (optional: brush ball of foot).
Ct 3 Step on ball of L foot, crossing front of R foot.
Ct 4 Step on R foot in place.
Ct 5 Hold.

The step is done in place (*en sitio*) and is audible.

Arms
Ct 6–4 Swing arms out slightly while changing to low 4th R front. Move head slightly from side to side, keeping even level, looking over arm in front.

Repeat, reversed.

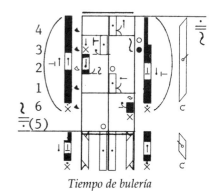

Tiempo de bulería

See *bulerías, bulería sencilla, chico, tiempo de.* See also Appendix: Basic Flamenco Rhythms.

---

[1] This term for "keeping time" in Spanish dance is similar to that used for a basic "time step" in tap dance, a "place step" in Hawaiian dance, or the American equivalent, "vamp," "marking," or "bridge" step.

TIEMPO DE FARRUCA *(tee-EHM-poh deh fah-ROO-cah)*
(Time marked to a *farruca* rhythm)

A simple time-marking step used at the beginning or between more complicated variations of a *farrucca*. The step travels only slightly backward, maintaining an even level of the body, and is accompanied by rhythmic finger
snapping *(pitos)*.

Beg pos Feet—1st parallel.
         Arms—Low 4th L front, facing front.

Ct 1 Beat ball of R foot beside L.
Ct 2 Extend R leg forward near floor.
Ct 3 Step very slightly back on ball of R,
        knee relaxed.
Ct 4 Step backward on L, finishing next
        to R.

        Repeat above several times.

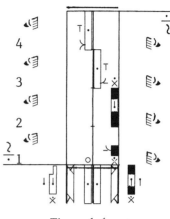

Tiempo de farruca

See *farruca, tiempo de.* See also Appendix: Basic Flamenco Rhythms.

TIEMPO DE JALEO *(tee-EHM-poh deh hah-LEH-oh)*
(Time marked with merriment)

This lighthearted, old-fashioned time-marking step, performed with much
charm *(salero)*, is seldom seen today.

Beg pos Feet—Parallel.
         Arms—Optional; female often lifts
         skirt to almost knee level.

Ct 1 Step R tightly crossed over L.
Ct 2 Step on ball of L behind R.
Ct 3 Step on R in place.
Ct 4 Lift L lower leg behind.

        Repeat all, reversed.

        The step is done in place *(en sitio)*,
        and the head maintains an even level
        throughout.

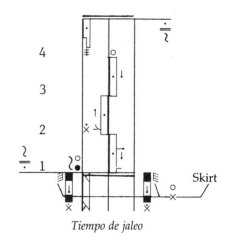

Tiempo de jaleo

See *jaleo, morisca andaluza, tiempo de.*

TIEMPO DE TANGO *(tee-EHM-poh deh TAHN-goh)*
(Time marked in a tango rhythm)

Beg pos Feet—1st.
           Arms—Low 4th L front (woman
           may hold skirt), head turned slightly
           to left.

  Ct 1   Step R side (leaving L leg to side).
  Ct 2   Drag L in, placing it behind R foot.
  Ct 3   Step L on ball of foot, crossing close
         behind.
  Ct 4   Stamp R in place (stamp on ct 4 is
         decidedly accented).

  Arms
  ct 1–2 Change to low 4th R front while turn-
          ing head slightly right.

          Repeat, reversed.

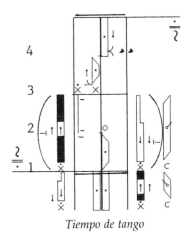

Tiempo de tango

See *rastreado, tango, tiempo de.*

TIENTO *(tee-EHN-toh)*
(Act of feeling)

There are two types of flamenco dances called *tientos*. The *tiento antiguo,* old
style, which is seldom seen today, originated in Cádiz with the Gypsies of
Puente Santa María and was performed in a slow, stately, solemn (*jondo,
grande*) style. When the music was quickened, it was called a *tiento canastero*
(basket weaver's dance).[1] This happy, popular dance (*baile chico*) is full of life.

See Appendix: Basic Flamenco Rhythms.

TIJERA CON VUELTA *(tee-HEH-rah cohn VWEHL-tah)*
(A scissor [kick] with a turn)

This step is widely used in many regional dances and is generally performed
on the ending of a musical phrase as an ending (*vuelta final*) of a dance.

[1] *Canasteros* refers to the Gypsies of Cádiz, weavers of baskets (*canastas*).

Beg pos Feet—Weight on L.
         Arms—5th, or between 2nd and 5th
         (*folklórico*).

Ct 6 Preparation—Lift R leg low in front
      and spring into air.
Ct 1 Land on R, lifting L leg low in front.
Ct 2 Step in place on L.
Ct 3 Step R tightly crossed over L.
Ct 4–6 Make one full turn left on balls of
        feet, ending in 3rd L front (*vuelta
        normal*).

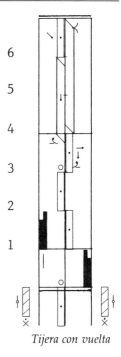

Tijera con vuelta

TIJERA DE ESCUELA BOLERA *(tee-HEH-rah deh es-CWEH-lah bo-LEH-rah)*
(A scissorlike movement of the *escuela bolera*)

This *tijera* constitutes only a small portion of a more involved combination (*compuesto*) of the *escuela bolera*.

Beg pos   Ct &   Ct a   Ct 1–2–3

Beg pos   Feet—4th R front, facing down-
          stage left.
          Arms—4th L up, chest inclined
          slightly toward audience, head facing
          downstage.

   Ct &   Brush R foot back almost touching R
          buttock; spring into air.
   Ct a   Land on R, kicking L foot back almost
          touching L buttock.
   Ct 1   Step forward on L into 4th.
   Ct 2–3 Hold.

          Repeat, reversed.

   Arms
   Ct &   Move R arm to 5th, turn to face
          downstage right, chest and head re-
          maining toward downstage.
   Ct a   Circle L arm out and down, passing
          through 2nd to 5th low front.
   Ct 1   Move L arm forward (ending in 4th R
          up), the reverse of beginning
          position.
   Ct 2–3 Hold.

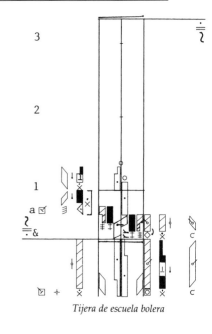

Tijera de escuela bolera

Ct: & a 1   2   3

TIJERA FOLKLORICA *(tee-HEH-rah folk-LOH-ree-cah)*
(A scissor [step] in regional style)

A regional step consisting of one forward kick followed immediately by another with the opposite leg, each passing the other in mid-air. Commonly referred to as a "hitch" kick.

Beg pos   Feet—Standing on R, knee slightly
          bent, L leg extended forward.
          Arms—Between 5th and 2nd
          (*folklórico*).

   Ct &   Spring into air.
   Ct 1   Land on L, extending R leg forward.
   Ct &   Spring into air.
   Ct 2   Land on R, extending L leg forward.

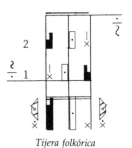

Tijera folkórica

The step is repeated several times
with varying degrees of energy and
height, depending on which regional
dance and/or music is being
performed.

See *media tijera*.

TIRADA *(tee-RAH-dah)*
(Distance, lapse of time)

In a Catalonian *sardana*, a specific phrase of music accompanying a combination, group, or series of typical long and short steps (*llargs y curts*). It is the
comprehension of and strict adherence to the various *tiradas*, rather than the
actual steps (*pasos*), that make the *sardana* both unique and difficult to execute
properly. As the Spaniards say, "Hay que saber matemáticas para poder bailar
la sardana" ("One must know mathematics to dance the *sardana*").

See *llargs y curts, sardana*.

TONADILLERA *(toh-nah-dee-LYEH-rah)*
(Female professional singer of light songs [*tonas*] especially popular in the
    1800s and early 1900s)[1]

While singing, the *tonadillera* would intermittently accompany herself with
castanets, making appropriate gestures and dancelike movements that were
the quintessence of wit and grace (*gracia*). The voices of famous *tonadilleras*
such as Lola Flores, Raquel Meller, and Pastora Imperio are preserved on
recordings.

See *aire, cante, copla, gracia, salero*.

TOQUE *(TOH-keh)*
(Touch, the playing of an instrument)

In guitar or castanet playing, a performer's skill or style of rendition. The term
can also apply to any regional instrument that is used to accompany dancing,
such as a tambourine, a flute, or a drum, each of which requires its own playing technique (*toque*). Guitarists and dance purists strive to preserve the purity of the *toque* in order to play true flamenco.

See *matiz*.

[1]The world-famous dancer La Argentinita (Concepción López) was for twenty years a dancing, whistling
tonadillera in the principal cities of South America and Europe before her talent as a concert dancer and her
genius as a choreographer were recognized.

TORCIDO *(tohr-THEE-doh)*
(A twist, bend, or turn)

Probably the dominant characteristic of Andalusian and flamenco dancing, namely, the torque or spiraling action of the chest and upper torso against the pelvis. This twist *(torcido)* is even further amplified by arm movements *(braceos)*, which seem to flow in nonstop circles and curves, reaching away from but always returning toward the body. This oppositional play of movements *(oposiciones)*, although basic and essential, is one of the most difficult techniques for the classically trained ballet dancer to acquire. Without *torcido*, Andalusian and especially flamenco dances have a wooden look. Without it all the steps *(pasos)* may be there, but the movement says nothing ("no dice nada").

See *borneo, oposiciones, paseo de panaderos.*

TORDIN *(tohr-DEEN)*
(A small bird)
Also called *salto tongo.*

This step resembles the vertical, about-face hopping action of the bird for which it is named. Similar to a classical ballet *tour en l'air*, this step is essentially a male dancer's step of the *escuela bolera*. Even its present-day double- and triple-tour variations were known and performed by the Basques, who are believed to have originated it years before it was adapted by the ballet world.

Beg pos	Feet—5th R front, knees slightly bent. Arms—Low 4th R front.
Ct &	Jump vertically, making one complete turn to right in air, changing arms to low 4th L front.
Ct 1	Land in 5th L front, knees slightly bent.
Ct 2	Straighten knees, but not rigidly.
Ct 3	Hold.

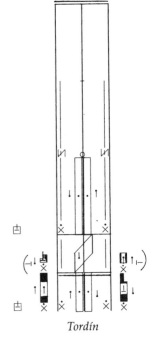

Tordín

TOREANDO *(toh-reh-AHN-doh)*
(Performing movements of a bullfighter)

As the art of bullfighting (*tauromaquia*) is based on form, agility, timing, and graceful maneuvers, the torero's basic body line and stance with a lifted chest and pelvis thrust forward are at times synonymous with those of a male dancer (*bailaor*). Although it is now considered somewhat dated, it was once customary for a soloist, usually a woman, to include at least one *paso doble* using *toreando* movements of a Spanish bullfighter. Among the most flamboyant (*vistoso*) movements used by these dancers were the following.

1. *La Verónica* is the fundamental manner of flourishing the cape (*capa*) to attract the bull's attention and to play with him before the *corrida* gets too far underway. Once the bull has charged and passed in response to this decoy, the torero gives an about-face (*vuelta por detrás*) to repeat the procedure in the reverse direction.

2. *La Media Verónica* is a suspended or cut *verónica*, an action of bringing the cape (actual or imaginary) close to or wrapped around the body with a circular movement of the hand as the imaginary bull passes in response to the movement. Other movements imitating the torero's manner of walking (*contoneo*) from the moment he enters the arena, holding his cap (*felucca*) high over his head to greet the presiding dignitaries, to the last victorious thrust of his sword, killing the bull (*suerte de matar*), were included in this short dramatic sketch (*bosquejo*), which was thoroughly appreciated as a lighthearted divertissement.

See *cimbrado, corrida, macho, quiebros, suertes, tauromaquia, vuelta torera.*

TRAJE DE COLA
See *bata de cola.*

TRAVESIA
See *cruza.*

TRENCITO *(trehn-SEE-toh)*
(Little train)

This is an easygoing, happy step. The small, quick staccato sounds imitate those of a little train as it goes chugging along its way. It is often done softly and invariably evokes applause. When performed by a capable artist, it is very effective, not only during a dance (often without music), but also as an exit step (*mutis*) accompanied by hand movements (*filigranas*) or cleverly devised skirt movements.

Beg pos	1st parallel, knees slightly bent.
Ct 1	Stamp R very slightly forward.
Ct &	Stamp L very slightly forward.
	Feet stay flat on floor between steps with weight evenly distributed as

Trencito

they alternately "shuffle" along in a
straight line. Stamps are done in
rapid succession (*corrida*) with absolutely no change of head level.

TRENZADOS *(trehn-THAH-dohs)*
(Braidings, intertwinings, caperings)

Steps which are jumped (*pasos saltados*) and which give a "braiding" effect
when being performed, such as *cuartas* and other beaten steps (*batidos*).

See *batidos, cuarta, lazos.*

TRONCADO
See *cortado.*

TXISTU *(CHEES-too)*
(Type of flageolet; Basque)

One of the principal instruments which carries the melody in accompanying
Basque dances. The player (*txistulari*) plays the *txistu* with one hand while simultaneously playing complicated rhythms with a stick on a drum (*tamboril*)
with the other.

VACIO *(vah-THEE-oh)*
(Vacant, void)

Vacío has two meanings: (1) a term synonymous with *destaque en dos tiempos*
(describing a step similar to a balletic *développé*), and (2) an *escuela bolera* term
describing a "nondanced" section within a dance or between dances in a suite
in which a soloist (or couple, usually alternating in a *robado* variation) simply
walks elegantly, either in time with the music or in silence, to the center of the
stage before beginning a variation. It is thus referred to as a blank (*vacío*) or
short span of time for the purpose of walking and presenting oneself, similar
to a balletic *pas allée.*

See *contoneo, destaque en dos tiempos, paseo de gracia, pavonear.*

VALONE *(vah-loh-NEH)*[1]
(An action of balancing)

The *valoné*'s "tilting" action, slowly from side to side, is akin to that of a *balanza* (literally, balancing scale or ropewalker's pole). The step is not unique to Spain and is easily recognized in folk dances of many countries.

Beg pos Feet—In 1st.
         Arms—Between 2nd and 5th
         (*folklórico*).

   Ct 1 Step R a small distance to side.
 Ct 2–3 Lift L leg slightly bent across standing leg, inclining torso a bit to left (standing heel may rise to half-toe; torso tilt may be eliminated).

         Repeat to opposite side.

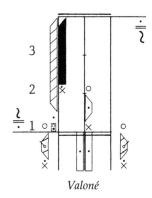

Valoné

VALONE A TIERRA *(vah-loh-NEH ah tee-EHR-ah)*
(A balancing, a tilting toward the ground [extreme backbend])

Term also implies two static poses described below.

Beg pos Feet—From previous action.
         Arms—Low 5th front.

   Ct 1 Step L forward, moving arms to 1st.
 Ct 2–3 Incline torso very far backward, back arched with head toward floor and turned slightly to right; lift R leg forward to hip height, knee slightly bent; move L arm over and slightly beyond head.

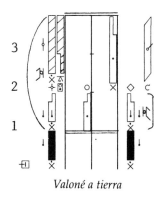

Valoné a tierra

Valoné a tierra, paso final, is sometimes used for a final pose of the old café dances in which the female dancer ended on one knee with the other leg extended forward on the floor, one hand on the floor, taking the torso's weight, the other arm extended to 2nd.

Valoné a tierra, paso final

[1]Not to be confused with *baloné* (although the letters v and b are often used interchangeably).

An even more spectacular ending was to carry it further, the dancer lying almost flat on her back in the same position, but with both arms extended to the sides in 2nd position. These poses of bygone days have been faithfully recorded in the etchings of Gustave Doré.

Valoné a tierra, paso final

See *cimbrado, parada, paso final,* figure 41.

VARIACIONES
See *diferencia.*

VARIEDADES
See *engaños.*

VERDIALES *(vehr-dee-AH-lehs)*
(Meaning uncertain)[1]
Also called *rondeñas* (in Ronda).

What the *sevillanas* is to Seville the *verdiales* is to Málaga. Like the *sevillanas,* it is also a group dance and is actually a lively version of *malagueña* usually accompanied by guitars, tambourines, violins, and homemade instruments. Because *verdiales* is a colorful, vivacious manifestation of joy accompanied by the rattle of castanets and songs that are positive and uplifting, they make favorite items in Spanish dance concerts and provide contrast to the more serious (*jondo*) flamenco dances.

VILLANO *(vee-LYAH-noh)*
(A rustic, peasant)

The name of an old country dance and tune. The term was also applied to a dance's origin or to the earthy or vulgar manner in which it was performed.

VISTOSO *(vees-TOH-soh)*
(Showy, colorful, with a flair)

A term describing a dancer's virtuosic style, beauty, or flamboyance.

VOLADA *(voh-LAH-dah)*
(Flying, flown)

When combined with the name of a step, it indicates that the step is to be performed in a flying or soaring manner, for example, *vuelta volada.* It can be compared to the balletic term *de volé.*

[1]Reportedly the dance owes its name to the *olivas verdiales,* olives which retain their green (*verde*) color when they are ripe.

VOLEO
See *puntapié*

VOLTERETA *(vohl-teh-REH-tah)*
(A tumbling, turning over, revolving action)

An action in *folklórico* dances usually performed by men in a showy *(vistoso)* and virile *(macho)* manner. *Volteretas* vary from turning in an upright position in the air to rollovers and somersaults. Such actions were common a thousand years ago and were performed by acrobatic clowns called *grotescos*.

See *vuelta volada*.

VUELTA *(VWEHL-tah)*
(A turn, revolution, rotation)

In Spanish dancing there exist many kinds of turns *(vueltas)* on one foot, both feet, and in the air. The term *vuelta* often requires a modifying word or phrase to identify a turn accurately and specifically, for example, *vuelta volada, vuelta quebrada,* or *vuelta de tornillo*.

See *en vuelta, giradas*.

VUELTA CIGÜEÑA *(VWEHL-tah thee-GWEH-nyah)*
(Stork turn)

A popular and one of the most spectacular *(vistoso)* turns used by flamenco dancers in which the ball of one foot is tapped on the floor and immediately lifted beside the standing knee, followed by a turn on the standing foot. It can be performed with the back erect or bent at the waist *(quebrada)*. It is not uncommon to see male soloists perform four, six, and eight such spinning turns.

See *cigüeña*.

VUELTA CONCLUSIVA
See *vuelta final*.

VUELTA CON DESTAQUE
See *destaque con vuelta*.

VUELTA DE CARACOL *(VWEHL-tah deh cah-rah-COHL)*
(A turn in a spiraling, winding pattern)

A dramatic pattern made by the flamenco dancer's long-trained dress *(bata de cola)* coiling about her legs as she slowly pivots in one spot *(en sitio)*. The step normally occurs well into the middle or second half of a dance. The female dancer *(bailaora)* audibly maintains the rhythm *(compás)*, often in silence, with the ball of the foot which pushes *(empuja)* and the heel *(tacón)* of the pivoting foot. It may be thought of as a turning pose, a *vuelta con figura*, in slow motion. It is often accompanied by appropriate counterpoint *(contratiempo)* on the castanets to create a theatrical effect.

Beg pos   Feet—Weight on R.
          Arms—Low 4th R front, chest turned
          slightly to left with head turned
          slightly right and torso tilted slightly
          forward.

   Ct   Optional.

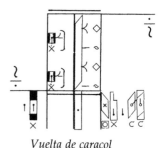

Vuelta de caracol

See *caracol, silencio*. See also Appendix: Basic Flamenco Rhythms.

VUELTA DE CIERRE
See *vuelta final*.

VUELTA DE FOLÍAS *(VWEHL-tah deh foh-LEE-ahs)*
(A turn of folly, jest, friskiness, madness; Hispanicized French *folie*)

According to Esquivel Navarro, dancing master of Seville (1642), this turn was
an exaggerated version of a *vuelta de pecho* and used in *folías,* a dance of Por-
tuguese origin. *Folías* was a popular street dance among the Spaniards on
feast days *(fiestas)*, much like the American Mardi Gras, when everyone is in
high spirits. On those occasions the *danza* was boistrous *(villana)* and frenzied.
French dancing masters later converted it into a dignified dance of gracious-
ness and élan, complete with castanets, called *folies d'Espagne*. It enjoyed great
popularity in the high society of eighteenth-century Paris. Its choreography is
available today through Feuillet notation.

See *vuelta de pecho*.

VUELTA DE HOMBROS *(VWEHL-tah deh OHM-brohs)*
(Turn of shoulders)

A simple turn *(vuelta normal)* in which partners facing each other *(enfrente)*
turn simultaneously in the same direction while leaning slightly forward.
Halfway through the turn their shoulders pass each other, appearing to touch,
before the dancers return to their starting positions. This *vuelta* is still seen in
some *fandangos*. One can see how a movement such as this can lead to body
contact and, if performed in a languorous or flirtatious manner, might well
have contributed to the reputation and eventual banning of the colorful but
"lascivious" *fandango*.

See *fandango*.

VUELTA DE JOTA ARAGONESA *(VWEHL-tah deh HOH-tah ah-rah-goh-*
   NEH-sah)
(A turn typical of the *jota* of Aragón)

Versions of this step occur in many regional (*folklórico*) dances. The energetic version described below is typical of *jota aragonesa*. It usually ends a musical phrase as partners turn on the spot (*en sitio*), ending facing each other and leaning slightly backward.

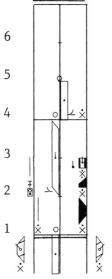

Beg pos	Feet—Weight on L foot. As a solo, face audience; as a duet, face partner. Arms—Between 2nd and 5th (*folklórico*).
Ct 1	Extent R leg low to side, bending both knees.
Ct 2–3	Circle R leg around inward toward L (with R foot lifted horizontally, almost in line with R knee), giving energy to complete one full turn (*vuelta*) on L high half-toe (*semi punta*). (Left knee is bent, and torso is almost half-seated [*asentado*] during this lively spin.)
Ct 4	Set R foot down next to L, both feet as high as possible on half-toes (*semi puntas*).
Ct 5–6	Hold, maintaining seated (*asentada*) and half-toe (*semi punta*) position facing partner.

Vuelta de jota aragonesa

See *jota*.

VUELTA DE PASOS (*VWEHL-tah deh PAH-sohs*)
(A turn of steps)
Also called *debolés*.

The movements of this step are not unlike balletic *chaînés*.

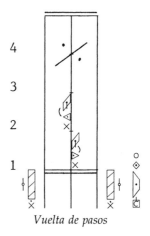

Beg pos	Feet—From previous action. Arms—5th or low 4th R front, eyes focus in direction one is traveling (here, to right).
Ct 1	Take step right on ball of R foot, making ½ turn to right.
Ct 2	Take step left on ball of L foot, making ½ turn to right.
Ct 3–4	Repeat ct 1–2.
	Make all steps close (not spaced apart). The above four counts make two complete turns (*vueltas*).

Vuelta de pasos

VUELTA DE PECHO *(VWEHL-tah deh PEH-cho)*
(Turn of the chest)

A turn involving a backbend in which the working foot is first crossed over the supporting foot while the chest *(pecho)* drops slightly forward, initiating a turn, as in *vuelta quebradita*. It is a step of the *escuela bolera*.

See *vuelta quebradita*.

VUELTA DE PIRUETA *(VWEHL-tah deh pee-roo-EH-tah)*
(A pirouette turn, a spinning action)

The action resembles a balletic *piqué tour*.

Beg pos   Feet—3rd.
          Arms—1st.

   Ct 1   Step R to right side, beginning to make complete turn right, opening arms to 2nd position.

   Ct 2   Step onto L half-toe *(semi planta)* to complete turn, beginning to return arms to 1st.

   Ct 3   Complete circle facing front with R foot in front of L ankle, bringing arms to 1st.

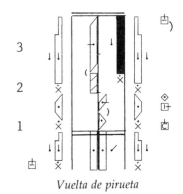

Vuelta de pirueta

VUELTA DE PIRUETA HACIA ADELANTE *(VWEHL-tah deh pee-roo-EH-tah*
   AH-thee-ah ah-deh-LAHN-teh)
(A pirouette or spinning action toward the front)

The turn described below is the version taught in the *escuela bolera*. The Spanish school Hispanicized the French term and considerably adapted the turn.

Beg pos   Feet—4th R front, facing downstage left, R knee bent, taking weight, L leg straight.
          Arms—Low in 4th R front, torso inclined slightly forward, head facing audience.

   Ct 1–2   Take 1¼ turns right on ball of R foot, finishing diagonally downstage right). At beginning of turn, quickly bring L foot to front of R shin, quickly changing arms to low 4th L front, bringing torso upright, head spots.

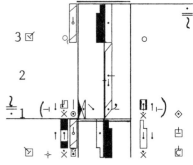

Vuelta de pirueta hacia adelante

Ct 3   (Facing downstage right) move L
front into 4th, bending leg taking
weight, keeping R leg straight, inclining torso slightly forward (reverse of
beginning position).

Repeat all, reversed.

VUELTA DE PIRUETA HACIA ATRAS *(VWEHL-tah deh pee-roo-EH-tah AH-thee-ah ah-TRAHS)*
(A pirouette or spinning action toward the back)

Although the term *pirouette* is familiar, the means of executing it in the *escuela bolera* style (as described below) is quite different.

Beg pos   Feet—5th R front.
Arms—Low 4th R front, head turned
slightly to right.

Ct 1   Touch R toe to side *(punto al suelo)*.
Ct 2   Close R to 5th back, head facing
front.
Ct &   Make one complete turn right on ball
of L foot, R coming quickly to front of
L shin; quickly change arms to low 4th
L front; head spots, ending slightly
turned to left.
Ct 3   Close R to 5th back.

Repeat to opposite side.

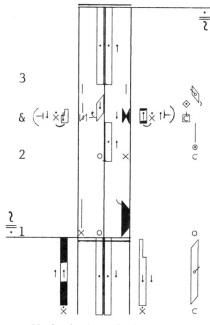

Vuelta de pirueta hacia atrás

VUELTA DE RIÑON *(VWEHL-tah deh ree-NYOHN)*
(Turn of the kidney [lower back])

This step is often incorrectly referred to as a *vuelta quebrada*. Its action re-sembles an exaggerated or distorted balletic *renversé cambré*.

Beg pos   Feet—4th R front.
          Arms—4th L up.

Ct 1–3   Begin making ¼ turn right while lift-
         ing R leg forward, circling it to side
         and back, ct 1; hop (or rise to *semi-
         planta*) slightly on L, ct 2; continue to
         circle R leg back, crossing tightly be-
         hind L foot, ct 3.

Ct 4–6   Continue turning right on balls of
         feet, passing through low back
         (*riñón*), completing one full turn
         (*vuelta por detrás*), ending with feet in
         3rd, R front. Return chest and head
         to normal.

Arms
Ct 1–3   Move arms through 2nd.
Ct 4–6   Move arms to 4th, R up, then
         through 1st to 4th, L up (beginning
         position).

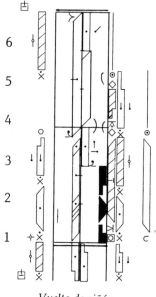

Vuelta de riñón

See *cimbrado, vuelta de folías.*

VUELTA DE RODILLAS (*VWEHL-tah deh roh-DEE-lyahs*)
(Turn on the knees)

This spectacular male turn on the knees in flamenco dance can be performed two ways. Some *bailaores* drop to one knee and start to turn on it as the other knee lowers next to it, completing the turn and finishing with the first knee drawn up and resting on the ball of the foot. Others perform the movement by doing a series (*corrida*) of half-turns, alternating from one knee to the other while traveling along the floor. These turns are not unlike those performed by male Tartar dancers of the Soviet Union.

See *corrida, rodillazo, vistoso.*

VUELTA DESCUIDA (*VWEHL-tah dehs-CWEE-dah*)
(A careless, unprepared turn)

This causal turn occurs mostly in regional (*folklórico*) dances.

Beg pos   Feet—Weight on R foot.
          Arms—Between 2nd and 5th
          (*folklórico*).

      Ct   Optional
           Make one full turn to right on ball of
           R foot, bending L knee, slightly re-
           laxed, behind, then bringing feet to-
           gether parallel (*paralelo*).
           The turn usually ends a musical
           phrase as partners turn in place (*en
           sitio*) and end facing each other.

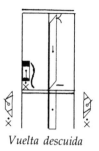

Vuelta descuida

VUELTA DE TORNILLO (*VWEHL-tah deh tor-NEE-lyoh*)
(A turn of the screw, a twisted turn)

This regional step is seen in dances of Valencia. The modest furling and unfurling of the women's skirts is caused by the twisting and untwisting screw-
like (*tornillo*) motion that makes this turn (*vuelta*) unique in Spanish regional
dance.

Beg pos   Feet—L foot well crossed over in
          front of R, knees slightly bent
          (crossed 2nd).   6
          Arms—Between 2nd and 5th
          (*folklórico*).   5

  Ct 1–3 Pivoting on balls of both feet, make
          one full turn right, dipping slightly   4
          (bending and straightening knees),
          ending in small crossed 2nd position   3
          with L foot crossed behind, again
          facing front.
  Ct 4–6 Reverse, making one full turn left,   2
          dipping slightly to end in a small
          crossed 2nd position with L leg
          crossed in front (having returned to   1
          beginning position, facing front).

          During the above action, the heels
          barely skim the floor.

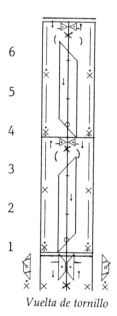

Vuelta de tornillo

VUELTA DE VALS *(VWEHL-tah deh VAHLS)*
(Turn while doing a waltz step)

As described below, this step is performed in the style of the eighteenth- and nineteenth-century *escuela bolera* and in ballet slippers (*zapatillas*). The same step can be equally effective when danced in high heels in contemporary works.

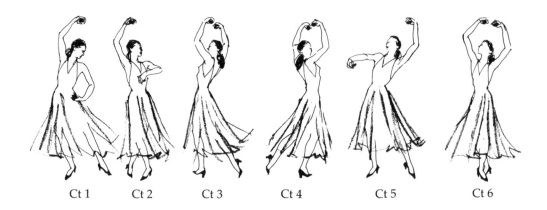

| Ct 1 | Ct 2 | Ct 3 | Ct 4 | Ct 5 | Ct 6 |

Beg pos Feet—5th R front.
         Arms—5th.

Ct 1 Step R to side.
Ct 2 Step L, crossing behind.
Ct 3 Step R, taking weight (beginning to make full turn right).
Ct 4 Step onto L, facing backstage (continue turning).
Ct 5 Step onto R (facing front), leaving L foot pointed to left side.
Ct 6 Slide L foot into 5th front.

Ct 1–5 Travel toward stage right.

Arms
Ct 1–3 Circle L arm out and down, passing through 2nd to 5th low front, turning head and inclining chest slightly toward same arm. Continue moving arm up midline of body, returning to 5th, returning chest and head to upright.
Ct 5–6 Circle R arm likewise out and down, passing through 2nd to 5th low front, turning head slightly toward arm and

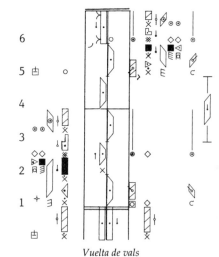

Vuelta de vals

inclining chest slightly away from
arm, moving arm up midline of body,
returning to 5th, returning chest and
head to upright.

See *escuela bolera.*

Ct: 1 2 3   4 5 6

VUELTA DE ZAMBRA *(VWEHL-tah deh THAM-brah)*
(Merrymaking, festive turn)

Of Moorish origin, this step is probably typical of steps of female dancers who
entertained at nocturnal revelries and fiestas called *zambras.* Originally performed barefoot, this slow, rhythmic turn is not unlike that of the Middle Eastern Dervish and the Marwar Nautch dancer of India. Technically speaking, it
might be called a *vuelta empujada,* or pushed turn. In America it is commonly
known as a paddle turn.

Beg pos Feet—Optional.
        Arms—Low 4th R front, torso in-
        clined to right side (slightly back),
        head turned slightly right.

  Ct 1 Begin pivoting slowly to right by
        stepping flat onto R foot.
  Ct & Push slightly *(empujar)* from ball of
        L foot behind R, briefly taking weight
        to free R. Keep knees bent through-
        out with body level low, head not
        rising and falling.
        Continue repeating above, pivoting in
        place *(en sitio).*

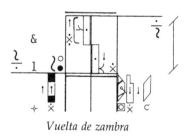

Vuelta de zambra

See *zambra.*

VUELTA EN CUATRO TIEMPOS *(VWEHL-tah ehn CWAH-troh tee-EHM-pohs)*
(A turn in four counts)

Beg pos   Feet—From any previous action.
          Arms—Optional.

Ct 1   Step R in place.
Ct 2   Step L in place.
Ct 3   Step R in place.
Ct 4   Step L feet together, facing front.

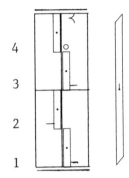

The above steps make one full turn to
the right in place *(en sitio)*. The step
often ends a phrase and can be silent
or audible. It is usually performed on
half-toe *(semiplanta)*, and at times
with stamps *(golpes)* on the flat foot
and usually ending a phrase of music
in even meter. Technically, as it is
performed in some regional and flamenco dances, the step might be referred to as a *vuelta plantada.*

Vuelta en cuatro tiempos

VUELTA EN TRES TIEMPOS *(VWEHL-tah ehn trehs tee-EHM-pohs)*
(A turn in three counts)

This step resembles a *pas de buret en vuelta,* but the term is not synonymous.

Beg pos   Feet—From previous action.
          Arms—Optional.

Ct 1   Step R in place.
Ct 2   Step L in place.
Ct 3   Step R in place, facing front.

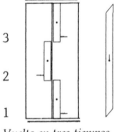

The above steps make one full turn
right in place *(en sitio)*, with heels
slightly off the floor. The step can be
silent or audible and is usually done
half-toe *(semiplanta)*, sometimes with
stamps *(golpes)* on the flat foot. It usually ends a musical phrase played in
¾ meter.

Vuelta en tres tiempos

See *vuelta en cuatro tiempos.*

VUELTA FIBRALTADA *(VWEHL-tah fee-brahl-TAH-dah)*
(An energized turn)

This step usually occurs at the end of a choreographic or musical phrase. It is a very showy (*vistoso*) step and is a favorite in eighteenth- and nineteenth-century dances such as *seguidillas machegas*. One can see various degrees of this action in many types of theater dance, including ballet, modern dance, musical comedy, and folk dance, where it is commonly referred to as a hitch kick.

Beg pos Feet—5th R front.
Arms—5th (see *braceo de escuela bolera*).

Preparation—Lift R leg forward, taking body into air.

Ct & Land on R foot, kicking L forward, higher than R, passing R in midair.
Ct 1 Cross L foot tightly over R at ankles feet parallel); circle arms out and down, passing through 2nd to 5th low front.
Ct 2–3 Make one full turn right, beginning on heel of L foot and toe of R foot, completing turn on ball of L, slipping R into 5th (see *vuelta por delante*), moving arms up midline of body, returning to 5th.

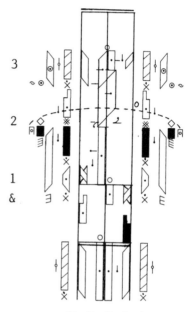

Vuelta fibraltada

The second kick (which occurs just before the downbeat, count 1) is always higher, since more force is expended than in the first, which triggers it; hence its name, *fibraltada*, or "energized." The movement is easily recognized in many Basque dances as a male step. It resembles a ballet *temps de flêche* (arrow step), meaning that the first leg movement acts as a bow releasing the second, an arrow. Some schools of ballet refer to it as *pas de basque*.

See *artasi-otsiko, vistoso*.

VUELTA FINAL *(VWEHL-tah fee-NAHL)*
(Final, last turn)
Also called *vuelta conclusiva* and *vuelta de cierre*.

A term used in folkloric dances for the turn (*vuelta*) which usually ends a musical phrase, a sung verse (*copla*), or the entire dance. A *vuelta final* frequently precedes a characteristic pose or a *bien parado*.

See *bien parado, vuelta y figura, vuelta y media*.

VUELTA GIRADA DE ESCUELA BOLERA *(VWEHL-tah hee-RAH-dah deh ehs-CWEH-lah boh-LEH-rah)*
(A revolving, gyrating turn of the *escuela bolera*)

A lyrical easy-going waltz movement especially suitable for female style.

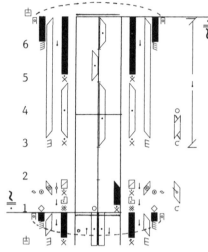

Beg pos	Feet—5th R front. Arms—5th low front; head does *not* spot sharply as in ballet but moves along freely with body as it turns.
Ct 1	Lift R leg across L (diagonally forward left), head slightly profile left, moving arms up midline of body to 5th.
Ct 2	Hold.
Ct 3–4	Step onto R, beginning full turn to right, circling arms outward, passing through 2nd and ending in 5th low front on ct 6.
Ct 5	Step onto L, continuing turn to right.
Ct 6	Step onto R, finishing turn, facing front.

Cts 3–6 travel to right during turn.

Repeat all, reversed.

Vuelta girada de escuela bolera

VUELTA NORMAL *(VWEHL-tah nohr-MAHL)*
(A standard turn)

This step, as illustrated below, is of the *escuela bolera*. In the classroom it is the first in a series of steps (*pasos*) and combinations (*compuestos*) typical of that style. However, it is frequently used in all styles of Spanish dance.

Ct 1   Ct 2   Ct 3

Beg pos Feet—3rd L front.
         Arms—5th.

Ct 1–2 Rise to half-toe (*semiplanta*), crossing
        R foot tightly over L, beginning to
        make left turn (*vuelta*) as arms circle
        outward through 2nd to low 5th front
        on ct 2.

Ct 3   Complete turn lifting arms vertically,
        following midline of body, returning
        to 5th.

        When this step is repeated in a move-
        ment to the side (*corrida de lado*), take
        a small preparatory step (&) to the left
        before each ct 1.

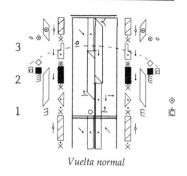

Vuelta normal

See *vuelta por delante*.

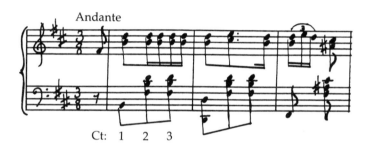

VUELTA PERDIDA
See *vuelta quebradita*.

VUELTA PLANTADA
See *vuelta en cuatro tiempos*.

VUELTA POR DELANTE (*VWEHL-tah pohr deh-LAHN-teh*)
(A turn by way of the front)

Most performers tend to overuse the *vuelta normal* (which is done on half-toe),
making it a cliché. The *vuelta* described below is subtle and, though difficult to
learn, is more dramatic and exciting. Once it is mastered at various speeds,
the action of the feet, skimming the floor in one spot (*en sitio*), is most effective.

Ct 1   Ct 2   Ct 3   Ct 4

Beg pos   Feet—3rd L front.
          Arms—Low 4th L front.

    Ct 1 Cross R tightly over L with weight
          evenly distributed.
 Ct 2–4   Make one full turn left, beginning
          turn on heel of R foot and toe of L
          foot, feet skimming floor; after ¾ of
          turn, feet will be parallel. Make last ¼
          turn with weight on ball of R foot,
          slipping into beginning position or
          4th (*planta natural*).

   Arms
    Ct 1 Change to low 4th R front.
 Ct 2–4   Gradually change to low 4th L front
          (beginning position).

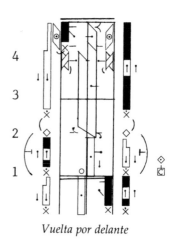

Vuelta por delante

See *vuelta normal, vuelta por detrás.*

VUELTA POR DELANTE Y POR DETRAS *(VWEHL-tah pohr deh-LAHN-teh ee
    pohr deh-TRAHS)*
(A turn by way of the front and the back)

Two turns, a *vuelta por delante* followed immediately by a *vuelta por detrás*. This combination, when repeated in a series (*corrida*), is visually most effective.

See *de frente por detrás*.

VUELTA POR DETRAS *(VWEHL-tah pohr deh-TRAHS)*
(A turn by way of the back [from behind])

The technique involved in this turn is exactly the same as that in the *vuelta por delante*. It is only the initial movement (the setting down of one foot behind the other) which makes it different. A parallel can be drawn with the balletic terms *dessous* and *dessus*.

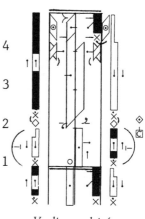

Beg pos   Feet—3rd R front, weight on L foot.
          Arms—Low 4th R front.

  Ct 1   Place R foot, tightly crossed, behind L, changing arms to low 4th L front.

Ct 2–4   Make one full turn R; begin turn on heel of L foot and toe of R, feet skimming floor. After ¾ turn feet will be in 1st parallel. In last ¼ turn on ball of L foot, slipping R into 3rd front and gradually changing arms to low 4th R front. Head spots front.

Vuelta por detrás

See *détourné, vuelta por delante*.

VUELTA QUEBRADA *(VWEHL-tah keh-BRAH-dah)*
(A broken, fractured turn)

The name is derived from the deep break in the spine during the turn. It can be performed slowly or in a rapid, staccato manner.

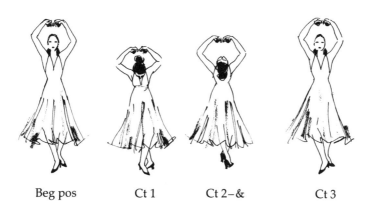

Beg pos   Ct 1   Ct 2–&   Ct 3

Beg pos   Feet—3rd R front.
          Arms—5th.

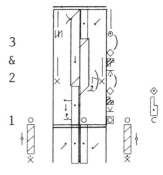

Ct 1   Bend forward at waist, crossing L foot
       over R at ankles.
Ct 2   Giving initial impulse to body and
       head, bend knees slightly, turning
       clockwise on the balls of both feet so
       that body bend (remaining in same
       direction) becomes deep backbend,
       keeping arms over forehead.
Ct &   Complete turn, head maintaining
       same level.

Vuelta quebrada

Ct 3   Return body to upright beginning
       position with feet in 3rd R front.

Ct: 1   2 &   3

VUELTA QUEBRADA DOBLADA *(VWEHL-tah keh-BRAH-dah doh-BLAH-dah)*
(A broken, doubled, folded turn)

This step is performed like a *vuelta quebrada* but with one knee bent and lifted forward as two rapid turns are made. The body, arms, and knee are folded, and the turn is doubled, hence its name. Although this turn is seldom seen, I have on several occasions witnessed as many as three such consecutive turns performed by both men and women. The step is invariably connected with flamenco.

See *cigüeña, vistoso, vuelta quebrada.*

VUELTA QUEBRADITA *(VWEHL-tah keh-brah-DEE-tah)*
(A small broken, fractured turn)

The term *quebradita* (small break) comes from the half-circle backbend during the turn, less exaggerated than that of the *vuelta quebrada*. When it is performed in a series as shown below, it travels in a path to one side (*corrida de lado*). When it is performed slowly, as in classical Andalusian dances, its effect is less extreme than that of a *quebrada*. However, its eighteenth-century innovator, Esteban Morales, reputedly died from performing the step to excess. It is sometimes called *vuelta de pecho* (turn of the chest) and, rarely, by its obsolete name, *vuelta perdida* (lost or misguided turn).

Beg pos   Ct 1   Ct 2   Ct 3

Beg pos Feet—3rd, R front.
         Arms—4th L arm up.

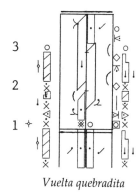

Ct 1   Bend torso to left, crossing ball of
       L foot over R as arms pass thru 2nd
       and exchange positions.

3

Ct 2   Give an initial impulse to the body
       and head, turning on balls of both
       feet to right and continuing turn,
       making a backbend as L arm con-
       tinues lifting and R arm lowering
       past face.

2

1

Ct 3   Return to beginning position but in-
       cline torso over R thigh.

Vuelta quebradita

See *vuelta de pecho*.

Ct: 1   2   3

VUELTA TORERA *(VWEHL-tah toh-REH-rah)*
(A torero turn)

This is basically a male dancer's movement.

Beg pos   Feet—1st parallel, touching each
          other.
          Arms—Low to right side (as if hold-
          ing bullfighter's cape), head turned to
          right, eyes cast low, pelvis thrust
          firmly forward, chest high, inclining
          right and arching back. Weight is
          thrust forward.

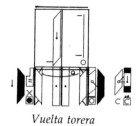

Vuelta torera

    Ct   Optional.

          Make one complete right turn on the
          ball of L foot, skimming floor with R
          sole. This is initiated by small thrust
          from upper torso and upper R arm.

See *paso de muleta, quiebros, tauromaquia, torcido, toreando.*

VUELTA VOLADA *(VWEHL-tah voh-LAH-dah)*
(A flying turn)

A showy (*vistoso*) folkloric jump turn made by stepping to one side and then
leaping onto the other foot while making a turn in midair. The movement resembles a *vuelta girada* of the *escuela bolera* or a balletic *tour jeté en tournant*. It is
often performed in folk dances, but in a freer, less exacting manner. It is one
form of *voltereta*.

Beg pos   Feet—3rd R front.
          Arms—2nd.

    Ct 1 Step R to side, beginning to make full
          turn right.
    Ct 2 Lift L leg while leaping into air to
          continue turn.
    Ct 3 Land on L foot with R leg extended in
          back, knee slightly bent.

   Arms
  Ct 1–2 From 2nd position move arms to low
          5th front and follow midline of body
          up to 5th.
    Ct 3 Hold.

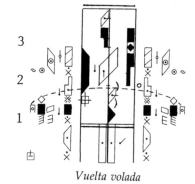

Vuelta volada

See *volada, voltereta, vuelta girada de escuela bolera.*

VUELTA VOLADA TEJIDA *(VWEHL-tah voh-LAH-dah teh-HEE-dah)*
(Flying turn woven)

This technically demanding *escuela bolera* movement resembles a balletic *grand
jeté dessus en tournant battu*.

Beg pos   Feet—3rd R front.
          Arms—2nd.

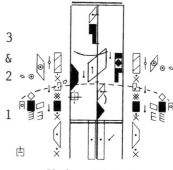

Vuelta volada tejida

Ct 1   Step R to side beginning to make full
        turn right.
Ct 2   Lift L leg while leaping into air to
        continue turn.
Ct &   Beat R leg against L while in air.[1]
Ct 3   Land on L foot with R leg extended in
        back, knee slightly bent.

Arms
Ct 1–2 From 2nd position, move arms to low
        5th front and follow midline of body
        up to 5th.
Ct 3   Hold.

See *volada, vuelta volada.*

VUELTA Y COLOCACION
See *vuelta y figura.*

VUELTA Y FIGURA *(VWEHL-tah ee fee-GOO-rah)*
(A turn and pose)
Also called (as in a *bolero*) *vuelta y colocación.*

As the name implies, the dancer makes a turn (*vuelta*), coming to a stop in a
well-chosen stance or pose (*figura*), displaying a striking body line. In classical
dance, *vuelta y figura* gives a charming effect. In flamenco it is used to dramatically punctuate the endings of phrases within a dance. Many renowned artists
have left a lasting impression by using this simple movement discriminately.

See *actitud, bien parado, caída, postura, remate.*

VUELTA Y MEDIA *(VWEHL-tah ee MEH-dee-ah)*
(A turn and a half)

This compound movement is a *vuelta por delante* immediately followed by placing the foot remaining in front directly behind the other and allowing the
body to continue turning in the direction in which it started (thus giving it the
extra half-turn).

See *bien parado, vuelta y figura.*

[1]During this extra beaten movement, while the body is airborne, the calves appear to interweave (*tejir*);
hence its name.

VUELTA ZAPATEADA *(VWEHL-tah tha-pah-teh-AH-dah)*
(A turn while producing rhythmic footwork)

The audible rhythm of triplets is made during a pivot on the ball of one foot which never leaves the floor (*en sitio*). The first two sounds are the ball and then heel with the free foot; the third sound is the dropping of the heel of the foot bearing the weight. The movement can be performed with musical accompaniment or in silence with accented rhythmic changes.

See *pica, solo de pies, tacón, vuelta.*

XINGO *(CHEEN-goh)*
(Rhythmic term; Basque)

This folkloric term is comparable to the Spanish term *llamada*.

See *cuatro pelos, llamada.*

YAUZIKA
See *muriska.*

ZALAMERIA DE HOMBROS
See *temblar los hombros.*

ZALEMA *(tha-LEH-mah)*
(Salaam, bow, curtsy; probably Moorish)

At nocturnal Moorish revelries (*zambras*) a female entertainer would begin and end a dance with an elaborate three-part gesture of greeting and respect to Allah, to the master of the house, and to all the invited guests. A similar introductory dance gesture of respect and acknowledgment exists in ballet as *pas révérence* and in East Indian dance as *guru vandanam*.

See *reverencia sencilla, saludo, zambra*.

ZAMBRA *(THAM-brah)*
(Moorish festival, merrymaking, revelry; From Arabic *samira*—Persian *zamira* [evening companion with lively conversation])

A pleasurable nocturnal open-air revelry of feasting, music, song, and poetry held on warm summer evenings and lasting until dawn. These favorite diversions, held in Seville after the fall of Córdoba, often presented artists of high intellectual caliber of Moorish, Jewish, and Christian faiths.

Today *zambra* is a flamenco woman's dance born in the caves of the Albaicín, the living quarters of the Gypsies of Granada, who have maintained it as one of the favorite showpieces in their performances for tourists. Although it has a slow, even, marked rhythm with a decided Eastern and sensuous character, it is considered, along with its accompanying music (*toque*) and song (*cante*), as *chico* (light). It is the most Arabic of flamenco dances and is often performed barefoot as the dancer accompanies herself with tiny, high-pitched finger cymbals (*crótalos*) similar to the Middle Eastern dancer's *zils* and, at times, with a large tambourine (*pandeira*).

See *crótalos, pandereta*.

ZAPATEADO *(tha-pah-teh-AH-doh)*
(Dance rhythms made with shoes; from *zapato*, shoe)

The term has two applications: (1) As technique, it refers to the rhythmic and counterrhythmic patterns made by any part of the shoe (*zapato*), including stamps (*golpes*); soft, brushing steps (*escobillas*); rhythmic heel beats (*taconeo*); and whatever toe-heel sound combinations the dancer can make with his shoes. (2) As a dance, it is usually a solo in ⅝ time in which the feet display this technique to the point of virtuosity, employing crescendos, diminuendos, and even brief intervals of silence. One of its unique characteristics is that it is the only flamenco dance traditionally performed without arm movements, although artists do appear who not only display but in program notes call attention to their ability to coordinate lyric and powerful arm movements (*braceo*) and hand claps (*palmadas*) while beating out a tattoo of counterrhythms with the feet. *Zapateado* is an Andalusian dance and has been the highlight of many concerts accompanied by a pianist. It is also considered a *baile intermedio* in the flamenco repertoire and is accompanied by guitar.

See *escobilla, taconeo*. See also Appendix: Basic Flamenco Rhythms.

ZAPATEADOR *(thah-pah-teh-ah-DOHR)*
(Early performers of rhythmic dancing)

This term was applied to special entertainers of the sixteenth century who traveled from village to village. They were accompanied by acrobats, tumblers, dancers, and actors and made a specialty act of rhythmic sounds with their shoes (*zapatos*). Under the most primitive outdoor situations they perfected their technique of rhythmically stamping their feet and slapping their soles (*zapatetas*) with such artistry that they were considered specialists and were engaged (according to old church records) in a separate category from dancers (*bailadores*). The *zapateadores* were the progenitors of those luminaries who were to follow over three centuries later such as El Raspao, Estampio, Escudero, and Carmen Amaya.

See *zapateta*.

ZAPATEO *(thah-pah-TEH-oh)*
(Making rhythmic sounds with the shoes or feet)

This term is used mostly in Hispanic folk dances throughout Latin America and Mexico for dances in which shoes, sandals, or bare feet are used to mark a repeated rhythm. The term is often used synonymously with the term *zapateado*.

See *zapateado*.

ZAPATETA *(tha-pah-TEH-tah)*
(A slap on the sole of a shoe during a leap, a jump)

A term used in folk dances, particularly the *jotas* of upper Aragón, in which the dancers (especially the men) leap into the air, throwing both legs to one side and striking the soles of their feet together. It also refers to slapping of the soles of the feet with the hands.

See *cabriola, zapateador*.

ZARANDEO *(thah-rahn-DEH-oh)*
(A moving to and fro, a shifting, a strutting)

A woman's body movement such as swaying of the hips. When the weight is on one foot, the hip is gently thrust out on the same side; then the same action is performed on the other side. It is typical of Gypsy dances and those with Moorish influence.[1] The *Natya Shastra*, the most authoritative treatise on East Indian dancing, written in Sanskrit between 200 and 2 B.C., mentions similar movements of the pelvis (*trika*) which for the most part have disappeared

---

[1] Moslem dogma forbade the practice of some Spanish dances, and the Koran prescribed that the moral way of performing certain dances was "with the women not stirring their feet so that their legs may not be seen." The specially draped shawl or scarf tied about women's hips (which was adopted by the nobility, as seen in Francisco Goya's paintings) was called a *zarandilla*.

from India's present-day dance but which may have been taken to Spain by India's migrating Gypsies. The term also refers to a shaking of the shoulders, as women would do when winnowing grain, another meaning of *zarandeo*.

See *zambra*.

ZARZUELA *(thar-THWEH-lah)*
(A type of Spanish musical comedy)

Although *zarzuelas* can range from a one-act comedy (*zarzuelita*) to a three-act serious drama, they have, like modern musicals, been choreographers' vehicles for staging all kinds of colorful national and folkloric dances interspersed with cheerful, lighthearted plots and scenes. Its name comes from a seventeenth-century hunting lodge called "Zarzuela" ("Brambles") situated in the royal domain of El Prado, outside Madrid.

ZINTZARRI *(tzeen-TZAH-ree)*
(Little bells; Basque)

Small metal bells (*cascabeles*) mounted on a pliable foundation, used by the male Basque dancer (*dantzariak* of Vizcaya). They are worn on each leg just below the knee and are similar to the bells worn the same way by Morris dancers and American Indians and the bells (*ghungooroo*) used in East Indian *kathak* dance.

See *pasos vascos básicos*.

Appendix: Basic Flamenco Rhythms
(Music for Guitar)

By
PETER BAIME

COMPASES BASICOS DEL BAILE FLAMENCO [1](com-PAH-sehs BAH-see-cohs dehl BAH-ee-leh flah-MEHN-co)
(Rhythmic, harmonic forms of flamenco dance)

Alegrías

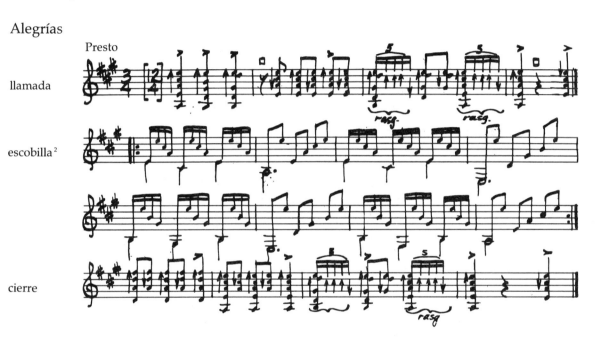

1. Musical examples written and arranged by Peter Baime. IP Revised August 1, 1986.
2. Example of *escobilla* written in *cifra*.

silencio

Bulerías

cierre

falseta

llamada/
desplante

Caracoles

Fandango de Huelva

Farruca

Guajira

cierre

Petenera

Rumba Flamenca

Sevillana

copla

Siguiriyas

Soleares

Tango

Tientos

Zambra

Zapateado

Selected Bibliography

Because of the paucity of technical literature on the subject of Spanish dance, much of the valid information in English and other languages is scattered and often disguised under misleading titles. Spanish dance is the product not of one culture and one country but of many. This is especially true in the multifaceted area of flamenco dance, which is inextricably united with singing (*cante*), history, view of life, and psyche.

The following references represent the most comprehensive list to date, gathered and researched over many years and found to be invaluable primary and secondary sources of information. Starred entries are primary sources.

Acevedo y Hyelves, Bernardo. *Vaqueros de Alzada en Asturias*. Oviedo, 1893.

Adams, N. B. *The Heritage of Spain*. New York, 1943.

Aguirre, Francisca. *La otra música*. Madrid, 1978.

Alcover, Antonio María. *Diccionari catala-valencia-balear*. Mallorca, 1930, 1964.

*Alford, Violet. "Ceremonial Dances of the Spanish Basques." *Musical Quarterly* [New York], July, 1932.

*———. *Dance and Song in Two Pyrenean Valleys*. London, 1937.

*———. "The Jota." *Dancing Times* [London], December, 1953.

*———. "Pepita's Spanish Dance." *Dancing Times* [London], November, 1936.

*———, and Rodney Gallop. *The Traditional Dance*. London, 1935.

Almendros Navarro, Carlos. *Todo lo básico sobre el flamenco*. Barcelona, 1973.

Almirall, V. "Consideraciones sobre los balls de gitanos del Valles." *Miscelánea folklórica* [Barcelona], 1887.

Amades Gelats, Juan. *Balls populars del Valles (Estret de la "Comarca del Valles")*. Barcelona, 1930.

———. "El ball de Torrent.·' *Anales del centro de cultua valenciana* [Valencia] 14 (1953).

*Amades, Joan. *La danza de moros y cristianos*. Valencia, 1966.

*Anderson, Ruth M. Exhibition illustrating dances of Spain at the Hispanic Society of America, New York, July, 1928–October, 1941.

———: *Galician Provinces of Spain: Pontevedra and La Coruna*. New York, 1939.

Andrade de Silva, Tomás. Introducción. *Antología del cante flamenco* [Hispavox recordings, explanatory booklet]. Madrid, 1958.

Aranguren, José Luis: "Moral y sociedad: La moral española en el siglo XIX." In *Cuadernos para el diálogo*. Fifth edition. Madrid, 1974.

Archivos Históricos de Toledo. Leg. 2, fol. 95, año 1631. Biblioteca Nacional, Madrid.

Arco, Ricardo del. *Notas de folklore alto aragonés*. Madrid, 1943.

Arévalo, José Carlos. "Gitanos en España: El precio de una integración." *Doctorama* [Madrid] 11 (1972).

*Armstrong, Lucile. *Dances of Spain*. Vol. 1 [south, central, and northwest]. London, 1950.

*———. *Dances of Spain*. Vol. 2, [Northeast and east]. New York, 1951.

Arnaudas Larrodé, Miguel. *La jota aragonesa: Una opinión sobre su origen, su forma musical y su ejecución*. Zaragoza, 1933.

Arraras, Soto, Fr. *Danzas e indumentaria de Navarra merinda*. Navarra, 1983.

*Asenjo Barbieri, Francisco. "Danzas y bailes de España en los siglos XVI y XVII." In *Ilustración española y americana*. 2 vols. Madrid, 1877.

*———. "Más sobre las danzas y bailes de España en los siglos XVI y XVII." In *Ilustración española y americana*. 2 vols. Madrid, 1878.

Atuna, M. *La corte literaria de Alhaquén de Córdoba*. Escorial, 1929.

Aubier, de Montherlant Brassai. *Seville en fête*. Paris, 1954.

*Barandiarán, Gaizka de, S. J. *Danzas de Euskalerri* [Dances of the Basque Country]. San Sebastián, 1969.

Barbiere, Francisco Ansejo. *Cancionero de los siglos XV y XVI*. Madrid, 1877.

———. *El teatro Real y el Teatro de la Zarzuela*. Madrid, 1877.

Barea, Arturo. *Lorca: The Poet and His People*. New York, 1949.

Barrios, Manuel. "Ese difícil mundo del flamenco." Universidad de Sevilla, 1972.

*Beaumont, Cyril W. *Antonio: Impressions of the Spanish Dancer*. London, 1952.

*Benn, David. "Flamenco Dancing and Dancers." *Ballet Today* [London], January– February, December, 1956.

Bercovici, Konrad. *The Story of the Gypsies* New York, 1928.

Bertram, Marcos Jesús. *De lo nuestro: La tonadilla y la danza*. Barcelona, 1915.

*Blasis, Carlo. "The Code of Terpsichore—The Spanish Dance." *American Dancer* [New York], March, 1937.

Blas Vega, José. *Temas flamencos*. Madrid, 1973.

———, and Manuel Ríos Ruiz. "Consideraciones sobre las orígenes del cante las tonás." In *Actas de la reunión internacional de estudios sobre los orígenes del flamenco*. Madrid, 1969.

Bleiberg, Germán. "El 'Informe secreto' de Mateo Alemán sobre el trabajo forzado en las minas de Almaden." *Estudios de historia social* [Madrid] 2–3 (1978).

Block, Martin. *Gypsies—Their Lives and Their Customs*. New York, 1939.

*Bobri, Vladimir. "What Is Flamenco?" *Guitar Review* [New York] 19 (1956).

*Bonilla, Luís. *La danza en el mito y en la historia*. Madrid, 1964.

Bonnin, Pere. "Los gitanos" *Mundo* [Barcelona], September 1, 1973.

*Borchard, Kent A. "Flamenco." *Viltis* [San Diego, Calif.], 1957.

Borrás Bermejo, Tomás. *Tam, tam: Pantomimas, bailetes, cuentos coreográficos mimo-dramas*. Madrid, 1931.

Borrow, George Henry. *The Bible in Spain*. London, 1843.

———. *Lavengro: The Scholar—the Gypsy—the Priest*. London, 1914.

———. *The Zincali; or, An Account of the Gypsies of Spain with an Original Collection of Their Songs and Poetry*. London, 1908.

*Borrull, Trinidad. *La danza española*. Barcelona, 1954.

*Bosch, Vicente. *Balls antics de Pallars*. Barcelona, 1907.

Botey, Françesc. *Lo gitano: Una cultura folk desconocida*. Barcelona, 1970.

*Bowers, Faubion. "The Preservation of the Dance in Spain." *Dance Magazine* [New York], April, 1952.

Brown, Irving. *Deep Song*. New York, 1929.

———. *Nights and Days on the Gypsy Trail*. New York, 1922.

*Brunelleschi, Elsa. "Classical Spanish Dances." *Dancing Times* [London], February, 1937.

*———. "English Dancers and Spanish Dancing." *Dancing Times* [London], November, 1924.

*———. "Spanish Dancing." *Dancing Times* [London], December, 1936.

*———. "A Table of Spanish Dances." *Dancing Times* [London], January, 1937.

Burgos, Antonio. *¿Andalucía tercer mundo?* Barcelona, 1974.

Burtnieks, J. A. "A Note on Flamenco Origins." *Guitar Review* [New York] 19 (1956).

Caballero, Fernán. *Escenas de costumbres*. Madrid, 1924.

*Caballero Bonald, José Manuel. *Andalusian Dances*. Barcelona, 1959.

———. Introduction. *Archivo del cante flamenco*. Barcelona, 1969.

———. *Luces y sombras del flamenco*. Seville, 1988.

———. *Vivir para contarlo*. Barcelona, 1969.

Caccini, G. S. *L'ultima parola sugli zingari*. Foligno, 1911.

Caffarena Such, Ángel. *Del cante andaluz, la saeta, la petenera.* Málaga, 1963.

*Cairón, Antonio. *Compendio de las principales reglas del baile.* Madrid, 1820.

*Calderón, Juan Rodrigo Jacinto. *Bolerología.* Philadelphia, Pa., 1807.

Campuzano, Ramón. *Origen, usos y costumbres de los gitanos y diccionario de su dialecto.* Madrid, 1851.

*Cansino, Angel. "Las Sevillanas." *American Dancer* [New York], November, 1936.

Cansinos Assens, Rafael. *La copla andaluza.* Madrid, 1976.

*Capdevilla, Manuel. *De la sardana.* Barcelona, 1925.

*Capmany, Aurelio. "El baile, la danza y el sarao." In Francisco Carreras y Candi, ed. *Folklore y costumbres de Espana.* Vol 2. Barcelona, 1934.

———. *El Bal i la danza popular a Catalunya: Historia, descripcio i ensenyamente.* Estudi folkloric de divulgació. Barcelona, 1948.

*———. *El ball popular a Catalunya: El contrapás.* Barcelona, 1922.

*———. *Com es balla la sardana: L'historia, la técnica, l'estética.* Barcelona, 1915.

*———. *La danza a Catalunya.* 2 vols. Barcelona, 1930, 1953.

*———. *La sardana a Catalunya.* Barcelona, 1948.

*———. *Un siglo de baile en Barcelona: Qué y donde bailaban los barceloneres el siglo XIX.* Barcelona, 1947.

Carlos de Luna, José. *El Café de Chinitas.* Madrid, 1942.

———. *El Cristo de los gitanos.* Madrid, 1942.

Caro Baroja, Julio. *Los moriscos del reino de Granada.* Madrid, 1976.

Carreras y Candi, Francisco, ed. *Folklore y costumbres de España.* 2 vols. Barcelona, 1931, 1934.

Castellá y Raich, Gabriel. "Igualada: Compasos o balls populars." *Revista Popular Catalana* [Barcelona], 1905.

Castellanos de Losada, Basilio Sebastián. *Discursos-históricos-arqueológicos sobre el origen, progresos y decadencia de la música y baile español.* Madrid, 1954.

Castro, Luis de: *El enigma de Bemugueti, la danza y la escultura.* Valladolid, 1953.

Charbonnel, Raoul. *La Danse.* Paris, 1899.

Chase, Gilbert. *Music of Spain.* New York, 1959.

Chávarri, Eduardo López. "La danza valenciana." *Revista musical catalana* [Barcelona] 28, 333 (September, 1931).

———. *Popular Spanish Music.* Barcelona and Buenos Aires, 1927.

Chejne, A. C. *Muslim Spain: Its History and Culture.* Minneapolis, Minn.: 1974.

Cimorra, Clemente. *El cante jondo: Orígen y realidad folklórica.* Buenos Aires, 1943.

———. *Los gitanos, húngaros y de otros países.* Madrid, 1953.

Cirlot, Juan Eduardo. *Diccionario de símbolos.* Barcelona, 1958.

Clebert, Jean-Paul. *The Gypsies.* New York, 1963.

Cobb, Stanwood. *Islamic Contribution to Civilization.* Washington, D.C., 1963.

Colocci, Adriano Amerigo, Marquis de. *Storia d'un popolo errante.* Turin, 1889.

Cora, Guido. "Die Zigeuner." In *Das Ausland.* Stuttgart, 1890.

*Cordelier, Susanne F. *La vie brève de La Argentina.* Paris, 1936.

*Corominas, E. *Lo contrapás.* Barcelona, 1918.

Cotareli y Mori, Emilio. *Colección de loas, bailes, jácaras y mojigangas desde fines del siglo XVI a mediados del XVIII.* Madrid, 1911.

———. *Historia de la zarzuela.* Madrid, 1934.

———. *Orígenes y establecimiento de la ópera en España hasta 1800.* Madrid, 1917.

*Cournand, Gilberte. *On La Argentina.* Press Extracts. Paris, 1928–36.

Covarrubias Orozco, Sebastián de. *Tesoro de la lengua castellana o española.* Madrid, 1921.

* *La Danse Espagnol. Revue choréographique de Paris* 2 (special number) (ca. 1950).

*Daubigny, Luis. *Libro de contradanza.* Seville, 1768.

*Davies, John Langdon. *Dancing Catalans.* London, 1929.

Davillier, Baron Charles. *Viaje por España.* Madrid, 1957.

Deleite y Piñuela, J. *El rey se divierte*. Madrid, 1935.

———. *También se divierte el pueblo*. Madrid, 1944.

*Del Río, Ángel. *Antonia Mercé, La Argentina*. New York, 1930.

*Del Río, Justo. *Danzas típicas burgalesas*. Burgos, 1975.

*Del Río Velasco, D. Justo. *Danzas típicas burgalesas*. Burgos, 1975.

*Dolmetsch, Mabel. *Dances of Spain and Italy from 1400 to 1600*. New York, 1975.

Domínguez Berrueta, Juan. "La jota aragonesa." In *Memoria enviada al Congreso Internacional de las artes populares*. Prague, 1928.

*Donostia, José Antonio de. "Danzas vascas." In *Memoria enviada al Congreso Internacional de Praga*. Prague, 1928.

*Dorcy, J. *Deux visages de la danse español*. Madrid, 1796.

D'ors, Eugenio. "Dialéctica de la guitarra." In *Nuevo Glosario*. Madrid, 1946.

Dozy, R. *Histoire des Musulmans d'Espagne jusqu'à la Conquête d'Andalousie (711–1110)*. Leyden, 1932.

*Draegin, Lois. "Fanning the Spanish Flame." *Dance Magazine* [New York], April, 1978.

Duff, Donald. "Flamenco." *Modern Music* [New York], May–June, 1940.

Durand-Viel, Ana María. *La sevillana: Datos sobre el folklore de la baja Andalucía*. Seville, 1983.

Echevarría Bravo, Pedro. *La canción andaluza*. Jerez, 1960.

Echevarría, F. *Cantos y bailes populares de Valencia con musica*. Valencia, 1912.

Ellis, Havelock. *The Dance of Life*. New York, 1923.

———. *The Soul of Spain*. New York, 1920.

Epton, N. C. *Andalucía*. London, 1968.

*Escudero, Vicente. *Arte Flamenco*. Madrid, 1959.

———. *Mi baile*. Barcelona, 1947.

———. *Pintura que baila*. Madrid, 1951.

*———. "What Is the Flamenco Dance?" *Dance Magazine* [New York], October, 1955.

*Esquivel de Navarro, Juan. *Discurso sobre el arte del danzado*. Seville, 1642.

Estébanez Calderón, Serafín (El Solitario). *Escenas andaluzas*. Madrid, 1955.

*Etxebaría y Goiri, J. L. *Danzas de vizcaya: Bizkai'ko dantzak* Bilbao, 1968.

Falla, Manuel de. *Escritos sobre música y músico*. Madrid, 1972.

Farmer, Henry. *History of Arabian Music*. London, 1929.

———. *The Legacy of Islam*. Oxford, 1931.

Fernández-Cid de Temes, Antonio. *Panorama de la música en España*. Madrid, 1949.

*Fernández Riego, Francisco. *Danzas populares gallegas. (Centro Gallego)*. Buenos Aires, n.d.

*Ferriol y Boxeraus, Bartolomé. *Reglas útiles para los aficionados a danzar*. Málaga, 1745.

Feuillet, R. A. *"Choreographie" ou l'art de décrire la danse*. Paris, 1701.

*Field, Alex. "Dancing Under the Spanish Republic." *Dance Observer* [New York], April, 1943.

*Fisher, Michael E. "Flamenco Rhythms and Forms." *Guitar Review* [New York] 19 (1956).

*Fogués, Francisco. "Los bailes de Carcagente [Valencia]." *Anales del centro de cultura valenciana*, January–March, 1933.

Ford, Richard. "Former Costumes of the Gypsies." *Manchester Literary Club Papers* [Manchester, Mass.] 2 (1876).

———. "Spanish Dances." Programs, 1904–1905, 1906–1907, 1915–16. Boston Symphony Orchestra Library.

Frazer, James. *The Golden Bough*. New York, 1922.

Frazer, Lilly Grove, Lady. "The Dance in Spain." In *The Badmington Library*. Vol. 10. London, 1907.

Gallop, Rodney. *The Book of the Basques*. London, 1930.

*———. "The Catalan Sardana." *Dancing Times* [London], May, 1936.

*Galmés, Antonio. *Bailes populares mallorquines.* Palma, 1952.
———. *Mallorca, Menorca, Ibiza Folklore.* Palma, 1951.
García Gómez, E. *Cinco poetas musulmanes.* Madrid, 1959.
———. *Poemas arabigoandaluces.* Madrid, 1959.
García Lorca, Federico. *Poema del cante jondo.* Buenos Aires, 1957.
———. *Teoría y juego del duende.* Madrid, 1968.
García Matos, Manuel. *Antología del folklore musical de España.* Madrid, 1957.
———. *Bosquejo histórico del cante flamenco.* Madrid, 1958.
———. "Cante flamenco, algunas de sus presuntos orígenes." In *Anuario musical.* Barcelona, 1904.
*———. *Danzas populares de España—Castilla la Nueva.* Madrid, 1957.
*———. *Danzas populares de España—Extremadura.* Madrid, 1964.
*———. *Danzas populares de España—Andalucía.* Madrid, 1971.
———. *Una historia del cante flamenco* [Hispavox Recordings, explanatory booklet]. Madrid, n.d.
*Gasch, Sebastián, and Pedro Pruña. *De la danza.* Barcelona, 1946.
Gómez-Tabanera, José Manuel. *El folklore español.* Madrid, 1968.
———. *Refranero español.* Madrid, 1959.
González, Palencia Ángel. *Historia de la España musulmana.* Barcelona, 1932.
González Climent, Anselmo. *Andalucía en los toros: El cante y la danza.* Madrid, 1953.
———. *Antología de poesía flamenca.* Madrid, 1961.
———. *Bulerías.* Jerez, 1961.
———. *Flamencología toros cante y baile.* Madrid, 1964.
———. *Oído al cante.* Madrid, 1960.
———. *Segunda bibliografía flamenca.* Málaga, 1966.
Goya, Carola. "Easter in Seville Most Spectacular Religious Festival in World Today." *New York Evening Post,* March 30, 1929.
*———. "Is It Spanish or Flamenco Dance?" *Dance Magazine* [New York], February, 1957.
Graham, Robert Bontine Cunninghame. *Aurora La Cujiñí, a Realistic Sketch in Sevilla.* London, 1898.
*Grahit y Grau, José. *Les Sardanes.* Estudio de la danza catalana. Gerona, 1915.
Grande, Felix. "Blanco spirituals." *Bibliografía.* Barcelona, 1977.
———. *Memoria del flamenco I: Raíces y prehistoria del cante.* Madrid, 1987.
———. *Memoria del flamenco II: Desde de café-cantante a nuestros días.* Madrid, 1987.
Grellmann, Heinrich. *Dissertation on the Gipsies: With an Historical Enquiry Concerning Their Origin and First Appearance in Europe.* London, 1807.
Groome, Francis Hindes. *Gypsy Folk Tales.* London, 1899.
———. *In Gypsy Tents.* London, 1880.
*Grosser Piéjus, Anne-Marie. "Flamenco." *World of Music* [Berlin–New York] 10, no. 4 (1968).
Grunfeld, Fredrick V. *The Spanish Style* [Time-Life Records, explanatory booklet]. New York, n.d.
Guest, Ivor. *Théophile Gautier on Spanish Dance.* Dance Chronicle: New York, 1987.
*Gyenes, Juan. *Ballet español.* Madrid, 1953; Berlin–New York, 1968.
Hamilton, Mary Neal. *Music in Eighteenth Century Spain.* Urbana, Ill., 1937.
Herrera Escudero, María L. *Trajes y bailes de España.* Madrid, 1984.
*Herrero, Bernabé. *Cante, baile y música española.* Madrid, 1957.
Herrero, Pedro Mario. *El campo andaluz.* Madrid, 1968.
Hilaire, Georges. *Initiation flamenco.* Paris, 1954.
Hobsbawm, Eric J. *Rebeldes primitivos.* Barcelona, 1974.
*Horosko, Marian. "Technique Spanish Dance: Where." *Dance Magazine* [New York], April, 1986.

*Horst, Louis. *Pre-Classic Dance Forms*. New York, 1940.

Imauddin, S. M. *Some Aspects of the Socio-Economic and Cultural History of Muslim Spain*. Leiden, 1965.

Infante, Blas. *El ideal andaluz*. Madrid, 1976.

*Inzenga y Castellanos, José. *Cantos y bailes populares de España*. Madrid, 1888.

Irving, Washington. *Tales of the Alhambra*. New York, 1970.

*Ishmael. "Spanish Dances." *Illustrated American* [New York], November 5, 1890.

*Ivanova, Anna. *The Dance in Spain*. New York, 1970.

——. "What Is Spanish Ballet?" *Dancing Times* [London], November–December, 1964, January, 1965.

*Iztueta, Juan Ignacio de. *Guipuzcoaco dantza*. San Sebastián, 1895.

*Jaque, Juan Antonio. "Libro de danzar de B. de Rojas Panteja." Manuscript, Biblioteca Nacional, Madrid, n.d.

Jobit, Mgr. Pierre. *El baile de los seises*. Paris, 1954.

Joel, Lydia. "The Gypsies of Granada." *Dance Magazine* [New York], November, 1956.

Jovellanos, Gaspar Melchor de. *Espectáculos públicos y su origen en España*. Granada, 1977.

*Kaz, Asya. "Traditions of Spain." *American Dancer* [New York], November, 1936.

*Keating, Franke. "Rebellious Catalan Spirit Surfaces in Folk Dancing. *New York Daily News*, July 30, 1978.

*Kinney, Troy. "The Dance in Spain." *Dance Magazine* [New York], March, 1929.

——, and Margaret West. *The Dance*. New York, 1914.

Krinkin, Alexandra V. "Vicente, Esto Es!" *Dance Magazine* [New York], February, 1955.

*Laborde, Alexandre de. "Spanish Dancing in 1808." *Dancing Times* [London], June–July, 1939.

Lafuente, Rafael. *Los gitanos, el flamenco y los flamencos*. Barcelona, 1955.

*Lagus, J. *Reglas para los bailes de salón*. Barcelona, 1890.

*Lalagia. *Spanish Dancing*. London, 1985.

*La Meri [Russell Meriwether Hughes]. *Spanish Dancing*. Pittsfield, Mass., 1967.

*——. "The Story of the Spanish Gypsy Dance." *Dancing Times* [London], January, 1936.

*Langdon-Davies, J. *Dancing Catalans*. London, 1929.

*Laplerya, J. *Bailes populares catalanes*. Barcelona, 1908.

Larria Palacín, Arcadio. *El flamenco en su raíz*. Madrid, 1974.

Lawson, Joan. *European Folk Dances*. London, 1953.

*Levinson, André. *La Argentina*. Paris, 1928.

*——. "The Spirit of the Spanish Dance." *Theatre Arts Monthly* [New York], September, 1925.

Lévi-Provençal, E. *La civilización árabe en España*. Madrid, 1969.

——. *España musulama*. Madrid, 1930.

Livermore, Ann. *Historia de la música española*. Barcelona, 1974.

*——. *A Short History of Spanish Music*. Bristol, 1972.

Llano, Aurelio de. *Del folklore asturiano: Mitos, supersticiones, costumbres*. Madrid, 1922.

*Llobet Busquets, Charles. *Bailes típicos y escudos de España y sus regiones*. Barcelona, 1929.

López Chávarri, Eduardo. *Música popular española*. Barcelona, 1927.

López de Meneses, Amanda. *La imigración gitana en España en el siglo XV*. Madrid, 1968.

López Rodríguez, Manuel. "Perfil flamenco de Falla." In *Versión literaria de Manuel de Falla*. Málaga, 1976.

Luna, José Carlos de. *De cante grande y cante chico*. Madrid, 1942.

——. *Gitanos de la Bética*. Madrid, 1952.

Luque Navajas, José. *Málaga en el cante*. Málaga, 1965.

Machado y Álvarez, Antonio. *Colección de cantes flamencos recogidos y anotados por De-*

mófilo. Seville, 1881; Buenos Aires, 1947.

Magri, Gennaro. *Trattato teorico-prattico di ballo*. Part 1. Naples, 1788.

*Manfredi Cano, Domingo. "Bailes regionales." *Temas españoles* [Madrid] 147 (1955).

———. *Cante y baile flamencos*. León, 1973.

———. *Geografía del cante jondo*. Madrid, 1955, 1964.

———. *Silueta folklórica de Andalucía*. Madrid, 1961.

*Manrique, Gervasio. "Castilla: Sus danzas y canciones." In *Revista de Dialectología*. Madrid, 1950.

*Marrero Suárez, Vicente. *El acierto de la danza española*. Madrid, 1959.

*———. *El enigma de España en la danza española*. Madrid, 1959.

*Martínez de la Peña, Teresa. *Teoría y práctica de baile flamenco*. Madrid, 1969.

Martínez Menchen, Antonio. "El flamenco hoy." *El Diario Montañes* [Santander], December 28, 1974.

Martín Moreno, Antonio. *Historia de la música andaluza*. Seville, 1985.

Martínez Torner, Eduardo. "La canción tradiccional española." In. Francisco Carreras y Candi, ed. *Folklore y costumbres de España*. Barcelona, 1944.

———. *Temas folklóricos: Música y poesía*. Madrid, 1935.

*Maspons y Labros, Francisco. "Ball de gitanos en lo Vallés." In *Folk-lore catalá*, v. Miscelánea folklórica. Barcelona, 1887.

Mas y Prat, Benito. *La tierra de María Santísima (Bailes de palillos y flamencos)*. Madrid, 1925.

*McBride, Harry A. "The Aurresku, Basque Dance in the Land of the Basques. *National Geographic*, January, 1922.

McDowell, Robert. "Gypsies: Wanderers of the World." *National Geographic*, January, 1970.

Matteo [Vittucci]. "Woods That Dance." *Dance Perspectives* [New York] 33 (1968).

Mercadal, J. García. *La jota aragonesa*. Madrid, 1964.

Mercé, Antonia [La Argentina]. "My Castanets." *Theater Arts Monthly* [New York], January, 1932.

*Michaut, Pierre. *Danse espagnol*. Paris, 1949.

*Minguet y Yrot, Pablo. *Breve tratado de los pasos de danzar a la española*. Madrid, 1764.

*———. *El noble arte de danzar*. Madrid, 1758.

Mitjana, Rafael. *La musique en Espagne*. Paris, 1920.

Molina, Ricardo. *Misterios del arte flamenco*. Barcelona, 1967.

———. *Obra flamenca*. Madrid, 1977.

———, and Antonio Mairena. *Mundo y formas del cante flamenco*. Seville, 1971.

Molina Fajardo, Eduardo. *El flamenco en Granada: Teoría de sus orígenes e historia*. Granada, 1974.

———. *Manuel de Falla y el cante jondo*. Granada, 1962.

Monleón, José. *Lo que sabemos del flamenco*. Madrid, 1967.

*Monsalvatje y Aleu. *La sardana: estudios curiosos sobre la historia y reglas con que debe bailarse la sardana según el sistema ampurdanés y el selvatá*. Olot, 1895.

Morca, Teodoro. "Technique: Spanish Dance, Part 1, Escuela Bolera." *Dance Magazine* [New York], February, 1986.

———. "Technique: Spanish Dance, Part 2, Flamenco." *Dance Magazine* [New York], March, 1986.

Muñoz, Mathilde. *Historia de Teatro Real, Madrid*. Madrid, 1946.

Navarro, José. "Los cantes de levante." *Flamenco* [Ceuta], July, 1975.

Negri, Cesare. *Nuove invenzioni di balli*. Milan, 1604.

Neville, Edgar. "La danza." In *El alma de España*. Madrid, 1951.

———. *Flamenco and Cante Jondo*. Málaga, 1963.

*Nielson, Rutgers. "Spanish Dancing of Today," *Dance Lovers Magazine [Dance]* [New York], April, 1925.

*Niles, Doris. "El Duende." *Dance Perspectives* [New York] 27 (1966).

Noel, Eugenio. *Escenas y andaluzas de la campana antiflamenca.* Valencia, 1914.

———. *Señoritos, chulos, fenómenos, gitanos y flamencos.* Madrid, 1916.

Noguera, Antonio. *Memoria sobre los cantos, bailes y tocatas populares de la Isla de Mallorca.* Palma, 1908.

*Nyssen, J. J. *Cuatros palabras sobre el baile.* Madrid, 1895.

Ocaña, Juan Sánchez. *Granada y sus gitanos.* Granada, 1963.

*Olazarán de Estella, Hilario. *Euskalerriaren Dartzak Muil-Dantza Baztan.* San Sebastián, 1925.

Olmeda, D. Federico. *Folk-lore de Castilla o cancionero popular* de Burgos. Seville, 1903; Burgos, 1975.

Orozco Díaz, Emilio. *Falla y Granada.* Granada, 1976.

Ortiz de Villajos, Cándido G. *Gitanos de Granada (la Zambra).* Granada, 1949.

Ortiz Echaqüe, José. *España: pueblos y paisajes.* Madrid, 1950.

———. *España: tipos y trajes.* Madrid, 1953.

———. *España mística.* Madrid, 1950.

Ortiz Nuevo, José Luis. "El Flamenco: ¿Cante del Pueblo?" *Cuadernos Hispanoamericanos* [Madrid] 279 (1973).

———. "El Pensamiento político del cante flamenco" *Triunfo* [Madrid], December 8, 1973.

*Ossorio y Gallardo, Carlos. *El baile.* Barcelona, 1902.

*Otero Aranda, José. *Tratado de bailes.* Seville, 1912.

*P., F. "Balls populares catalans: Dansa y ball del cinia castelltersol (Descripción coreográfica y transcripción musical)." *Revista Musical Catalana* [Barcelona], March, 1904.

Pabanó, F. M. *Historia y costumbres de los gitanos.* Barcelona, 1915.

Palencia, Isobel de. *El traje regional de España.* London, 1926.

*Pauer, E. "The Dances of Spain." *Monthly Musical Record* [London], September 1, 1872.

Pedrell, Felipe. *Cancionero musical popular español.* Vol. 2. Barcelona, 1948.

Pematín, Julián. *El cante flamenco.* Madrid, 1966.

*Peters-Rohse, Gisela. "Jazz und Flamenco in tanzerischer Verbindung." *Tanzarchiv* 328 (May, 1980).

Plata, Juan de la. *Flamencos de Jerez.* Jerez, 1961.

Pohren, Donn E. *The Art of Flamenco.* Jerez, 1984.

———. *Lives and Legends of Flamenco.* Seville, 1987.

———. *A Way of Life.* Madrid, 1980.

Pritchett, V. S. *The Spanish Temper.* New York, 1954.

Puente y Brañas, Ricardo. "Romerías y bailes de Galicia." *Museo Universal,* 1860.

*Puig, Alfonso. *El arte del baile flamenco.* Barcelona, 1977.

———. *Ballet y baile español.* Barcelona, 1951.

Pujol, F., and J. Amades. *Diccionari de la dansa i dels instruments i sonadors.* Barcelona, 1939.

Quièvreux, Louis. *Art flamenco.* Brussels, 1959.

———. "Flamenco and the Flamencos." *Guitar Review* [New York] 20 (1956).

Quiñones, Fernando. *De Cádiz y sus cantes.* Madrid, 1974.

———. *El flamenco, vida y muerte.* Barcelona, 1972.

Quintana, Berthe B., and Lois Gray Floyd. *¡Qué Gitano! Gypsies of Southern Spain.* New York, 1972.

*Raffé, W. G. "Folk Dance is . . . Basque, Fuori & Dantza." *Dance Magazine* [New York], October, 1948.

Ramírez Heredia, Juan de Diós. *Nosotros los gitanos.* Barcelona, 1972.

———. *Vida gitana.* Barcelona, 1973.

Rehfisch, Farnham. *Gypsies, Tinkers and Other Travelers*. London and New York, 1975.

Reinbeck, Emil. *Die Zigeuner*. Salzkotten, 1861.

Rennert, Hugo Albert. *The Spanish Stage in the Time of Lope de Vega*. New York, 1963.

Rey, Agapito. *Cultura y costumbres del siglo XVI en la península ibérica y en la Nueva España*. Mexico, 1944.

Ribera y Tarragó, Julián. *Music in Ancient Arabia and Spain*. London and Stanford, Calif., 1929.

———. *La música andaluza medieval en las canciones de los trovadores, troveros y minnesinger*. Madrid, 1925.

———. *La música de la jota aragonesa*. Madrid, 1928.

Rice, Cyril. *Dancing in Spain*. London, 1931.

*———. "Spanish Dancing In 1932." *Dancing Times* [London], October–November, 1932.

*Riego, Fernando del. *Danzas populares gallegas*. Buenos Aires, 1950.

*Riggs, Arthur Stanley. "Some Spanish Dances." *Century Magazine* [New York], January, 1912.

Ríos Ruiz, Manuel. *Introducción al cante flamenco*. Madrid, 1972.

———. *Tiempo íntimo*. Madrid, 1975.

Roberts, Samuel. *The Gypsies: Their Origin, Continuance and Destination; or, The Sealed Book Opened*. London, 1842.

Rodríguez Gómez, Fernando (El de Triana). *Arte y artistas flamencos*. Madrid, 1952.

Rodríguez Marín, Francisco. *El alma de Andalucía*. Madrid, 1929.

———. *Cantos populares españoles*. Seville, 1882.

Romero, Vicente. "Close-Up of Flamenco." *Dance Magazine* [New York], November, 1962.

Rosa y López, Simón de la. *Los seises de la catedral de Sevilla: Ensayo de investigación histórica*. Seville, 1904.

Rossy, Hipólito. *Teoría del cante jondo*. (Granada, 1974).

*Roxo de Flores, D. Felipe. *Tratado de recreación instructiva sobre la danza: Su invención y diferencias*. Madrid, 1793.

Sachs, Curt. *World History of the Dance*. New York, 1937.

*Sagaseta, Miguel Ángel. *Danzas de Valcarlos*. Pamplona, 1977.

*Sainz de la Maza, Regino. "Spanish Dancing Yesterday and Today." *Guitar Review* [New York] 19 (1956).

Salas Viu, Vicente. *Música y creación musical*. Madrid, 1966.

Salazar, Adolfo. *La música en España*. Buenos Aires, 1953.

Sales Mayo, Francisco de. *Los gitanos, su historia, sus costumbres, su dialecto*. Madrid, 1869.

*Saleta, H. *Escenas vibereñas: Las jotas aragonesa y navarra a orillas del Ebro, Arga, Egea y Aragón*. Zaragosa, 1898.

Salillas, Rafael. *Hampa: Antropología picaresca*. Madrid, 1898.

Salom, Andrés. *Didáctica del cante jondo*. Murcia, 1976.

Sánchez, María Helena. *Documentación selecta sobre la situación de los gitanos españoles en el siglo XVIII*. Madrid, 1977.

———. *Los gitanos españoles: El período borbónico*. Madrid, 1977.

Sanchez Romero, José. *Castilla, la copla, el baile y el refrán*. Madrid, 1972.

San Román, Teresa. *Vecinos gitanos*. Madrid, 1976.

Santos, Jaime. *Insider's Guidebook to Flamenco*. Madrid, 1966.

*Sanz, Don Gregorio. "Arte de baylar." In *Enciclopedia metódica*. Madrid, 1791.

Sassone, Felipe. "La jota, himno, danza y oración de la raza." In *Blanco y negro*. Madrid, 1934.

Sawa, Alejandro. *Iluminaciones en la sombra*. Madrid, 1977.

*Schneider, Marius. *La danza de espadas y la tarantela*. Barcelona, 1948.

*Sevilla, Paco. "El baile." *Jaleo* [San Diego, Calif.], April–June, 1979.

*Shawn, Ted. "Dancing in Spain." *Dance Magazine* [New York], March, 1926.

Shergold, N. D. *History of the Spanish Stage from Medieval Times Until the End of the Seventeenth Century.* Oxford, 1967.

Simonet, F. S.: *Sacada de los autores arabigos.* Granada, 1827.

Simson, Walter. *History of the Gypsies.* London, 1965.

Sinclair, Albert Thomas. "Gypsy and Oriental Music." In *Journal of American Folklore.* Vol. 20. New York, 1963.

Smith, Laura Alexandrine. *Through Romany Songland.* London, 1889.

Solis, Ramón. *Flamenco y literatura.* Madrid, 1975.

Soriano Fuertes y Piqueras, Mariano. *Música árabe-española.* Barcelona, 1853.

Starkie, Walter. "Cante Jondo, Flamenco and the Guitar." *Guitar Review* [New York] 20 (1956).

———. *Casta gitana.* Barcelona, 1956.

———. *Don Gitano (Don Gypsy).* New York, 1937.

———. "The Eternal Dances of Spain." *Irish Statesman* [Dublin], August 3, 1929.

———. *The Gypsy in Andalusian Folk-Lore and Folk-Music.* London, 1935.

———. *The Road to Santiago.* New York, 1957.

———. *In Sara's Tents.* London, 1953.

———. *Spain: A Musician's Journey Through Time and Space.* Geneva, 1958.

———. *Spanish Raggle-Taggle—Adventures with a Fiddle in North Spain.* London, 1934.

Suárez de Salazar, Juan Bautista. *Grandezas y antigüedades de la isla y ciudad de Cádiz.* Book 4. Cádiz, 1610.

Subira, José. *Historia de la música.* Barcelona, 1947.

———. "El paisaje, las canciones y las danzas de Cataluña." *Nuestro Tiempo* [Madrid], 1921.

Teres, Elías. "Testimonios literarios para la historia del cante flamenco (1750–1850)." In *Actas de la reunión internacional de estudios sobre los orígenes del flamenco.* Madrid, 1969.

Terry, Walter. "Spanish Dancing in America." *Dance Magazine Annual.* New York, 1968.

———. "What Ever Became of Spanish Dance?" *New York Times,* August 23, 1981.

Thompson, A.G., "The Dance of the Aurresku." *South African Dancing Times,* [Johannesburg], June, 1938.

———. "The National Dances of Spain." *South African Dancing Times* [Johannesburg], January, 1938.

Torrano Soier, Gines. *Bailes típicos de la region murciana.* Murcia, 1984.

Triana, Fernando el de. *Arte y artistas flamencos.* Madrid, 1952.

Tuñon de Lara, Manuel. *La España de siglo XIX y la España del siglo XX.* Barcelona, 1974.

*Udaeta, José de. *Flamenco.* Hamburg, 1964.

Vallador, F. *Apuntes para la historia de la música en Granada.* Granada, 1972.

Vanzo, Sue. "The Art of Flamenco." *Viltis* [San Diego, Calif.], May, 1979.

Varela, Silvari. "Asturias: Su música y danza populares." *Alhambra.* [Granada] 20 (1917).

Vechten, Carl van. *The Music of Spain.* New York, 1918.

Vélez, Estéban. *Danzas vascas.* Madrid, 1952.

Vigo, Enrique. *Alpec de Balls populars de Pallars.* Barcelona, 1909.

Ville, F. de. *Tziganes.* Brussels, 1956.

Vincent, Bernard. "La cultura morisca." *Historia* [Madrid], October 16, 1977.

Vuilliere, Gaston: *La Danse.* Paris, 1898.

*Walsh, T. "The Dancers of Spain." *Theatre Magazine* [New York], October, 1906.

Watt, Montgomery. *Historia de la España islámica.* Madrid, 1970.

Webb, G. E. C. *Gypsies: The Secret People.* London, 1960.

Wedeck, H. E. *Dictionary of Gypsy Life and Lore.* New York, 1973.

*Widner, Winifred. "The Dancing Basques." *Dance Observer* [New York], June–July, 1957.

Wild, Roger. "La danse et tauromachie." *Formes et Couleurs,* [Lausanne] 4 (1948).

*Wingrave, Helen and Robert Harrold. *Spanish Dancing.* Kent, 1972.

Wishaw, Bernard, and Ellen Wishaw. *Arabic Spain.* London, 1912.

Yoors, Jan. *The Gypsies.* New York, 1967.

———. *The Gypsies of Spain.* New York, 1974.

Zamora, Florentino y Ortega, Luís. "Cien fichas sobre técnica de la danza y del baile." *El Libro Español* [Madrid] 16 (April, 1959).

———. and J. L. Díez Poyatos. "Cien fichas sobre técnico de la danza y del baile." *El Libro Español* [Madrid] 18 (June, 1959).

Zern, Brook. "Flamenco: For the Purist It's a Ritual Not a Spectacle." *New York Times,* November 19, 1972.

Specialized Periodicals

Jaleo, newsletter devoted to spreading art, culture, and enjoyment of flamenco, published by Jaleistas, The Flamenco Association of San Diego, Box 4706, San Diego, CA   92104.

Journal of the Gypsy Lore Society, scholarly journal unquestionably the most reputable source concerning Gypsy customs, language, and folktales, published by University Library, Liverpool.

Index

Full definitions are indicated by bold-faced numbers, which are listed first in entries.